When it comes to coaching defensive football, Kenny Ratledge is second to no one. He is one of the most innovative and creative coaches I have had the privilege of being around in all levels of football. His tireless work ethic and the effort he puts into stopping all types of offenses are what separates him from everybody else. I was fortunate to play under Coach Ratledge for four years. His game planning skills and in-game adjustments are without a doubt the best in the business. To this day, I call upon Coach Ratledge for any questions or concerns that I may have concerning the schematics or fundamentals of defensive football.

Daniel Cotter
Defensive Backs Coach/Special Teams Coordinator
University of the Cumberlands

Kenny Ratledge is one of the best coaches that I have ever been around. I had to coach against Coach Ratledge for many years, and his defenses were the best at scheme, technique, and fundamentals. I would highly recommend this book to any coach.

Scott Meadows
Head Football Coach
Pigeon Forge (TN) High School

Kenny Ratledge's 4-3 defense was as difficult to prepare for as a calculus exam. Read this book, and it will help you learn how to play winning defense.

Graham Clark
Head Football Coach
Dobyns-Bennett High School (TN)

The Complete 4-3 Defensive Playbook

Kenny Ratledge

COACHES
CHOICE™

ISBN: 978-1-60679-320-6
Library of Congress Control Number: 2014950781
Book layout: Cheery Sugabo
Cover design: Cheery Sugabo
Front cover photo: ©Scott Terna/Cal Sport Media/ZUMAPRESS.com

Coaches Choice
P.O. Box 1828
Monterey, CA 93942
www.coacheschoice.com

Dedication

I would like to dedicate this book to my family. Thanks to Debbie, Patrick, and Laura for all your support.

Acknowledgments

I would like to give special thanks to my typist and daughter, Laura Ratledge. Also, I would like to thank my son and computer guy, Patrick Ratledge. Thanks for all your help!

Contents

Introduction

The title of this book may seem a little pretentious. It is not meant to be. The definitions of complete include "to make whole" and "having no part lacking." I feel those definitions describe this book. Any coach on any level can take this book and install a complete defensive system from its contents. Coaches can consult this playbook to handle any situation that might arise in implementing a defensive system. This book has the answers to the test. Chapter 1 focuses on the first thing a coach must consider when installing a defense: what does he want the defense look like? What are to be its attributes and characteristics? Chapter 2 establishes a system on fingerprinting the offense. An important part of any defensive playbook or system is the verbiage and nomenclature used to communicate with other defensive coaches and players. Defenses don't exist in a vacuum. Everything that is done defensively is tailored to defensing an offensive football team. This book establishes an easy to understand vocabulary to describe an opponent's personnel, personnel groupings, formations, shifts, and motions, to name a few. Chapter 3 establishes a defensive vocabulary and system. It illustrates how the positions are named, huddle procedure, substitution packages, gap labels, and alignment labeling, to name a few. This language is used to enable the different defensive groups to interact. From that point, schematics are detailed. Fronts are illustrated in Chapter 4, as well as base zone coverages in Chapter 5. Chapter 6 explores three eight-men-in-the-box man coverages. Chapter 7 develops stunt coverages. Chapter 8 deals with peel blitzes. Goal line defense is explored in Chapter 9. Chapter 10 illustrates the mustang package. Mustang is the 3-3-5 change-up. Chapter 11 covers situational defensive football, which includes time-affiliated situations such as Big Ben defense, four-minute offense, and two-minute offense. Also included in Chapter 11 are kick safe defenses and how to defend surprise formations such as the swinging gate and much more. Positional technique play is covered in Chapters 12 through 14. Chapter 12 covers line play, Chapter 13 illustrates linebacker play, and Chapter 14 explores secondary play. Chapter 15 gives tips on how to plan and implement a defensive practice plan and drills. These drills are tailored to the schemes and strategies included in the playbook. Chapter 16 has a list of defensive calls, strategies, and wrinkles found in the playbook. A coach can take this checklist after he has studied the upcoming opponent and can select the calls, schemes, stunts, and coverages that would be effective against the next opponent. Finally, a glossary is included. This glossary has the definitions to coaching points, techniques, and calls in the playbook.

1

Philosophy and Motivation

No playbook—offensive, defensive, or special teams—would be complete without a section dealing with philosophy and motivation. Before a coach looks at schematics and X's and O's, he must establish how he wants the defensive team to generally look. What values is the coach looking for? What are the fundamental assumptions or beliefs of the defense? What is the mindset that will make the defense successful? This section sets in stone the mindset or attitude needed to be successful. Philosophically, players and coaches should be on the same page. This section should be the compass or North Star to keep everyone working in the same direction. Teams that work at cross purposes will fail. What is expected from players and coaches? How should the game be played? What are the defensive goals and objectives? In an effort to answer those questions, this chapter will explore the following:

- Defensive philosophy
- Characteristics of a physical defense
- What the defensive team should be known for
- What is expected from players and coaches
- What makes a defense great
- Down-and-distance goals
- Play competency
- Defensive progression
- Principles of contact

- Great pursuit
- Elements of hustle
- What it takes to create turnovers
- Sudden change situations
- What is average
- Mental errors
- Defensive practice objectives
- Player enthusiasm

No matter the defensive structure (e.g., 4-3, 3-3, 4-2, 3-4, bend but don't break, or get-after-their-butt defense), these items are very important elements.

Defensive Philosophy

The number-one objective of any defense should be to stop the run, which is done by being very aggressive and physical. Defenses must be technique-sound, which will allow it to be gap-sound with run fits and foster sound coverages on the back end. Effective defenses mix in zone and man coverage along with blitz packages. The secondary must have highly effective man coverage skills, which enables the defense to load the box to stop the run and make the quarterback a target in the pass game. Great defenses have relentless pursuit because they understand angles and have a burning desire to get to the ball. Successful defenses have great communication skills so everyone will be on the same page. No man can be an island. Mental mistakes cannot be tolerated. Mental mistakes happen because of a lackadaisical attitude or poor practice habits. Players must play the defense called. Each defender must do his job. Defenders must play fast; they must play hard! They must be great tacklers and seek to punish and intimidate ballcarriers. They should seek to turn the ball over by attacking the ball, which will set up the offense or allow a defensive score.

Physical Defense

The essence of winning defense hinges on the ability and desire to outhit the opponent. More times than not, the most motivated and toughest team wins. Defensively, the two most important elements that affect the outcome of a game are striking and tackling. Have the philosophy that the defense will consistently stuff blockers and knock ballcarriers back. "Knock the pile backwards!" must be the motto.

Basic Principles of Physical Defense

- *Be quick:* Beat the opponent to the punch. Be strong and explosive.
- *Play low:* The low man wins. Develop leverage by using large muscle groups.

- *Strike:* Defeat the blocker with quickness and leverage.
- *Pursue relentlessly:* Physical defenses get to the ballcarrier as quickly as possible, and they get there in a bad mood.
- *Use good tackling fundamentals:* Keep the eyes up and open, keep the tail down, bend the knees keeping a good base, hit upward, and grab cloth. The face or shoulder should be on the ball. Tackle at ball level, hitting through the opponent. Make the football a target. Contact the near number of the ballcarrier, and slide the head across. Punish the ballcarrier.

What the Defense Should Be Known For

When people look at the defensive team, what do coaches and players want them to see? When someone reads a game account in the newspaper of a game, what mental picture do coaches and players want people to have? Following is a list of attributes to be instilled in the defensive unit:

- Play with pride.
- Play physically and mentally tough.
- Attack the line of scrimmage.
- Swarm to the ball.
- Be great tacklers.
- Play as a team.
- Execute when the pressure is on.
- Play with confidence.
- Be great communicators.
- Be fundamentally sound.
- Know what to do: alignment, assignment, and responsibility.
- Be great hustlers. The will to win is sometimes more important than the skill to win. A defensive player's worth is directly proportional to his distance from the football.
- Don't commit selfish penalties. Pre-snap and selfish penalties cannot be tolerated.

What Is Expected of Players

What do you, as the coach, expect from your players? What attributes and characteristics do you want them to possess? Some players may see the coach-player dynamic as adversarial. You, as the coach, must make it clear to the player what your expectations are and why you ask him to do the things you do. The player must believe that the coach has his best interest at heart and wants him to be the best player he can be. Coaches prepare players for game situations that will test their mettle. Coaches should expect players to do the following:

- Be mentally tough.
- Give great effort.
- Finish every play or practice rep.
- Be able to run and move.
- Be goal-oriented in running program. Players should know why they are conditioning. Quoting the great philosopher and poet, Bruce Springsteen, "The door's open, but the ride it ain't free." Players must pay the price to be successful.
- See light at the end of the tunnel. Players must know why they are being conditioned. Vince Lombardi said, "Fatigue makes cowards of us all." Fatigue causes mental errors, loafs, lack of toughness, and surrender.
- Be competitive.
- Be disciplined.
- Be coachable.
- Be consistent.
- Be dependable.
- Be committed.
- Be willing to invest time, not spend time.
- Learn from mistakes. Move on!
- Play with confidence.
- Be a warrior.

What Is Expected of Coaches

Coaches have to get across the point that they and the players are on the same team. Players must understand that the coach is a benefactor and not an adversary because coaches will demand players do things they may not want to do. Motivation, after all, is getting people to do work that may not want to do or give all-out effort when they may not want to. Coaches who demand discipline and sacrifice must demonstrate that they also are willing to sacrifice. It cannot be a one-way street! Coaches must not only "talk the talk, but must walk the walk." Effective coaches will do the following:

- Let players know what they are doing right and what they are doing wrong.
- Praise what players do correctly and correct mistakes. They will be honest with players.
- Do their best to help players improve as a football player and a person.
- Be well-prepared for practices and games to give players a chance to be successful.
- Be excited and enthusiastic.

Great Defense

When fans think of great defenses, they may have a mental picture of what that adjective means. Older fans may have a flash back to the "No-Name Defense" of the Dolphins and the "Steel Curtain" of the 1970s. Present-day fans may think of the Steelers, Patriots, or the Ravens. All great defenses have the following characteristics:

- *Give maximum effort:* Eleven men giving maximum effort every play of every game. Players supply this part.
- *Display toughness:* If players aren't physical, they can't play. Tennis might be a better fit. It takes courage to tackle.
- *Create togetherness:* Everyone has to trust the guy next to him. Players should trust each other to carry out assignments.
- *Develop great fundamentals:* Players learn how to play the game. Coaches supply this aspect.
- *Win the first down:* The defense allows only three yards or less on first downs.
- *Dominate the third down:* The defense must get off the field.
- *Win the field position battle:* The defense plays on the opponent's side of the field.
- *Limit YAC:* The defense keeps yards after contact on running plays and yards after catch on passes to a minimum.
- *Create turnovers.*
- *Score on defense.*

Down-and-Distance Goals

Every endeavor should have a goal or objective. Defenses must have a mindset or approach for every down. If a defense can meet the following goals for each down, it will be successful. Whenever teams scrimmage during spring ball and fall camp, they can incorporate down-and-distance and objectives in the huddle call. Doing so will make players focus and build a down-and-distance mindset. By the time a team starts the season, each player is indoctrinated to the point that down-and-distance calls are superfluous. Each player will know the situation and the goal:

- *First down:* Hold the offense to three yards or less.
- *Second down:* Hold the offense to half or less needed for first down.
- *Third down:* Get off the field.
- *Fourth down:* Take it personal.

Play Competency

Following are the three levels or stages of each football play. Practice progressions and schedules should be implemented with these levels in mind. Install protocol should take these steps into consideration.

- *Level One:* Alignment, assignment, stance, and first step. Three of these things occur before the ball is snapped. Of those three, two are mental. If coaches spend too much time on alignment and assignment, the defensive scheme may be too complicated.

- *Level Two:* Breaking on balls, taking on blocks, angles, and so forth. This step happens after Level One when the ball is snapped.
- *Level Three:* Interception, fumble, big hit, tackle, and such. This step is how a play ends. Levels Two and Three are post-snap. These levels should be the focus of practice time. Working on the first step plus Levels Two and Three requires teaching fundamentals and technique. The majority of precious practice time should be spent on those areas.

Defensive Progression

Following is the natural progression from pre-snap to the conclusion of the play. Valuable practice time should be spent on the following areas:

- Stance
- Attack—take on blocks
- Neutralize—control blocks
- Separate—escape blocks
- Run to the ball
- Tackle

Principles of Contact

There is an old saying that tackling is 90 percent desire and 10 percent technique. The following information covers the 10 percent technique. The listed coaching points will serve to enhance effective tackling technique. Players will become more effective and physical tacklers using these principles. Good hard tackling serves to further the goal of having a physical football team. A by-product of teaching proper tackling techniques and having those coaching points written in a playbook is to help the coach with the liability issue.

Tackling Phases

Come to Balance Phase

- Adjust stride relative to tackling situations.
- Sink the hips.
- Keep the back flat.
- Keep the head up.

Contact Phase

- Use same-side foot and shoulder on contact.
- Keep the knee in front of the ankle.

Rhythm of Contact Phase

- Roll off the front foot.
- Wrap on contact.
- Lift and run through contact.

Great Pursuit

All great defensive teams are classified as a gang tackling, aggressive, get-after-it unit, which has a sic 'em mentality. Players must understand that "want to" is the most important ingredient in pursuing the ball. Great pursuit doesn't require:

- Athletic ability
- Tremendous strength
- Scheme

    All great pursuit requires is:
- Tremendous effort (Have ball obsession.)
- Tail busting
- Getting off the ground (The ground is a hot stove.)
- Proper angles
- Not overrunning the play (Play inside-out or outside-in, whatever the assignment calls for.)
- Tackling with a purpose

What It Takes to Pursue

- Desire is the number-one requirement. If players want to, they can.
- Pursuit is foremost a mental task. Players should visualize making great plays.
- Physical conditioning is a necessity. Vince Lombardi said, "Fatigue makes cowards of us all." Players must be in shape to pursue.
- Speed, speed, speed. Players need to think fast. Knowing assignments can speed a player up or slow him down if he doesn't know them. Players need to improve physical speed, especially in the off-season.
- "Play fast, play hard" should be the players' motto.

Elements of Pursuing Correctly

- Defenders play responsibility first.
- Defenders take good angles to the ball.
- Again, desire is the number-one requirement.

What Pursuit Does

- Intimidates opponents
- Eliminates big plays
- Covers up mistakes
- Makes a unit a great defensive team
- Increases a team's chances of winning

Elements of Hustle

This section deals with the characteristics of what hustle looks like. This list can be used to grade a player when breaking down practice or game film:

- Change of speed
- Turning and bursting to the ball (Players should have a three-step change of speed.)
- Not being passed by another positional player
- Getting off the ground (The ground is a hot stove.)
- Making the hit on the ballcarrier
- Being in the picture when the film stops

Elements of a Loaf

The following traits of non-hustle can be used to identify players who have not bought into the balls-to-the-wall mentality:

- No change of speed
- Not turning and bursting to the ball
- No three-step change of speed
- Getting passed by another positional player
- Staying on the ground when knocked down
- Turning down a hit on the ballcarrier
- Not in the picture when the film stops

Loaf Prevention

An antidote to non-hustling is illustrated in Figure 1-1. This figure illustrates the hustle course. Loafs can be graded each game, selected scrimmages, or unit work, and if a player falls into any of the six elements of a loaf, the defensive team will run the hustle course one time per loaf. A scoop-and-score element can be added at the end. Understand that if a team loafed double-digit times, they probably got beat. Hustle is a habit!

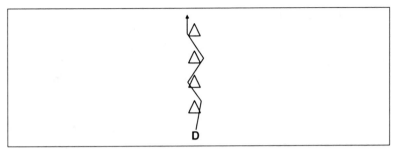
Figure 1-1. Antidote to non-hustling

Turnovers

Turnovers, for the most part, just don't happen. Occasionally, the ball might fall in a team's lap, but 99 percent of the time defenses are going to have to fight like heck to get the ball out. Following is the mental frame of mind and physical skills players need to turn the ball over. Practice time must be spent to hone the skills needed.

What It Takes Mentally for a Player to Create a Turnover

- Think turnovers. Creating turnovers is foremost a mental process.
- Believe. Make the football a target. If a player wants to create a turnover, he can.
- Be aware of turnover opportunities.
- Expect to create a turnover.

Turnover Techniques

- Practice fumble strip drills.
- Attempt to get a helmet or shoulder pad on the ball when making a tackle.
- Second man always goes for the ball. Leverage the tip of the ball.
- Practice interception drills. Catch the ball at the highest point.
- Practice tip drills. Be alert and ready to react.

What a Turnover Does

- Creates momentum
- Discourages opponents
- Gives the defense an opportunity to score
- Gives the offense an opportunity to score
- Makes a defensive team great

Interception Return Procedure

Having an organized interception return can win football games. Defenders should have a systematic procedure in place on interceptions to maximize the benefits to be gained. Instead of having a chaotic response, the defense has a great chance to score if an interception protocol is in place.

- An effective return rule is to return the ball to the nearest numbers. If the interception is in the middle of the field, the defender should return to the right.
- The defender should get the ball in the outside arm as soon as possible. He should not fumble it back to the opponent.
- The defender intercepting the ball will start up the field and then cut to the near numbers.
- The nearest defender blocks the intended receiver. He is the one most likely to make the tackle. The defensive line is responsible for blocking the quarterback. The quarterback is the second leading tackler on interceptions.
- Defenders return the ball at least 30 yards in practice.
- Defenses can score if everyone will hustle to the nearest numbers and pick out an opponent. Defenders should not clip, and should not throw an unnecessary block if the interceptor is on his way. They should not block below the waist.
- The defender should yell "Oskie" on an interception.
- If two defenders are covering one receiver, the one who is in position to intercept should yell, "Me, me!" This means "my ball." The other defender is ready for a deflected ball, to block, or to help in any way. By doing so, the defenders will not knock each other off, and will also increase interception chances.

Sudden Change Situations

Teams that win the turnover battle usually win the game. That is a given. However, how a team reacts to giving up the ball is also crucial. This section gives a winning approach to a sudden change situation. The prudent coach will incorporate sudden change situations into the practice schedule. Sudden change is the real test of a great defensive team. The score is 7-7 in the fourth quarter, and the defense has just stopped the opponent's offense on the defense's own 28-yard line. Defensive players have just sat down on the bench, they feel good and relieved. They have done their job and sure could use the rest. All of a sudden, the opponent's fans go crazy. The offense has just fumbled the ball back to the opponent. This is a sudden change situation! Is the defense going to feel sorry and roll over, or are they going to be aggressive? What must the defense do?

Sudden Change Definition

What is the definition of sudden change?

- After a fumble
- After an interception
- After a blocked punt or field goal
- After a long kickoff return or punt return
- After a failed fourth-down play

Sudden Change Coaching Points

- The defense should huddle up on the sideline before it goes back into the game.
- Defenders must gain control of their thoughts and get ready to play.
- Players should get other teammates mentally ready. Players cannot have a defeatist attitude or criticize the offensive team.
- Defenders must accept the challenge and remember that stopping the opponent now will give the psychological advantage to the defense.
- Each player must be determined to make the play.

What to Expect on the Next Offensive Play After a Turnover

- Long pass
- Trick play

Characteristics of Being Average

Obviously, being average is not desirable. Players should avoid being average. Average means:

- Getting blocked
- Staying blocked
- Making a tackle with "help"
- Slowing the runner while allowing him extra yardage
- Not carrying out assignments because a player misinterpreted what he saw
- Getting tired
- Not hustling
- Permitting a big offensive play
- Falling or slipping down

Mental Errors

Mental errors are inexcusable. Players must be able to concentrate on assignments and carry those assignments out on each and every play. Mental errors happen when players have a lack of concentration and a lax attitude during the week of preparation for the game. Concentration, self-pride, and team confidence are the best ways to combat any chance of a mental error. Players must refuse to allow anything or anyone to disturb or distract concentration. They should avoid being the weak link and letting down their teammates.

Practice Objectives

Games are truly won or lost in practice. What are practice expectations? Following are some worthy expectations for players:

- Effort is the number-one expectation. Effort has nothing to do with ability.
- Players should practice the way they expect to play on game day.
- Players should get better every day. Players don't stay the same. A player either gets better or worse. Players should not waste a practice or rep.
- Players should narrow their vision. They must see only what concerns them; they must not see too much.
- Players should practice full speed and be enthusiastic.
- Players should have a willingness to hit (i.e., be a big dog, not a puppy).
- Players should finish every play.
- Players should not play down to the scout team.
- Players should give maximum effort in every drill. A player can rest while waiting in line.
- Players should exaggerate lowness during practice (i.e., be a knee-bender).
- Players should not get lazy.
- Players should communicate. Players had better get the call. They must talk pre- and post-snap.
- Players should practice strips on ballcarriers and receivers.
- Players should collision receivers that come through their assigned zone.
- Players should go full-speed through the ball on passes. They should return interceptions for 30 yards.
- Players should learn something every practice. They must have and know the objectives of each practice: what is the goal?
- Players should focus on daily, weekly, and seasonal goals.

Player Enthusiasm

What It Takes to Be Enthusiastic

- Is the player having fun? If a player is not having fun, he may be in the wrong sport.
- Mental discipline will get players into the right frame of mind.
- Players can't be enthusiastic if they lack confidence.

How to Play Enthusiastically

- Give maximum effort in every drill and play. Develop good practice habits.
- Players should be positive. They should encourage teammates. They should want to be someone teammates want to be around.
- Give all to the team. Don't hold back.
- Celebrate with teammates after a big hit, turnover, or big play.

What Enthusiasm Does

- Motivates teammates
- Gets the fans behind the team
- Discourages and intimidates opponents
- Makes the defense great

2

Fingerprinting the Offense

Included in every playbook should be a breakdown of the opposing side of the football. Offensive playbooks should include an overview of defenses, their characteristics, personnel, coverages, and so forth. Conversely, defenses should generically break down offensive schemes. This chapter will establish a uniform nomenclature to describe an opponent's offensive personnel, personnel groupings, formations, shifts, motion, blocking schemes, pass trees, pass protections, and such. This nomenclature will allow coaches to communicate with other coaches and players in a clinical setting as well as on the sideline during a game with bullets flying and time is of the essence. The ultimate language would be to use as much terminology as possible from the defensive team's offensive system. This would allow carryover from one side of the ball to the other. Included in Chapter 2 are the following:

- Offensive personnel groups
- Offensive player identification
- Formation identification
- Backfield identification
- Numbering eligible receivers
- Receiver deviations
- Receiver motions
- Shifts
- Run actions
- Pass actions

- Receiver passing tree
- Tight end passing tree
- Running back passing tree

Offensive Personnel Groups

This system allows defensive coaches to identify the offensive personnel group in the game. Knowing the type of offensive personnel in the game will allow defensive coaches to make an educated guess as to the type of formation and play they will see so the defensive coach can match defensive personnel with offensive personnel and craft an effective defensive call. Backs are listed first, with tight ends listed second. Subtract the number of backs and tight ends from five, and that number will tell coaches and players the number of receivers. Example: 21 personnel = 2 backs, 1 tight end, 2 receivers. Refer to Table 2-1.

Grouping	Backs	Tight Ends	Receivers
00	0	0	5
01	0	1	4
10	1	0	4
11	1	1	3
12	1	2	2
13	1	3	1
20	2	0	3
21	2	1	2
22	2	2	1
23	2	3	0
30	3	0	2
31	3	1	1
32	3	2	0

Table 2-1. Offensive personnel groups

Offensive Player Identification

Each offensive position should be given a name, which allows the defense to identify a particular offensive player.

Regular Personnel (Figure 2-1)

F: Fullback
QB: Quarterback

T: Tailback
X: Split end
Y: Tight end
Z: Flanker (off the line receiver)

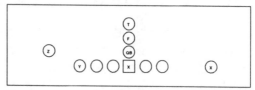
Figure 2-1. Regular personnel

Substitute Back and Receiver Designations

H: Third back in a three-back set
R: Fourth receiver
S: Third receiver
U: Second tight end
V: Third tight end

Formation Identification (Figures 2-2 through 2-13)

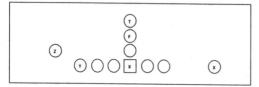
Figure 2-2. Pro

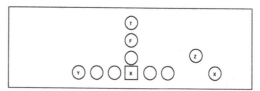
Figure 2-3. Slot

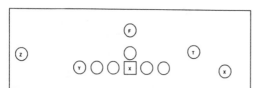
Figure 2-4. Spread

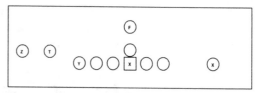
Figure 2-5. Trey

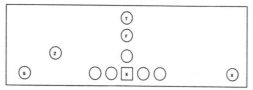
Figure 2-6. Three wides

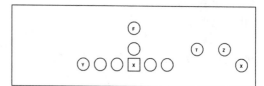
Figure 2-7. Trips closed

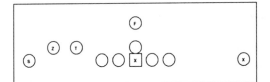

Figure 2-8. Trips open

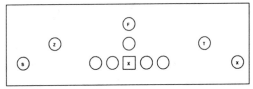

Figure 2-9. Doubles

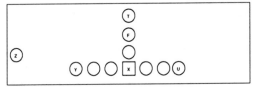

Figure 2-10. Flanker

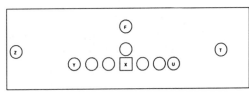

Figure 2-11. Tech

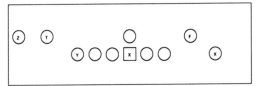

Figure 2-12. Empty trey

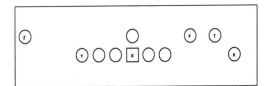

Figure 2-13. Empty spread

Backfield Identification

Numbers are used to show back alignments. A single number is used for one-back sets. A double-digit number is used for two-back sets, and, obviously, three digits tag a three-back set. Figure 2-14 shows the possible positioning of backs. Figure 2-15 gives an example of identifying a one-back set. This is a gun 2 set. A weak I set (54) is shown in Figure 2-16. Figure 2-17 shows a power I three-back set (234).

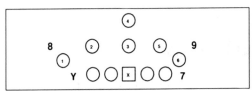

Figure 2-14. Possible positioning of backs

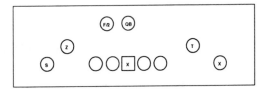

Figure 2-15. Gun 2 set

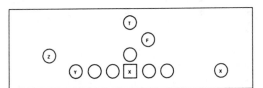

Figure 2-16. Weak I set (54)

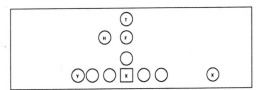

Figure 2-17. Power I three-back set (234)

Numbering Eligible Receivers

Numerically labeling eligible receivers is desirable when discussing coverage responsibilities. Eligible receivers are numbered outside-in from the widest to the center (Figure 2-18). Different offensive maneuvers, however, can affect a particular receiver's number. Motion can change a receiver's number. In case of motion, the defense will have to recount. Receivers in close proximity will require a banjo call. A banjo call is an alert between defenders that receivers may cross. The defense will have to sort it out post-snap. Figure 2-19 illustrates how offensive personnel can change numbers post-snap. F can be #2 or #3, depending upon his and Y's release. A banjo call would alert the defense to this possibility. Stacked receivers also present a counting problem. In Figure 2-20, the defense must sort it out as the receivers release. The defense must also have a system for stacked receivers who distribute to the same side. In Figure 2-21, the receiver closest to the line of scrimmage is given the smaller number.

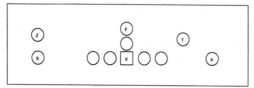

Figure 2-18. Eligible receivers numbered outside-in from the widest to the center

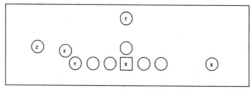

Figure 2-19. Number change post-snap

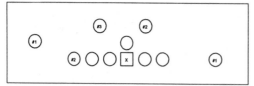

Figure 2-20. Stacked receivers numbering

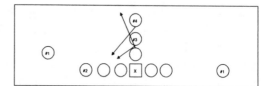

Figure 2-21. Same-side stacked receivers numbering

Receiver Deviations

Receivers don't always align in "normal" positions. They will vary their alignments for a variety of reasons. Adjusting position might gain the offense an advantage on a pass release or blocking assignment. Following are some receiver alignment deviations. Figures 2-22 through 2-24 show the X-receiver's abnormal alignments. X's normal alignment is seven or more yards from the offensive tackle. Figure 2-22 shows X over. X aligns on the same side as Y. Figure 2-23 illustrates X tight. X aligns one yard or less from the offensive tackle. Figure 2-24 illustrates X nasty. X aligns two to six yards from the offensive tackle. Figures 2-25 through 2-29 show Y's possible alignments. Y's normal alignment is one yard outside the offensive tackle and on the line of scrimmage. Figure 2-25 shows Y off. Y aligns outside the offensive tackle, but off the line of scrimmage. Figure 2-26 shows Y nasty. Y lines up two to five yards from the offensive tackle. Figure

2-27 shows Y flex. Y is six or more yards from the offensive tackle. Figure 2-28 signifies YOZ. Y aligns outside Z. Figure 2-29 shows Y backfield. Y lines up in the backfield at a running back position. Figures 2-30 through 2-32 shows Z's deviations. Z's normal alignment is seven or more yards from Y. Figure 2-30 illustrates Z wing. Z is one to two yards outside the offensive tackle off the line of scrimmage. Figure 2-31 illustrates Z close. Z lines up three to six yards outside the offensive tackle. Figure 2-32 shows Z backfield. Z lines up in a backfield position.

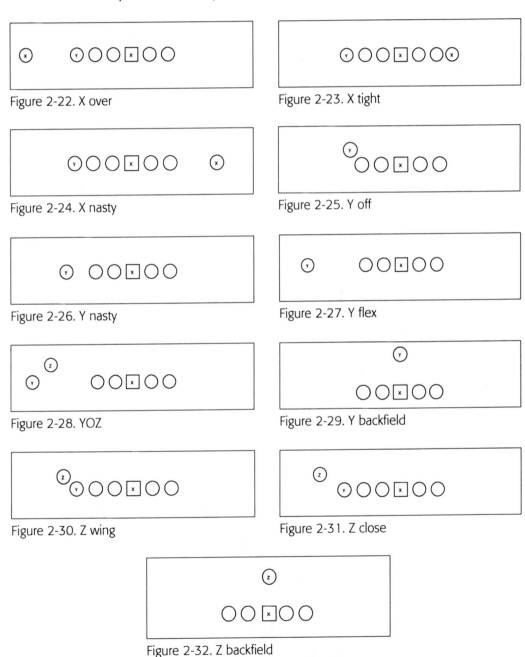

Figure 2-22. X over

Figure 2-23. X tight

Figure 2-24. X nasty

Figure 2-25. Y off

Figure 2-26. Y nasty

Figure 2-27. Y flex

Figure 2-28. YOZ

Figure 2-29. Y backfield

Figure 2-30. Z wing

Figure 2-31. Z close

Figure 2-32. Z backfield

Motion

Nomenclature for motion must be established. Motion forces the defense to adjust whether it is in man or zone. Different types of motion are explored and each offensive position has a label should they be the motion man. Motion is tagged by position.

Across-the-Ball Motion (Figure 2-33)

F: F across
R: R across
S: S across
T: T across
U: U across
V: V across
X: X across
Y: Y across
Z: Z across

Figure 2-33. Across-the-ball motion

Motion Past the Offensive Tackle With Intentions on Blocking a Defender in the Box (Figure 2-34)

F: Fap
R: Rap
S: Sap
T: Tap
U: Pap
V: Vap
X: Jap
Y: Yap
Z: Zap

Figure 2-34. Motion past the offensive tackle

Motion Across the Ball With Depth (Figure 2-35)

F: Farc
R: Rarc
S: Sarc
T: Tarc
U: Parc
V: Varc
X: Jarc
Y: Yarc
Z: Zarc

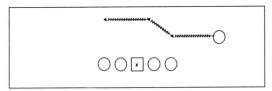

Figure 2-35. Motion across the ball with depth

Motion In, Then Out, and Then Back Across the Ball (Figure 2-36)

F: Fig
R: Rig
S: Sig
T: Tig
U: Pig
V: Vig
X: Jig
Y: Yig
Z: Zig

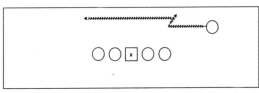

Figure 2-36. Motion in, then out, and then back across the ball

Motion to the Fringe of the Tackle Box (Figure 2-37)

This motion is usually used to block the end-of-the-line defender, crack a second-level defender, or run a crossing route. Also, it can be used on zone-type plays to the opposite side.

F: Fing

R: Ring

S: Sing

T: Ting

U: Ping

V: Ving

X: Jing

Y: Ying

Z: Zing

Figure 2-37. Motion to the fringe of the tackle box

Motion From the Backfield (Figure 2-38)

F: Fon, followed by snap formation (For example, Fon to trey. If F motions but stays in the box the motion is called shuffle and then the backfield set. For example, shuffle to weak I.)

R: Room

S: Soom

T: Ton, followed by snap formation (For example, Ton to spread.)

U: Poom

V: Voom

X: Joom

Y: Yoom

Z: Zoom

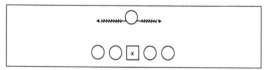

Figure 2-38. Motion from the backfield

Motion In and Back Out (Figure 2-39)

F: F Orbit
R: R Orbit
S: S Orbit
T: T Orbit
U: U Orbit
V: V Orbit
X: X Orbit
Y: Y Orbit
Z: Z Orbit

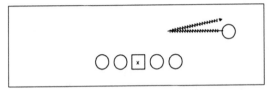

Figure 2-39. Motion in and back out

Motion Away From the Core of the Formation (Figure 2-40)

F: F out
R: R out
S: S out
T: T out
U: U out
V: V out
X: X out
Y: Y out
Z: Z out

Figure 2-40. Motion away from the core of the formation

Back-in-the-Box Motion (Figures 2-41 and 2-42)

This motion doesn't leave the tackle box.

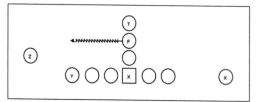

Figure 2-41. Fly motion to the tight end or strength side

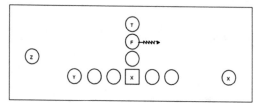

Figure 2-42. Peel motion away from the tight end or strength side

Shifts

Offensive maneuvers may include offensive skill players lining up in one place, and then moving to another. This technique is used to cause defensive confusion or recognition problems. Figures 2-43 though 2-45 show a variety of pre-snap movements from one position to another. Figure 2-43 has a tight end trade from one side to another. Figure 2-44 illustrates a two or more offensive men movement pre-snap, which is called scramble. Scramble followed by motion is called scatter (Figure 2-45).

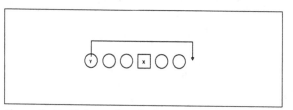

Figure 2-43. Tight end trade from one side to another

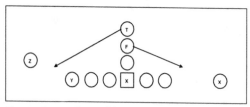

Figure 2-44. Scramble

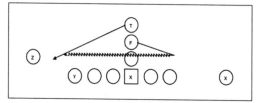

Figure 2-45. Scatter

Run Actions

Action to the tight end is called flow run (Figure 2-46). Action away from the tight end is called flood run (Figure 2-47). Backs going in opposite directions on the snap is called a divide run (Figure 2-48). When both backs start in the same direction, and then the ballcarrier redirects usually accompanied by pulling linemen, is called a counter run (Figure 2-49).

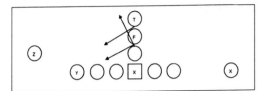
Figure 2-46. Flow run

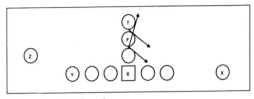
Figure 2-47. Flood run

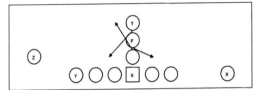
Figure 2-48. Divide run

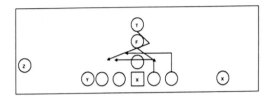
Figure 2-49. Counter run

Pass Actions

Following are the various pass actions most teams have in their playbook.

60 Series (Figures 2-50 through 2-55)

The quarterback executes roll or sprint passes.

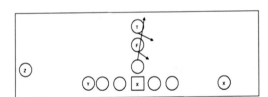
Figure 2-50. 61—half roll to the openside

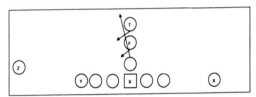
Figure 2-51. 62—half roll to the closed side

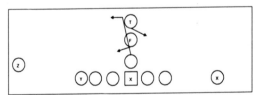
Figure 2-52. 66—backs divide with pull up to the closed side

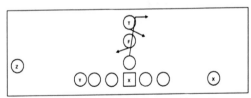
Figure 2-53. 67—backs divide with pull up to the openside

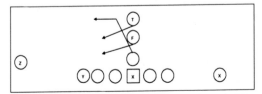
Figure 2-54. 68—full sprint to the closed side

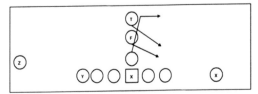
Figure 2-55. 69—full sprint to the openside

100 Series: Play-Action Passes (Figures 2-56 through 2-58)

The quarterback throws a pass after a run fake.

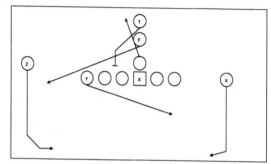

Figure 2-56. Fire: Play-action strong with the quarterback in the box and the tight end on a drag

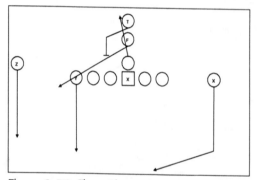

Figure 2-57. Flow: Play-action strong with the quarterback in the box and the tight end on a seam

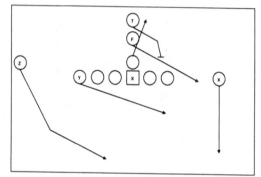

Figure 2-58. Flood: Play-action weak with the quarterback in the box and the tight end on a drag

200 Series (Figure 2-59)

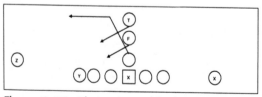

Figure 2-59. Play-action with the quarterback leaving the box

300 Series: Boots (Figures 2-60 through 2-63)

Boots are play-action passes with the quarterback going opposite the run fake.

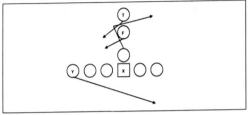

Figure 2-60. Power boot

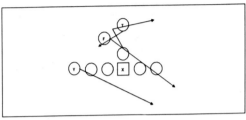

Figure 2-61. Packer boot

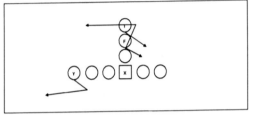

Figure 2-62. Belly boot

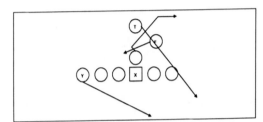

Figure 2-63. Niner boot

400 Series (Figure 2-64)

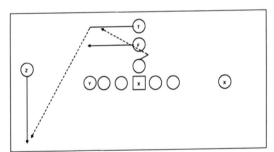

Figure 2-64. Running back throws off run action

500 Series: Screens (Figure 2-65)

The first digit identifies the play as a screen. The second digit identifies the back or receiver. If the back is the recipient of the screen, give the number of his position. If a receiver is involved, give his designation. The third digit gives the point of attack. Since most screens are attempted behind the line of scrimmage, list the point of attack using run hole designations. Also, identify the screen with descriptive terms such as slip, quick, read, flare, middle, bubble, and such.

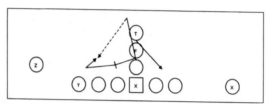

Figure 2-65. 538 slip screen

600 Series: Dashes (Figures 2-66 through 2-71)

Dash passes occur when the quarterback drops straight back then rolls or sprints to the corner.

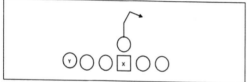

Figure 2-66. 631—three-step dash to the openside

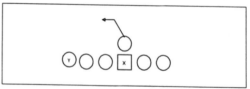

Figure 2-67. 632—three-step dash to the closed side

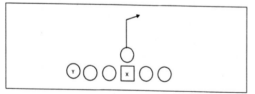

Figure 2-68. 651—five-step dash to the openside

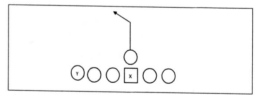

Figure 2-69. 652—five-step dash to the closed side

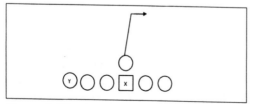

Figure 2-70. 671—seven-step dash to the openside

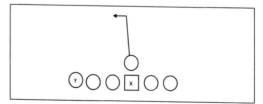

Figure 2-71. 672—seven-step dash to the closed side

800 Series: Level-Three Passes (Figures 2-72 through 2-80)

The quarterback drops straight back on his pass drop.

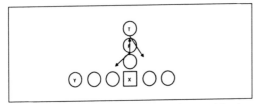

Figure 2-72. 830—three-step drop with the backs on a divide

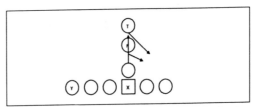

Figure 2-73. 831—three-step drop with the backs to the openside

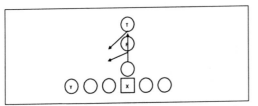

Figure 2-74. 832—three-step drop with the backs to the closed side

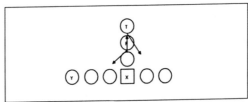

Figure 2-75. 850—five-step drop with the backs on a divide

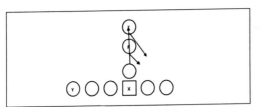

Figure 2-76. 851—five-step drop with the backs to the openside

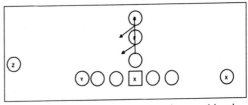

Figure 2-77. 852—five-step drop with the backs to the closed side

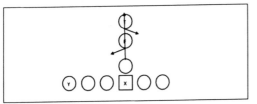

Figure 2-78. 870—seven-step drop with the backs on a divide

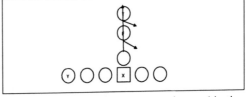

Figure 2-79. 871—seven-step drop with the backs to the openside

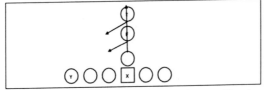

Figure 2-80. 872—seven-step drop with the backs to the closed side

Receiver Passing Tree

This section displays the basic routes for the receivers. Figure 2-81 illustrates routes for X and Z. Z illustrates outside routes. Also, the skinny post route is shown. X illustrates inside routes. Also, X illustrates a snag route. Z could run the same routes.

A: Outside quick
B: Out
C: Comeback
D: Corner
E: Skinny post
F: Takeoff
G: Inside quick
H: Slant
I: Snag
J: Hook curl
K: In
L: Post

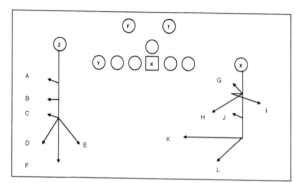

Figure 2-81. Receiver passing tree

Tight End Passing Tree

Y is shown running outside routes, and U is illustrated on inside routes (Figure 2-82).

A: Flat
B: Out
C: Corner
D: Takeoff
E: Cross
F: Hook curl
G: In
H: Post

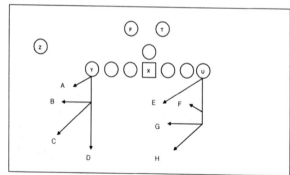

Figure 2-82. Tight end passing tree

Running Back Passing Tree

F shows inside cuts, while T demonstrates outside cuts (Figure 2-83).

A: Angle
B: Cross
C: In
D: Post
E: Takeoff
F: Flare
G: Option
H: Out
I: Wheel
J: Corner

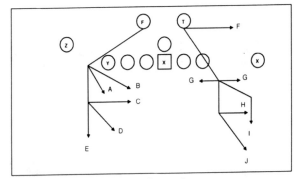

Figure 2-83. Running back passing tree

3

Defensive System and Terminology

This chapter deals with the basic setup and workings of the defense used in this playbook. These pre-snap organizational issues include the following:

- Defensive personnel identification
- Substitution packages
- Gap labeling
- Alignment labeling
- Huddle procedure
- Communicating defensive checkoffs
- Close (strength declarations) rules
- Defensive practice notes

Defensive Personnel Identification

The base front is a 4-3 configuration. The two defensive tackles and two defensive ends are designated left and right tackles and ends. Unless the defense can gain a match-up advantage, there will be no flip-flop. For stunt purposes, when the offense breaks the huddle and Mike makes the strength call, the end to the strength call becomes Stud and the tackle to the call becomes tackle. The end away from the call is designated as the end, and the tackle away from the call is tagged as the nose. The outside linebackers do flip-flop. The outside linebacker to the call is Will. The weakside outside linebacker is Sam, and the middle linebacker is Mike. Many defensive systems denote Will as the weak outside linebacker and Sam as the strong outside linebacker. Many of the concepts in this playbook reflect a Monte Kiffin influence, including player identification. The safety to the call is the strong safety, while the safety to the weakside is the free safety. Figure 3-1 illustrates defensive positions with a left call. Following are positions and the symbols that will be used through the remainder of this playbook:

- S: Stud (end to the call)
- T: Tackle (tackle to the call)
- N: Nose (tackle away from the call)
- E: End (end away from the call)
- W: Will (outside linebacker to the call)
- M: Mike (middle linebacker)
- S: Sam (outside linebacker away from the call)
- SS: Strong safety (safety to the call)
- FS: Free safety (safety away from the call)
- C: Corner (The corner to the right would be the right corner, and the corner to the left would be the left corner.)

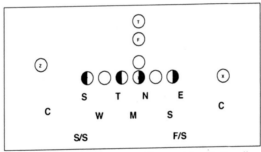

Figure 3-1. Defensive positions with a left call

Substitution Packages

- *Nickel:* Defensive back for Will
- *Dime:* Defensive back for Sam
- *Quarter:* Defensive back for Mike
- *Mustang:* 3-3-5 look. A fifth defensive back, Rover, comes in for a defensive lineman.
- *NASCAR:* Four speed rushers are used on the defensive line. It may consist of four ends or a mix of linemen and linebackers.

Gap Labeling

Gaps are areas between offensive linemen (Figure 3-2). Following are gap definitions and the type of offensive plays commonly used to attack those gaps:

- *A gap:* Area from the near leg of the center to the outside leg of the guard. Commonly used plays in this area are traps, cutbacks, midline option, isolations, and draw-type plays.
- *B gap:* Area from the outside leg of the guard to the outside leg of the tackle. Plays tailored for this area include zone plays, veer options, and isolations.
- *C gap:* Area from the outside leg of the tackle to the outside leg of a tight end. If there is no tight end, the area would extend to the nearest receiver. Plays used in this area include power-type plays and is the domain of counters.
- *D gap:* Area from the outside leg of the tight end all the way to the sideline or the nearest receiver. The intention of the offense here is to outflank the defense. Plays include quick pitches, sweeps, lead options, sprint passes, and reverses.

Figure 3-2. Gap labeling

Plus gaps are to the strength call, with minus signifying gaps away from the strength. Designations change if a defender is backside of a play. These gaps are considered cutback gaps. For example, on a flow run in cover 2, Sam is responsible for cutback B. (Figure 3-3). Gaps are assigned for every defensive front. Gap designations assign gap, option, force, fill, cutback, and pass rush responsibilities. Defenders must understand that their gap may expand or contract according to the offensive blocking scheme. For example, a reach block on a 3 technique would serve to widen the B gap, while a down block by the guard would cause the 3 technique to squeeze to the A gap.

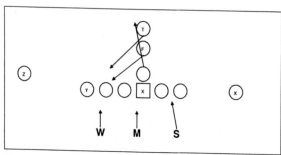

Figure 3-3. Cutback B

Alignment Labeling

Alignments are given numerical designations, which gives defensive linemen reference points for their alignments and also gives them gap assignments (Figure 3-4). These designations can also be used for two-point players such as linebackers and safeties. Simply add a 0 to the alignment for those players. For example, if Will lines up off the ball on the outside shoulder of the offensive tackle, he is in a 50 technique. Shades include outside, inside, and head-up alignments.

Figure 3-4. Alignment labeling

Outside Shades

- *1 technique:* Shade on the center. If to the call, the defender will be in a plus 1 shade. If the shade is to the weakside, he is referred to as a minus 1 shade.
- *3 technique:* Defender's inside foot splits the guard's crotch.
- *5 technique:* Defender's inside foot splits the tackle's crotch.
- *9 technique:* Defender's inside foot splits the tight end's crotch.

Inside Shades

- *2 technique:* Defender's outside foot splits the guard's crotch.
- *4 technique:* Defender's outside foot splits the tackle's crotch.
- *7 technique:* Defender's outside foot splits the tight end's crotch.

Head-Up Alignments

Only two head-up alignments are used to play technique. Head-up alignments are also used with slants.

- *0 technique:* Head-up on the center. Used in the mustang package. From the 0, the nose can two-gap or slant.
- *6 technique:* Stud is head-up on the tight end. Used with the Ohio front, rifle call in goal line, and to butch the tight end.

Numbering is the same on both sides of the ball. The base rule on alignment is the defender's designated foot is down the offensive man's crotch. However, there are nuances to each shade assignment. A wide adjustment puts the defender's designated foot on the offensive lineman's foot and not the crotch. A jet call places the defender's outside foot outside the offensive man's foot. This places the defender in a pass rush mode. These variations are used for a variety of reasons. Talent level, scouting report, down-and-distance, and game situation are all reasons to vary the shade.

Huddle Procedure

There are as many huddle protocols as there are coaches. The huddle procedure described in this section is a hanging huddle. This informal, yet efficient, structure allows the defense to better play no-huddle or uptempo offenses. Figure 3-5 illustrates the hanging huddle. In this huddle structure, Mike faces the defense as he gets the call from the sideline. Mike is the prime communicator. He will give the offensive personnel grouping, front, stunt, and coverage. If Mike is not clear or unsure of the sideline call, he will tap his facemask. If any player is unsure of Mike's call, he will tap his facemask and yell, "Check, check!" Will and the strong safety will line up to the left. Sam and the free safety will line up to the right. The corner away from the defensive bench will search the opponent's sideline for trick plays. The corner to the defensive bench looks to the sideline for instructions. The strong safety will give the down-and-distance. All players know the goal for the down-and-distance situation:

- *First down:* Hold the offense to three yards or less.
- *Second down:* Hold the offense to half the yardage needed for a first down or less.
- *Third down:* Get off the field.
- *Fourth down:* Take it personal!

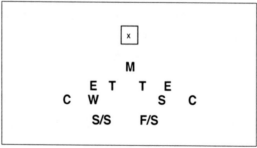

Figure 3-5. Hanging huddle

Will and Sam will eyeball the offensive tackle to their side in the huddle for tackle over formations. Mike gives the strength call as the offense breaks the huddle. Even though it is Mike's job to make the strength call, it is everyone's responsibility to know the strength call. Mike will make a right or left call to denote strength. As Mike verbally makes the call, he will also point to the strongside. After Mike makes the strength call, he will call out the backfield set. The corners will verbally and visually communicate the number of receivers to their side. For example, with two receivers to the right side, the right corner will say "two right" and show two fingers. The free safety will call out the formation.

Example of Huddle Communication

In the huddle:
- Strong safety: "First and 10"
- Mike: "21, over 8, over 8"
- Everyone claps and says, "Black shirts."

At the line of scrimmage:
- Mike: "Right, right—I, I"
- Right corner: "Two right" (showing two fingers)
- Free safety: "Pro right"
- Everyone checks for tips (e.g., stances, splits, etc.).

Note: Everyone should be familiar with the defensive signals.

Communicating Defensive Checkoffs

Defense would be so much easier if defensive coaches could make a call and the offense would come out in a vanilla look. That isn't reality in today's game. A great majority of the time, the defense is going to have to adjust the call or in some cases change the call completely. Defenses, as a result, must be able to efficiently and smoothly communicate. Following is a short list of defensive responsibilities regarding checkoffs:
- Will and Sam must read their offensive tackle in the offensive huddle so the defense has early recognition of unbalanced or tackle over sets.
- Everyone is responsible for recognizing "exotic" formations and front or coverage changes.
- Linebackers and secondary give verbal and visual signals. Everyone must be on the same page. Eliminate any possible errors by having players talk to each other.
- Mike must make any front adjustment. He calls "Check it," and gives the new call twice.
- All changes must be made quickly. This requires concentration and communication by everyone. There are no secrets on defense!

Close Rules

Effective strength declaration is paramount to good defense. The defense must not allow the offense to gain an advantage because of unsound positioning of the defense. Strength declaration is Mike's responsibility. Mike will make a right call for strength to the right, and a left call when formation strength is to the left. As a basic rule, if all things are equal, he should declare strength to the wideside of the field. If things are equal and the ball is in the middle of the field, he should declare to the defense's left because most offenses are right-handed. Close calls can vary according to the defensive package. Following are defensive packages and their respective close rules:

- *Cover 8:* To the tight end. If no tight end, go to receiver numbers.
- *Cover 2:* To the tight end. If no tight end, go to receiver numbers.
- *Cover China:* To the tight end. If no tight end, go to receiver numbers.
- *Cover black:* To the tight end. If no tight end, go to receiver numbers.
- *Cover 0:* Declare to receiver numbers.
- *Cover 4:* With Will, Mike, Sam, free safety, and strong safety stunts, declare to the tight end. If no tight end present, go to receiver numbers.
- *Cover 4:* Cobra and viper stunts. Go to receiver numbers.
- *Peel blitzes:* Declare to receiver numbers.
- *Goal line:* Tight end and wing.
- *Mustang:* Declare to receiver numbers.

   Note: Always declare to a 3x1 or 3x2 set.

Defensive Practice Notes

Following are some principles and fundamentals that should be followed when establishing foundationally sound practice organization:
- Fundamentals are more important than schemes. Schemes are no good if players can't run, defeat blocks, and tackle.
- Use two-a-days to master physical techniques. The mental aspect of the playbook should already be installed before donning pads.
- Use fast tempo-type practices. This tends to make practice flow, increases functional conditioning, and maximizes repetitions. Also, it prepares the defense for up-tempo offenses.
- Walk-through is better than board work.
- Review the tougher looks (e.g., empty, tight bunch, quads, etc.).
- Quiz players. Use oral and written tests on alignment and assignment.
- Coach effort. Demand great effort. Reward hustle, and punish loafs.
- Emphasize the importance of individual roles. Foster a mindset of: "Do your job!"
- "Play fast; play hard" should be the motto.

4

Fronts

This chapter will serve to illustrate the base defensive fronts used in the playbook. Included will be individual line stunts, coordinated line stunts, and lane exchanges. Base pass rush concepts are explored as well as pass rush techniques and stunts. The chapter ends with the ultimate get-after-the-quarterback package: the green package. Following are the base defensive fronts used in the playbook.

Base Fronts (Figures 4-1 through 4-7)

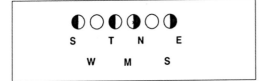

Figure 4-1. Over

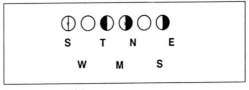

Figure 4-2. Ohio

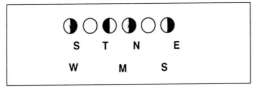

Figure 4-3. Oregon

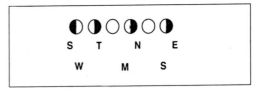

Figure 4-4. Wide

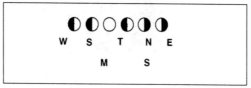

Figure 4-5. Under

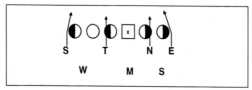

Figure 4-6. Green, automatic jet

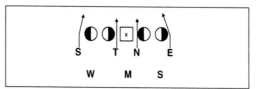

Figure 4-7. Yellow, automatic jet

G Fronts (Figures 4-8 through 4-12)

The over, Ohio, Oregon, wide, and under fronts can be tagged with a G call. This tag changes the 1 technique to a 2 technique.

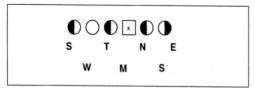

Figure 4-8. Over G

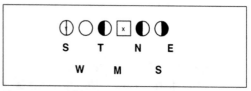

Figure 4-9. Ohio G

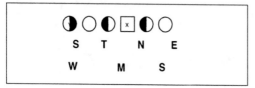

Figure 4-10. Oregon G

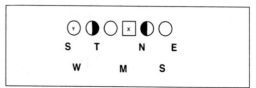

Figure 4-11. Wide G

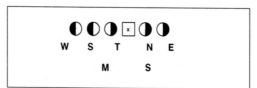

Figure 4-12. Under G

Line Games

Defensive linemen may align in a particular shade and, on the snap, slant to another gap. This technique is called a stick (Figure 4-13). Sticks are an integral part of the stunt package. A stick is a one-gap move. On a stick, the attack step is short and quick at a 40-degree angle. The heel on the backside foot stays behind the toe (square step). The defender's eyes go to the near hip of the offensive man he is sticking to. If play flow is inside the stick, the defender will flatten and take a good pursuit angle. Should play flow be outside the stick, the defender will "bumper car" to a good pursuit angle. The defender, on a stick, will go under any base, reach, or pass set. If the offensive man is blocking down, the defender will close off his hip, looking to attack and spill. A two-gap stick is called a long stick (Figure 4-14). A three-gap move is called a big stick (Figure 4-15).

Figure 4-13. Stick

Figure 4-14. Long stick

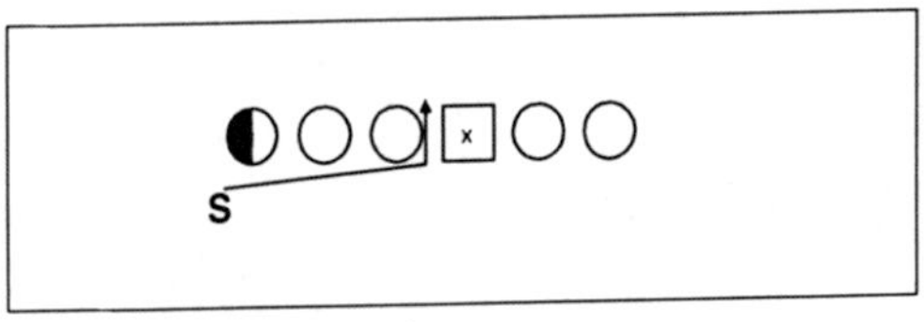

Figure 4-15. Big stick

One-Man Line Stunts (Figures 4-16 through 4-24)

The following individual lineman stunts may or may not include a linebacker insert or be part of a coordinated stunt.

Figure 4-16. Stud

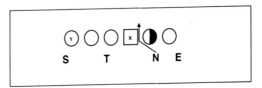

Figure 4-17. Blast

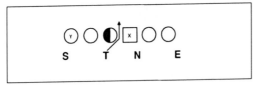

Figure 4-18. Spike

Figure 4-19. Nail

Figure 4-20. Hammer

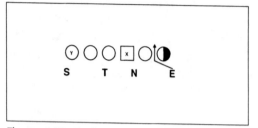

Figure 4-21. End

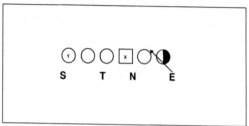

Figure 4-22. End it

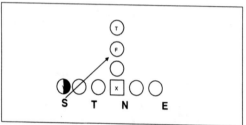

Figure 4-23. Fullback

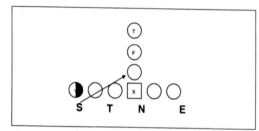

Figure 4-24. Quarterback

Coordinated Line Stunts (Figures 4-25 through 4-30)

The following stunts include more than one defensive lineman and may or may not include linebackers or secondary members:

- *Pirate* (Figure 4-25): The nose will wrap and assume cage responsibility to the strongside on pass plays.
- *Robber* (Figure 4-26)
- *Pistol* (Figure 4-27): The Stud is on an end it.
- *Switch* (Figure 4-28)
- *Stab* (Figure 4-29)
- *Cram* (Figure 4-30)

Figure 4-25. Pirate

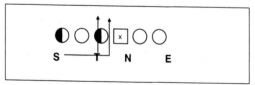

Figure 4-26. Robber

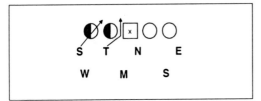

Figure 4-27. Pistol

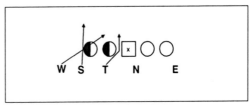

Figure 4-28. Switch

Figure 4-29. Stab

Figure 4-30. Cram

Change-Ups (Figures 4-31 through 4-37)

The following plays are not stunts per se, but are change-ups in line charges:

- *Jet* (Figure 4-31): All linemen are on an upfield charge.
- *Gap* (Figure 4-32): The linemen align in the gap to the shade side and get vertical.
- *Heads* (Figure 4-33): The tackles align head-up and stick to the called front.
- *Heads Over Call* (Figure 4-34)
- *Heads Under Call* (Figure 4-35)
- *Opposite* (Figure 4-36): The linemen align in the opposite shade and stick to the called front. This figure shows an over opposite call.
- *Radar* (Figure 4-37): The linemen align in a two-point stance, move around, and attack the called alignment. This figure shows a radar over call. Any front or stunt may be tagged with a radar call.

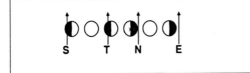

Figure 4-31. Jet

Figure 4-32. Gap

Figure 4-33. Heads

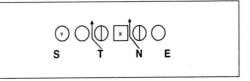

Figure 4-34. Heads over call

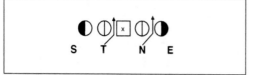

S T N E

Figure 4-35. Heads under call

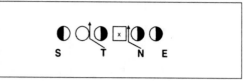

S T N E

Figure 4-36. Opposite

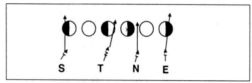

S T N E

Figure 4-37. Radar

Pass Rush Objectives

Obviously, a major responsibility for defensive linemen is to rush the passer. As in any endeavor, attitude is crucial. The correct attitude must be instilled and nurtured by the coach. The coach must define success. If players think the only definition of pass rush success is a sack, a lot of players are going to be disappointed. Players must understand that success can mean many things. Following is a list of possible successful objectives for rushers:

- Squeeze the quarterback's area. The ends attack his upfield shoulder. The tackles attack the near number. Force him closer to another rusher.
- Don't allow the quarterback to go to the second receiver.
- Force him out of the launch point. However, contain an athletic quarterback.
- Force the quarterback to throw on the run.
- Make the quarterback aware of pressure.
- Make the quarterback lose confidence in his protection.
- Inside rushers push the pocket to reduce the quarterback's ability to step up. Outside rushers force the quarterback to step up.
- Sack the quarterback.
- The ultimate contribution is the trifecta. Sack the quarterback, make him fumble, and scoop and score.

Even if a rusher cannot get to the quarterback, he can still be beneficial to an effective pass rush. A rusher simply getting his hands up is a benefit to the rush. The objectives when getting the hands up include:

- Divert the quarterback's attention.
- Bat the ball down.
- Tip the ball for an interception.
- Force a bad throw.

- Force the quarterback to tuck the ball and run.
- Force elevation of the pass.
- Make the quarterback move his feet, which throws off his timing.
- Throw off the receiver's timing.
- Obstruct the quarterback's vision.

Even if the pass is delivered, there can still be positive results for the defense if defensive linemen disengage and aggressively pursue the ball. The objectives when covering after the ball is thrown include:

- Create intimidation.
- Knock the ball loose from the receiver.
- Get big hits.
- Gang tackle.
- Get in position to block for an interception.

Pass Rush Tips

Anticipation is crucial. Players should know the down-and-distance situation and the game plan. Field position and down-and-distance are tipoffs. Immediate pass recognition predicated on offensive movement comes from effective game preparation. What moves first? In some cases, a quarterback's body part may move just prior to the snap. For example, the quarterback may move his foot just before the snap. Some quarterbacks will open their hands just before the center-quarterback exchange. Players should also watch for the blocker's head to pop up (high helmet). Quickness and decisiveness of the initial move is crucial to the pass rush. Coordination of the rusher's hands, feet, and head movements are paramount. Rushers must keep momentum going toward the passer without any lost motion. A one-move, one-counter mindset is crucial since rushers seldom have time for multiple moves. The clock is ticking. Rushers should be quick and decisive on their initial pass rush move. Effective rushers get their hands inside the blocker while keeping their shoulders forward of the feet to prevent the blocker from getting under the rusher's pad level. An effective rusher never shows his numbers. Rushers must never get hat-to-hat with the blocker, their face mask should be under the opponent's face mask, and rushers must not give up their chest to the blocker. Linemen should keep their eyes on the quarterback, while hands, head, and feet get them there. A competent rusher runs through the quarterback and tackles him high. Cage players make the quarterback step up by staying on the quarterback's upfield shoulder. The tackles attack the near number. If the rusher hasn't reached the quarterback, he should get his hands up as the quarterback starts to throw. He should stay out of the blocker's middle by working half man on the blocker and pressure the blocker's outside shoulder while staying in the assigned rush lane. Working down the middle of the protector turns into a strength tactic, which takes time. The clock is running, and a rusher has no time to wrestle with the blocker. Pass rushers must understand that the right arm works with the right leg, and the left arm works with the left leg. They must close the critical area with speed and quickness, allowing no separation between rusher and blocker by making pass rush moves at an arm's distance. The offensive man's only ally is distance. The pass rusher must run straight lines, keeping his feet, weight, and upper body going forward (i.e., advance—don't dance). Rushers should try to make offensive linemen move their feet, but once a lineman makes a stand, they use their leverage to defensive advantage (i.e., if the blocker pushes, the defender pulls, or if the blocker pulls, the defender turns him). Sound pass rushers take advantage of offensive pass sets. The following are effective ways to attack various pass block techniques:

- *Soft deep set:* The defender should use an early power rush.
- *Hard set (blocker pops up):* The defender should make the blocker move his feet. Speed moves or a run-around are good. Also, the blocker is open to a push-pull move.
- *Head or shoulders are down:* The defender should use a quick swim.
- *Leaps forward:* The defender should use a quick swim or run-around.
- *Deep setter:* The rusher should use a power move. Also, the blocker can be beaten inside using a spin, hump, or foot fake.
- *Chaser:* The defender should run around the blocker.
- *Rider:* The defender should get low and speed rush. However, he shouldn't be ridden past the quarterback.
- *Sets and cuts:* This technique is employed by shorter offensive players or on three-step passes. Effective use of hands by the rusher is crucial. The defender should use a limp-leg technique, and get the hands up. The ball is coming out quick on the three-step drop.

As a basic rule, rushers should use finesse moves on power blockers, and use power moves on finesse blockers.

Pass Blocker's Pressure Point

Rushers should see the pressure point of the blocker, which is the inside or outside shoulder of the blocker, depending upon which lane the defender is attacking. Tips on attacking the blocker's pressure point include the following:

- The rusher should keep his hands inside the blocker's hands.
- The rusher never stops his feet. He always works north and south. He should not chop his feet or bring them back to parallel.
- The rusher should rid himself of the lineman when he turns. He should stay tight to the blocker (half man). Once the rusher disengages from the blocker, he should accelerate to the quarterback.
- If the blocker sets short and soft, the rusher should use a power rush.
- The rusher should feel the pressure point of the blocker. If he leans, the rusher pulls. If he squats, the defender pushes.

- Versus a hold, the rusher should grab his wrist and lift and follow with a rip move.
- When being driven past the quarterback by the blocker, the rusher should use the blocker's momentum to crossface with a club and rip inside or discus spin. Also, at the quarterback depth the rusher can use a power rush by pointing his toes toward the quarterback and bull rushing. Counter pass rush moves are automatic at the quarterback level. The worst place to be is behind the quarterback.

Speed Rush Tips

Speed rushers should have a big first step with a four-yard spot behind the blocker as the target spot. The rusher will decide at that point which move to use. This is the critical area. If the rusher gets to the target spot and he is deeper than the blocker, he should continue on with a speed move. To do this, the rusher should simply take his inside hand and press the blocker's hand down and turn the corner. The goal of a speed rush is to turn the shoulders of the blocker, which weakens his ability to stay strong. Rushers should plant "the seed of speed." When the blocker becomes concerned about a speed rush, he is open to other pass rush moves. Rushers can use speed, alignment, and technique to turn the shoulders of the blocker. If the rusher can get hip-to-hip with the blocker, he has a decided advantage. Anytime the hips are even and the rusher is facing the quarterback, the blocker should not be able to prevent the rusher from bursting to the quarterback without an obvious holding infraction. The previous information on pass play has been in generic form. These tips are applicable to this or any other defensive system. The remainder of this chapter deals with specific techniques and information for this playbook.

Pass Rush Concepts

For every defensive call, there will be well-defined cage responsibilities. Cage players must reach the quarterback and squeeze the pocket, making the quarterback step up. Cage defenders must be very careful when using an underneath path on a blocker on a pass rush move (a spin move, for example). The defense must have solid cage with pressure calls since most quarterbacks try to escape outside. The quarterback cannot be allowed to escape; cage players must make him stay in the pocket and take the hit. In peel packages, the cage player will jump flare routes on the way to the quarterback. There will also be inside pressure lanes on both sides of the ball. These lanes will be filled according to the defense, stunt, or pressure called. All pass rushers must understand the concept of balance and containment. Defenders cannot be freelancers. Everyone must know his responsibility and execute it.

Base Rush Lanes

Figure 4-38 shows base rush lane concepts. The tackles get an inside push by attacking the quarterback's inside number. The ends make the quarterback step up by attacking the quarterback's upfield shoulder. A point concept is used when rushing the quarterback. The defender responsible for cage attacks the quarterback's upfield shoulder. The inside rushers aim for the near number of the quarterback. On a five-man rush, the cage player has the upfield shoulder. The #2 defender has the near number, and the #3 rusher in the fit attacks the quarterback's nose.

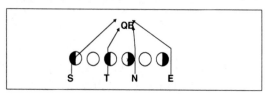

Figure 4-38. Base rush lane concepts

Two-Way Go

Figure 4-39 illustrates the two-way go concept. This concept allows a 3 technique defender to pass rush inside or outside the offensive guard. This serves to enhance his ability to get to the quarterback.

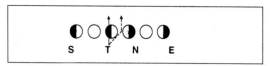

Figure 4-39. Two-way go concept

Cage From a 3 Technique (Zone Blitz)

The nose must be aware that, with no one rushing outside, the offensive tackle will look to seal him inside. The drop end—a deuce player—can assist by faking a rush before he drops (Figure 4-40).

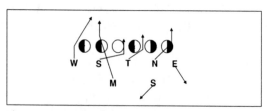

Figure 4-40. Cage from a 3 technique (zone blitz)

Natural

This concept allows the end to the 1 technique side to go inside on his pass rush with the 1 technique working to cage. This allows the end some wiggle room to beat the offensive tackle, who cannot predict that the end always has cage. Also, this scheme gives the nose some leeway because he will usually be double-teamed by the guard and the center (Figure 4-41).

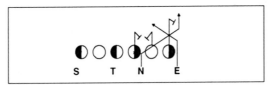

Figure 4-41. Natural

Pass Rush Stunts (Figures 4-42 through 4-50)

These games are designed specifically to rush the passer. On any lane exchange, the defender making the first move is termed the penetrator, and the second man is called the flasher. The penetrator will aim for the near hip, pin the hip, and push upfield in that gap. Players should communicate with each other. Everyone must be on the same page. Players should know who has cage responsibility.

- *Twist* (Figure 4-42): The tackle goes first with the nose wrapping around. The tackle reads the center's shoulders and can turn up in either A+ or A– gap. The nose will read the guard's shoulders and can end up in either A+ or B+ gap.
- *Tango* (Figure 4-43): Tango is a reverse twist with the nose going first.
- *Pick* (Figure 4-44): The ends are the penetrators with the tackles flashing. This stunt is executed on the snap. The pick can be run to both sides, strong, or weak. Also, this stunt can be run delayed. It is executed after linemen get upfield.
- *Pop* (Figure 4-45): The tackles go first, and the ends go second. This stunt also occurs on the snap. It can be run to both sides, strong, or weak. Pop also can be run on a delayed basis.
- *Change* (Figure 4-46): Change is a pick to the weakside and a pop to the strongside.
- *Over Mirror* (Figure 4-47): This scheme is a great way to flush the quarterback. All linemen stick inside with a linebacker or defensive back running down the quarterback.
- *Over Pirate Wrap* (Figure 4-48): This stunt is a three-man change-up. The end and tackle will execute a Pirate stunt with the nose on an automatic wrap.
- *Under Pirate Wrap* (Figure 4-49)
- *Mixer* (Figure 4-50): Both ends are on inside sticks, and both tackles assuming cage duties to the opposite side.

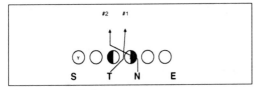

Figure 4-42. Twist

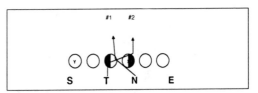

Figure 4-43. Tango

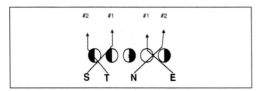

Figure 4-44. Pick

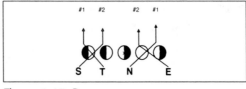

Figure 4-45. Pop

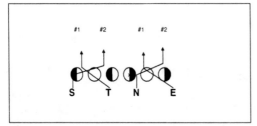

Figure 4-46. Change

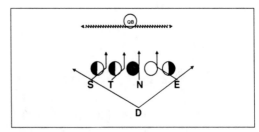

Figure 4-47. Over mirror

Figure 4-48. Over pirate wrap

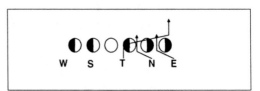

Figure 4-49. Under pirate wrap

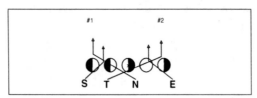

Figure 4-50. Mixer

Green Package Stunts (Figure 4-51 through 4-62)

The green package is a designed get-after-the-quarterback package and is even more effective with lane exchanges.

- *Base Green Alignment* (Figure 4-51)
- *Green Pick* (Figure 4-52): The ends go first with the tackles going second. A delayed pick call has the ends sticking on their second step. A timing device they use is to mentally say, "One, two, cha-cha-cha." Tackles work to cage after color crosses their face.
- *Green Pop* (Figure 4-53): The tackles go first, and the ends go second.
- *Green Delayed Pop* (Figure 4-54): The tackles go first, and the ends go second.
- *Green Twist* (Figure 4-55): The tackle goes first with the nose going second.

- *Green Tango* (Figure 4-56): The nose executes his move first and the tackle second.
- *Green Read Twist* (Figures 4-57 and 4-58): The tackles read the turn of the center. The tackle opposite the center's turn goes first, and the second tackle can go under or over the center. In Figure 4-57, the center is turning toward the nose. With this look, the tackle goes first. In Figure 4-58, the center is turning toward the tackle. With this look, the nose goes first.
- *Green Spike* (Figure 4-59): The tackle sticks. The nose will wrap on a pass.
- *Green Nail* (Figure 4-60): The nose sticks. The tackle will wrap on a pass.
- *Green Double Spike* (Figure 4-61): Both tackles stick.
- *Green Pick Strong* (Figure 4-62): A pick is run to the strongside with the weakside on a jet. Conversely, out of the green package, pick weak, pop strong, and pop weak can be run.

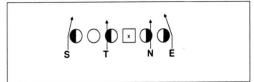

Figure 4-51. Base green alignment

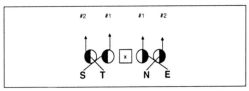

Figure 4-52. Green pick

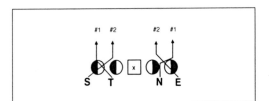

Figure 4-53. Green pop

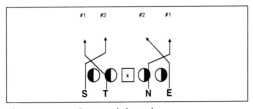

Figure 4-54. Green delayed pop

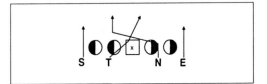

Figure 4-55. Green twist

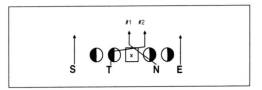

Figure 4-56. Green tango

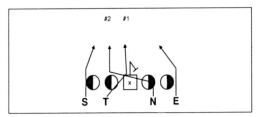

Figure 4-57. Green read twist—center turns toward nose; tackle goes first

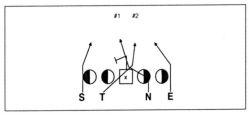

Figure 4-58. Green read twist—center turns toward tackle; nose goes first

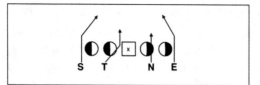

Figure 4-59. Green spike

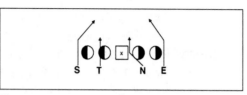

Figure 4-60. Green nail

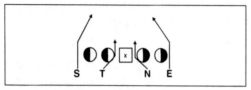

Figure 4-61. Green double spike

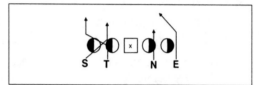

Figure 4-62. Green pick strong

5

Zone Coverages

This chapter breaks down the coverages that use a base four-man rush and drop seven defenders into coverage. Included in this chapter are cover 2, cover 8, and cover 3. Cover 8 is the base coverage used in the playbook. Each coverage will include the following:

- An overview with strengths and weaknesses for each coverage
- Alignment, techniques, and keys
- Run and pass responsibilities
- Run fits
- Motion adjustments
- Coverage variations
- Coaching points

Cover 2

The first coverage illustrated is cover 2. Cover 2 is a five-under, two-deep zone. The corners are rolled up with a five-yard vertical alignment on the receiver with a redirect on the receiver. An over front is used the majority of the time in cover 2 (Figure 5-1). Figure 5-2 shows the back seven alignment.

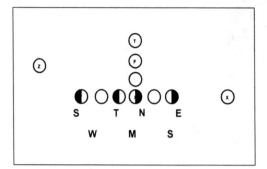

Figure 5-1. Over front

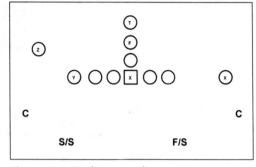

Figure 5-2. Back seven alignment

Strengths of Cover 2

- Takes away the flats
- Handles four verticals
- Is good versus three-man combination routes
- Disrupts the two-receiver pass game
- Disrupts timing between the quarterback and the receivers
- Protects the corners' ability
- Gives the rush more time to get to the quarterback
- Takes away the speed of the receiver

Weaknesses of Cover 2

- Cover 2 is not as effective against the run. Only seven defenders are in the box against a pro set.
- Safeties are not inherently involved in defending the run game.
- Vertical holes along the sidelines are vulnerable.
- Middle of the field is weak with #3 vertical.

Additional Information

- Defenders will close to the tight end. Against no tight end, they will declare to receiver strength.
- Defenders will always close to the three-receiver side in a 3x1 formation.

Alignments for Formations in Cover 2
(Figures 5-3 through 5-14)

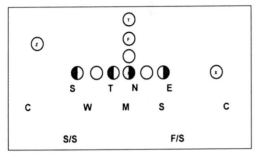

Figure 5-3. Pro

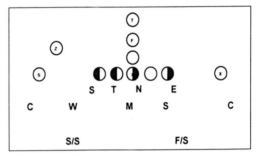

Figure 5-4. Slot

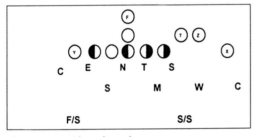

Figure 5-5. Spread

Figure 5-6. Three wides

Figure 5-7. Trips closed

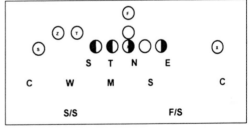

Figure 5-8. Trips open

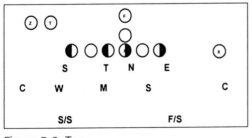

Figure 5-9. Trey

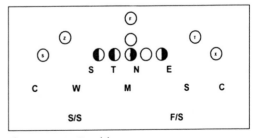

Figure 5-10. Doubles

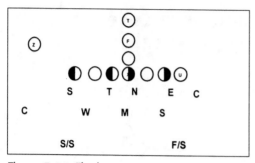

Figure 5-11. Flanker

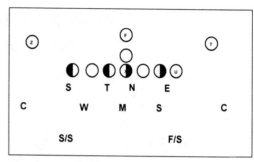

Figure 5-12. Tech

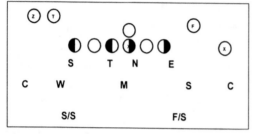

Figure 5-13. Empty trey

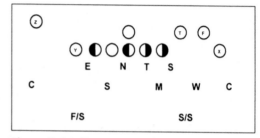

Figure 5-14. Empty spread

Linebackers make all the adjustments in cover 2. Following are linebacker alignment rules.

Base Rules

Will: 50
Mike: +10
Sam: 50

Slot Rules

Will: A+
Mike: B–
Sam: Halfway between #2 and the end man on the line of scrimmage (EMLOS)

Spread Rules

Will: 50
Mike: +10
Sam: Halfway between #2 and the end man on the line of scrimmage (EMLOS)

Trips Rules

Will: Splits #2 and #3
Mike: 30
Sam: 30

Doubles Rules

Will: Halfway between #2 and the end man on the line of scrimmage (EMLOS)
Mike: +10
Sam: Halfway between #2 and the end man on the line of scrimmage (EMLOS)

Run Fits for Cover 2

Flow Run (Figure 5-15)

Will: A+ to C+. Spills.
Mike: A+ to the ball. Spills.
Sam: Cutback B–
Strong safety: Alley when he reads uncovered linemen downfield
Free safety: Alley through the strong safety when he reads uncovered linemen downfield
Onside corner: Force
Offside corner: Cutback to cutoff

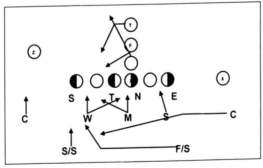

Figure 5-15. Flow run

Flood Run (Figure 5-16)

Will: A+ to C+
Mike: B− to A+
Sam: B−. Spills.
Strong safety: Alley through the free safety when he reads uncovered linemen downfield
Free safety: Alley when he reads uncovered linemen downfield
Onside corner: Force
Offside corner: Cutback to cutoff

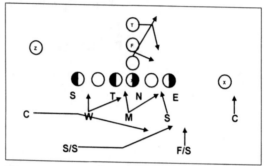

Figure 5-16. Flood run

Divide Run (Figure 5-17)

Will: C+ to A+
Mike: A+ to C+
Sam: B−
Secondary: Treats as a flow run.

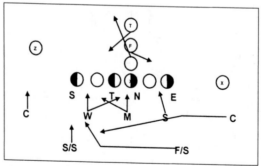

Figure 5-17. Divide run

Cover 2 Adjustments to a Slot Set

Versus slot sets, the closed side corner will make a dead call and align 1x LOS off the tight end. A dead call tells the Stud and tackle to execute a pirate stunt. Figure 5-18 shows defensive reaction to a flow run. Will and Mike are over the top with Sam on a carry-fold technique. The playside corner is the force player. The backside corner plays cutback to cutoff. The strong safety aligns at seven yards depth and fits over the top, which is called a ram technique. The free safety will run the alley after he works parallel through the strong safety's alignment. Flood run responsibilities are illustrated in Figure 5-19. Will is quick to B– with Mike spilling B–. Sam has D–. The playside corner forces the ball with the backside corner chasing flat, trying to catch the play from behind. The strong safety plays ram and is over the top. However, the strong safety is a little slower because he has reverse responsibility. The free safety keys the triangle and is an alley player.

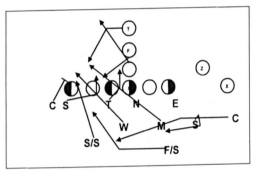

Figure 5-18. Defensive reaction to flow run

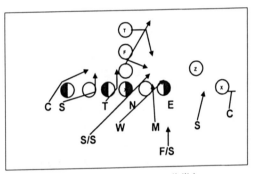

Figure 5-19. Flood run responsibilities

Cover 2 Line Stunts

Over Pirate (Figure 5-20)

This stunt is automatic with a dead call versus a slot set. It can also be used as a change-up. On a flow run, all linebackers are over the top, with the secondary executing normal cover 2 responsibilities. Against a flood run, Sam will spill, Mike will be quick to B–, and Will can either be over the top or play backside the pirate stunt. Again, the secondary will be in cover 2. Versus a pass, the nose will wrap and assume cage responsibility.

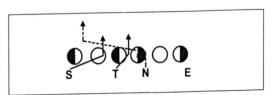

Figure 5-20. Over pirate

Over End (Figure 5-21)

The end will stick to B–. Versus a pass, the nose will wrap and assume cage responsibilities. On a flow run, Will and Mike will play base rules, but Sam will have cutback C– instead of cutback B–. A flood run will have Will responsible for cutback A–, and Mike will be quick to C–. Sam will assume C– responsibilities and will spill the play. The secondary will have normal cover 2 rules.

Figure 5-21. Over end

Over Spike (Figure 5-22)

The tackle will stick A+. The nose will wrap against a pass. This call enables the defense to have a built in twist stunt versus a pass. Against flow runs, Will has C+ and Mike can play over the top because A+ gap is filled. A spike frees up Sam to play over the top on flow runs because the tackle assumes cutback responsibilities. However, Sam should be ready to fall back to the backside on a drastic cutback or bend back play. A flood run has Mike and Sam playing normal. Depending upon the game plan, Will may be over the top or he may play backside the tackle. The secondary plays cover 2.

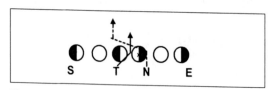

Figure 5-22. Over spike

Cover 2 vs. Play-Action, Dash, and Sprint Passes

Fire Pass (Figure 5-23)

Will: 2 match. Carries #2, listening for an in call from the corner. With an in call, he will build a wall on #1.

Mike: 3 match. Plays the shallow hole and will drive on a checkdown.

Sam: 2 match. Plays dig to drag.

Safeties: Get eyes to #1. If #1 is outside the corner, the safety will have to expand.

Onside corner: Squeezes #1, looking for #2. Takes flat and up routes man-to-man.

Offside corner: Squeezes #1, looking for #2. Drives on a tight end on the drag if he is in the flat.

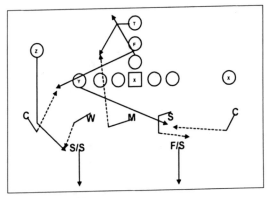

Figure 5-23. Fire pass

Flow Pass (Figure 5-24)

Will: 2 match. Takes the fullback in the flat.
Mike: 3 match; middle run-through on the tight end
Sam: 2 match. Takes the tailback on a checkdown.
Safeties: Get eyes to #1. If #1 is outside the corner, the safety will have to expand.
Onside corner: Sinks with #1, and drives on #2 late.
Offside corner: Sinks with #1

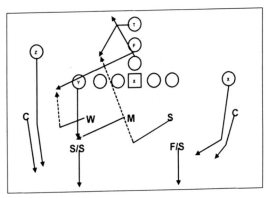

Figure 5-24. Flow pass

Flood Pass (Figure 5-25)

Will: 2 match. Looks for dig to checkdown.
Mike: 3 match. Jumps the tight end on a drag.
Sam: 2 match. Takes the fullback in the flat.
Safeties: Get eyes to #1. If #1 is outside the corner, the safety will have to expand.
Onside corner: Sinks on #1, then drives on the fullback.
Offside corner: Sinks on #1.

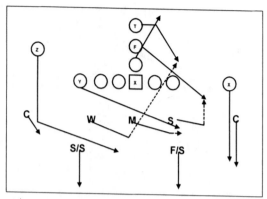

Figure 5-25. Flood pass

Waggle (Figure 5-26)

Will: 2 match. Takes the tailback on a checkdown.
Mike: 3 match. Collisions and runs with the tight end. Will be ready to recage the quarterback.
Sam: 2 match. Hangs between the fullback and the tight end.
Safeties: Get eyes to #1. If #1 is outside the corner, the safety will have to expand.
Onside corner: Sinks on #1, then drives late on the fullback.
Offside corner: Sinks with #1.

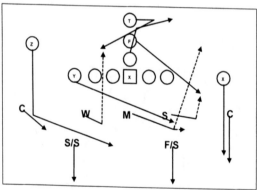

Figure 5-26. Waggle

Sprint Passes (Figures 5-27 through 5-29)

Flat defender: Holds the deep comeback route by #1.
Onside linebacker: Plasters #2 (takes him man-to-man).
Mike: 3 match with a possible recage on the quarterback
Offside linebacker: 2 match. Looks for a screen or crosser.
Onside safety: Cover deep

Offside safety: Remains alert for a throwback.
Offside corner: Remains alert for a throwback.

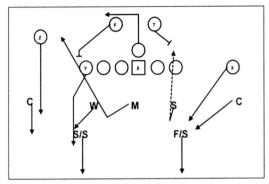

Figure 5-27. Flow dash

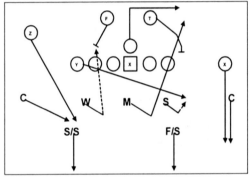

Figure 5-28. Flood dash

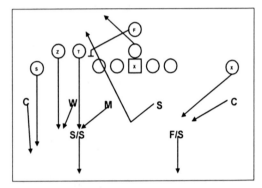

Figure 5-29. Sprint pass

Cover 2 Motion Adjustments
(Figures 5-30 through 5-37)

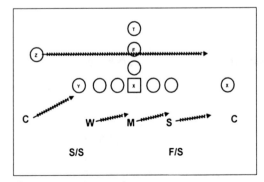

Figure 5-30. Pro to slot

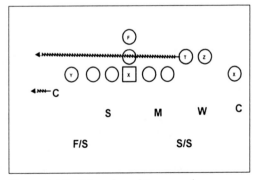

Figure 5-31. Trips closed to spread

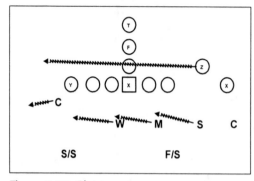

Figure 5-32. Slot to pro

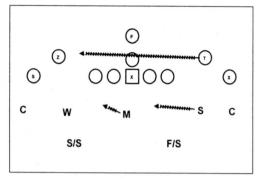

Figure 5-33. Doubles to trips

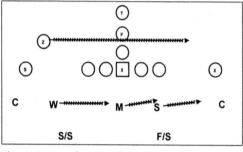

Figure 5-34. Three wides ZAC

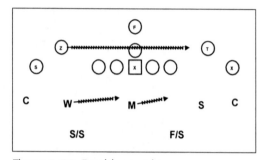

Figure 5-35. Doubles to trips

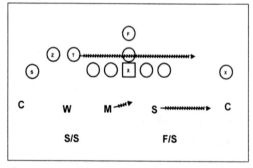

Figure 5-36. Trips open to doubles

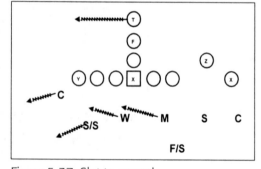

Figure 5-37. Slot to spread

Cover 2 Coaching Points—Linebackers

Mike

Against pro sets, Mike will carry the tight end through the hole, which is called a middle run-through. If the tight end runs a flat or drag, Mike will sit down and look for crossers. Mike will have middle run-through on three-wide sets. Mike will carry #2 if he is on an inside route. Versus 2x2 sets, Mike opens up to #3 and sprints to the deep hole. Against 3x1 sets, Mike reads from #3 to #2. He will give a banjo call to Will if #2 and #3 are close on alignment and there is a chance they might cross paths on their distribution. If #2 or #3 are in the seam, Mike will carry him. If #2 and #3 disappear, Mike will sit down and look for crossers.

Will and Sam

With #2 vertical, Will and Sam disrupt and ride his inside hip, playing low shoulder. The only time the outside linebacker will come off the seam is when he gets an in call from the corner. With an in cut by #1, the backer will build a wall on #1. With a smash call, the backer will drive inside-out on #1, building a wall.

Cover 2 Coaching Points—Secondary

Safety Coaching Points

The safeties align 12 yards deep on the edge of the box. They key the triangle for a run-pass read. However, they should think pass first. Safeties play over the top of vertical routes and must be able to midpoint multiple receivers. They read the ball to #1. #1 will let the safety know if he will be stretched on passes, especially if the receiver releases outside the corner. If #1 is outside the corner, the safety will play to outside the hash. If #1 is on an inside release, the safety will squeeze to inside the hash. If #2 is no threat or he blocks, the safety will lean to #1. Versus running plays, the safeties attack the alley when they read offensive linemen downfield. When in the alley, the safety should be ready to overlap the corner. On runs away, they rotate through the other safety before inserting into the alley. With a receiver in the middle, they hold the half (middle read) and break on the long arm of the quarterback. With no middle read, safeties check #1 to the offside. On a smash route, they get over the top of #2's flag-out. With #1 on an in route, they get on top of #2's vertical or corner route. The strong safety's ram technique against the slot set requires him to align seven yards deep over the offensive tackle. On a pass play, the safety will work the innermost part of the zone if there is no threat from the tight end. On flow runs, the strong safety plays over the top to D+ after taking two shuffle steps. The strong safety plays over the top on flood runs, but is responsible for reverse because the corner is chasing flat.

Corner Coaching Points

Corners line up on the outside shoulder of #1 at a depth of five yards, turned at a 45-degree angle to the ball. From that point, the corners will read the three-step drop. They will communicate the release of #1 if he isn't vertical (e.g., smash, in, etc.). Corners reroute #1 and run with him on any deep route spying #2. If #1 releases inside, they squeeze him as far as possible, looking for #2. On an inside release, they squeeze #1 and look for #2 on an out or corner route. If so, they gain depth at a 45-degree angle. On an inside release, the corners give the linebacker an in call. If #1 tries a boundary release, they use a hook technique. With the hook technique, the corner will post the receiver with the outside arm and drive him outside. The corner will drop his hips and throw his inside elbow toward the quarterback, blocking the receiver from getting up the boundary and looks for #2. If #2 is inside, the corner continues to get depth. If #1 is inside and #2 runs a wheel, the corner takes him man-to-man, which is called the wheel rule. Against a sprint pass, the frontside corner will plaster #1, while the backside corner will gain depth and defend the innermost part of the zone. The corner should be in position to undercut a backside throw.

Corner Dead Technique

The corner to the tight end against a slot set aligns one yard outside the tight end and on the line of scrimmage. He will give a dead call. From that point, the corner will play flat-footed, gaining no depth. Versus a flow run, the corner will aggressively force the ball. Against flood runs, he will chase flat because the strong safety has reverse responsibility. Versus passes, the corner has the flat looking for leakers or crossers.

Corner Slant Technique

Backside of a 3x1 set, the corner aligns 1x5 inside the receiver. Since the corner will have no inside help from Sam, he is susceptible to a slant. This alignment will better enable him to break on any inside route.

Corner Force Techniques

The corner has a toolbox full of force techniques so the receiver won't be able to zero in on one particular technique. Following are three force techniques:
- *Speed:* The corner will simply out run the receiver inside and force.
- *Outside in:* The corner will escape quickly outside the block and force.
- *Outside fake:* The corner will move upfield, making the receiver commit, and then beat him inside with an inside move. On runs away, the corner gives ground and holds position on the receiver for play pass. After identifying a run away, he will take a cutback to cutoff angle.

Cover 2 Variations

Following are a variety of tweaks and variations of the cover 2 package.

Cover 2 Man (Figure 5-38)

Will: #2 man
Mike: #3 man
Sam: #2 man
Corners: #1 man
Safeties: Deep half zone

Cover 2 man is a five-under, two-deep man-to-man defense. Mike will close to the tight end. If there is no tight end, Mike will declare to receiver strength. Various fronts may be used. Underneath defenders Will, Mike, Sam, and the corners use an inside alignment on the receivers and use a trail technique. With a trail technique, defenders will deny an inside release by the receivers by jamming them and playing low shoulder on him. Defenders stay low shoulder and key the receiver's inside hip. They match his angle on cuts. Underneath defenders can undercut routes because they have deep help from the safeties. The safeties supply deep help and have force responsibility. Against running plays, the safeties must give a run call because the underneath defenders have their backs to the ball.

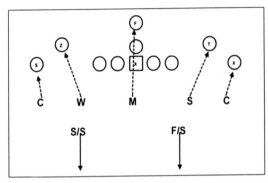

Figure 5-38. Cover 2 man

Cover 2 Loose (Figure 5-39)

This coverage is used in third-and-long-yardage situations or near the end of the half or game. With this coverage, the underneath defenders loosen and drop to the line to gain and sit down. They keep the ball inside and in front, tackling the receiver short of the line to gain.

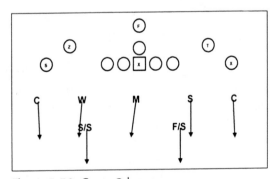

Figure 5-39. Cover 2 loose

Cover 2 Middle (Figure 5-40)

A Tampa 2 look, cover 2 middle is used late in the half or game. The outside linebackers Will and Sam loosen and get depth. Mike will align deeper and run to the deep hole. A defensive back can be substituted for Mike. The safeties will widen and are able to play the hole behind the corners more efficiently because, with an extra defender in centerfield, the top of the coverage will have a three-deep configuration. Corners will get extra depth giving up short routes. The ends will widen and jet, containing the quarterback by keeping him in the pocket. The ends must not allow the quarterback to extend the play by scrambling. The nose will drop over #3, replacing the Mike. The 3 technique will spike to balance the rush.

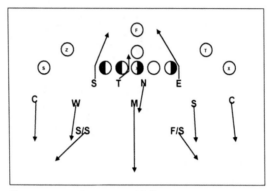

Figure 5-40. Cover 2 middle

Cover 2 Lurk (Figure 5-41)

Cover 2 lurk is a five-under, one-deep, lurker (robber) man-to-man coverage. Mike will close to the tight end. If there is no tight end, Mike will declare to the receiver strength. The strengths of this coverage include deep and shallow hole players, the lurker can jump crossing and misdirection routes, spy on an athletic quarterback, or double a designated receiver. Figure 5-42 shows the lurker spying on the quarterback. Underneath defenders follow cover 2 man rules to determine their assigned receiver. Underneath players' lurk techniques include assuming a press position and, with a receiver taking an outside release, taking shuffle steps and cutting off deep routes. With an inside release, they jam and ride the receiver's outside shoulder, maintaining an outside and high shoulder position. They will squeeze seam routes and carry them to the deep hole player. Outside linebackers will not chase shallow crossers, but will hold and look for a crosser from the opposite side. If no crosser shows, they zone up and read the quarterback. As a basic rule, the strong safety is the lurker. If the lurker is game planned to double a designated receiver, the safety to the side of the receiver will be the lurker and the remaining safety will be the deep hole player. The lurker will take the first shallow crosser with Sam's side taking first priority. Versus 3x1 formations, the lurker will look for the crosser coming from the strongside. The strong safety will align in A+ against an aligned empty or rock down on motion to empty to help out on the quarterback draw. The lurker has force to both sides. He must turn in all outside runs.

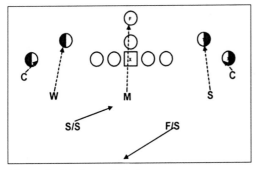

Figure 5-41. Cover 2 lurk   Figure 5-42. Lurker spying on the quarterback

Cover 2 Cone (Figure 5-43)

Safeties and corners double #1 inside-outside. The corner assumes an outside shade on #1 and reroutes him inside. If #1 releases inside, the safety will jump him with the corner gaining depth and backing up the safety for a double move. Should #1 take an outside release, the corner will play him low shoulder, and the safety will zone up and read the quarterback. Linebackers follow cover 2 man rules.

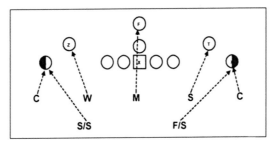

Figure 5-43. Cover 2 cone

Cover 2 Deuce (Figure 5-44)

The safeties and the backer on #2 will double #2 inside-outside. The primary defender will align head-up on #2 at a depth of five yards. If #2 releases outside, the primary defender will man-turn and play low shoulder. With an outside release, the safety will zone up and read the quarterback. If #2 releases inside, the safety will jump him, and the primary defender will back him up for a possible double move. If #2 is in the backfield, the primary defender will lock down on him, and the safety will play a normal half-field technique.

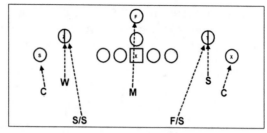

Figure 5-44. Cover 2 deuce

Cover 2 Mike (Figure 5-45)

Everyone plays normal cover 2 man rules except Mike and the strong safety. This coverage is used to give Mike help on #3. If #3 runs a vertical route, the strong safety will double him. If #3 runs an out or in cut, the strong safety will zone up and read the quarterback with Mike single covering #3 man-to-man.

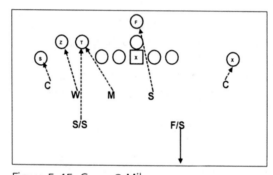

Figure 5-45. Cover 2 Mike

Cover 2 Trap (Figure 5-46)

This coverage is used to double a designated receiver short-deep. The primary defender forces the receiver outside and settles in the flat or curl area and reads the quarterback. The safety to the designated receiver's side takes over, using inside leverage. The other safety assumes hole responsibilities.

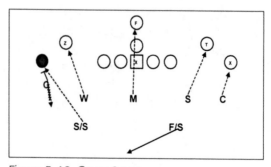

Figure 5-46. Cover 2 trap

Cover 2 Swipe (Figure 5-47)

Will and Sam: #1 man under
Mike: #3 man under
Safeties: #2 man under
Corners: Bail to half field

Cover 2 swipe is an exotic coverage that can give the quarterback a difficult time making his progression reads. The defense will show a cover 2 shell and on the snap jump into a variation of cover 2 man coverage. All underneath defenders use a trail technique. Versus motion, the defenders will bump to make it look like cover 2. A variety of fronts or line stunts can be used.

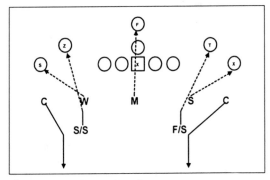

Figure 5-47. Cover 2 swipe

Cover 2 Checks

At times, the defense may want to check out of another coverage into a two-deep look. Reasons can vary from defensive confusion to an offensive set that may give problems to the huddle call defense. For example, the defensive coordinator may not want to run man coverage against the bunch set illustrated in Figure 5-48. Following are the code or check words for possible checks:

- *Tampa:* Over cover 2
- *Toledo:* Green cover 2
- *Tucson:* Over pirate cover 2
- *Baseball:* Over end cover 2

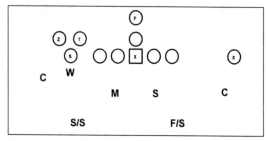

Figure 5-48. Bunch set

Cover 8 (Quarters Coverage)

All defenses in this playbook originate from this coverage shell. Cover 8 is a rush-four, drop-seven concept.

Strengths of Cover 8

- A nine-man front is possible versus running plays.
- The defense constricts as the offense constricts and expands as the offense expands.
- It offers great run support because the safeties are near the line of scrimmage.
- The free safety and strong safety are mirrored positions as well as Will and Sam.
- Coverage ends up with four deep versus four verticals.
- It has three defenders over two receivers against a doubles formation.
- The quarterback sees the same 8 shell pre-snap on each play. He must diagnose the coverage post-snap.
- Short routes are handled aggressively. Corners can be more aggressive because of over-the-top help. Linebackers can be more involved on short routes, screens, and checkdowns.
- Coverage allows the linebackers to be more aggressive on runs because the safeties handle cutbacks.
- Coverage is a disguised double-robber coverage with the capability to double outside receivers.
- Coverage unfolds differently against different routes. Defensive reaction will not look the same, but will develop differently depending upon the route.

Weaknesses of Cover 8

- Safeties can be influenced by play-action passes.
- Corners aren't guaranteed post help.
- Trips sets require a major adjustment.
- The defense must get quarterback pressure off a base four-man rush.

Additional Information

- Read is the base call.
- Linebackers and safeties play run first and react to pass unless in an obvious passing situation.
- Defenders will close to the tight end. Against no tight end, they will close to receiver strength.
- Defenders will always close to the three-receiver side in a 3x1 set.
- Once receivers distribute, underneath coverage is locked. Defenders play tight man in a zone. The defense doesn't cover grass.

Alignments for Formations in Cover 8 (Figures 5-49 through 5-60)

Figure 5-49. Pro

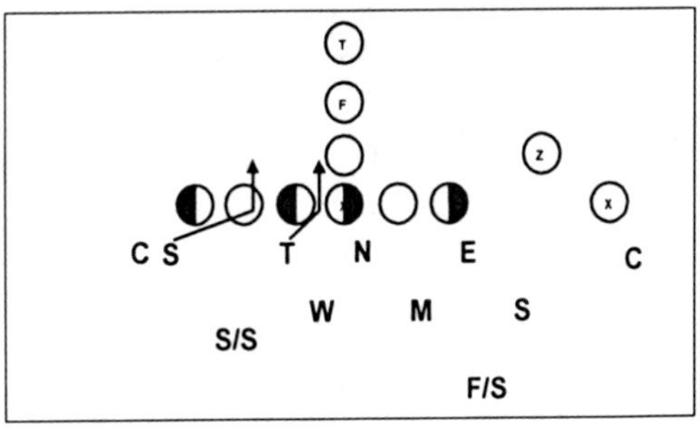

Figure 5-50. Slot

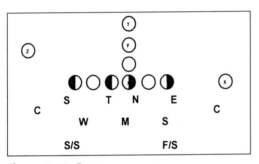

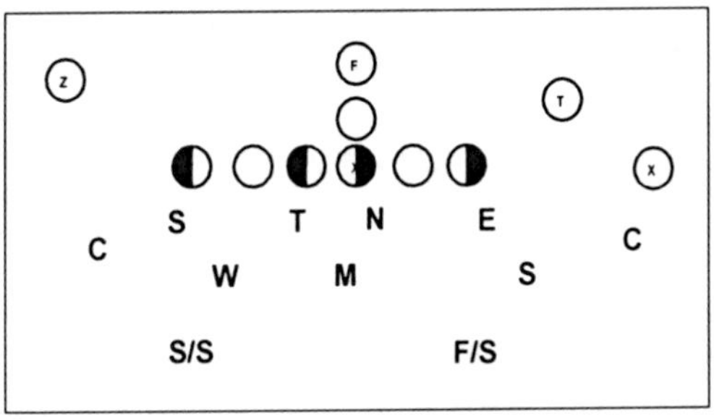

Figure 5-51. Spread

Figure 5-52. Three wides

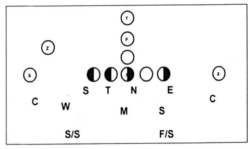

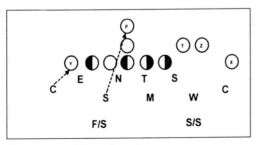

Figure 5-53. Trips closed

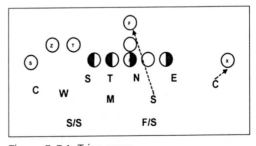

Figure 5-54. Trips open

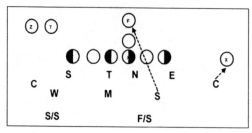

Figure 5-55. Trey

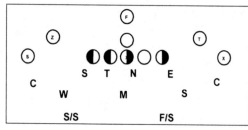

Figure 5-56. Doubles

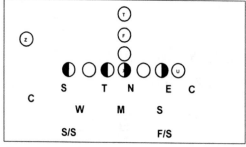

Figure 5-57. Flanker

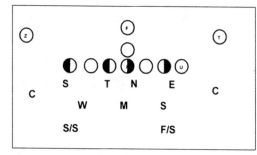

Figure 5-58. Tech

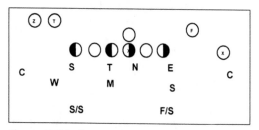

Figure 5-59. Empty trey

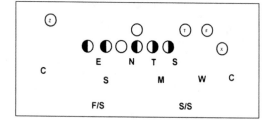

Figure 5-60. Empty spread

Linebackers make all the adjustments in cover 8. Linebacker adjustments in cover 8 and cover 2 are the same.

Run Fits for Cover 8

Flow Run (Figure 5-61)

Will: C+. Spills.
Mike: C+
Sam: A+
Strong safety: Stacks with Stud.
Free safety: Stacks with the end.
Onside corner: Secondary contain
Offside corner: Cutback to cutoff

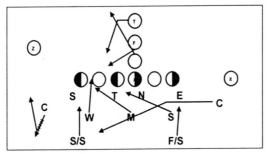

Figure 5-61. Flow run

Flood Run (Figure 5-62)

Will: A+

Mike: B−

Sam: B−. Spills.

Strong safety: Stacks.

Free safety: Stacks.

Onside corner: Secondary contain

Offside corner: Cutback to cutoff

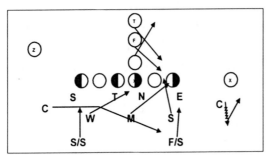

Figure 5-62. Flood run

Divide Run (Figure 5-63)

Will: C+

Mike: A+

Sam: B−

Strong safety: Stacks.

Free safety: Stacks.

Onside corner: Secondary contain

Offside corner: Cutback to cutoff

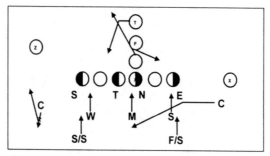

Figure 5-63. Divide run

Cover 8 Adjustments to a Slot Set

Cover 8 adjustments to a slot set are basically the same as in cover 2. Later in this chapter, cover 8 match will be discussed. This serves to give the offense a different look in a slot set. Also 8 match is very good against teams that like to motion to slot or motion from slot to pro. The same line stunts used with cover 2 are also effective in cover 8.

Cover 8 vs. Play-Action, Dash, and Sprint Passes

Fire Pass (Figure 5-64)

Will: 2 match. Runs the stripe, and takes the fullback in the flat.

Mike: 3 match. Zones over the tailback. Will be alert for a checkdown.

Sam: 2 match. Reads high helmets from the offensive linemen, and recognizes the tight end on a drag.

Strong safety: Zones the quarter. Reads high helmets from the offensive line.

Free safety: Zones the quarter if he reads high helmets from the offensive linemen. If he bites on the play-action, he can help on the tight end on the drag.

Corners: Man on #1

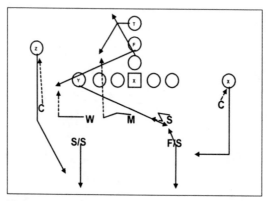

Figure 5-64. Fire pass

Flow Pass (Figure 5-65)

Will: 2 match. Takes the fullback in the flat. Runs the stripe.

Mike: 3 match. Carries the tight end.

Sam: 2 match. Zones over the tailback. Will be alert for a checkdown.

Strong safety: Takes the tight end man.

Free safety: Reads high helmets, and zones the quarter.

Corners: Man on #1

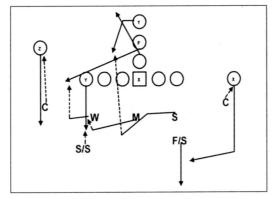

Figure 5-65. Flow pass

Flood Pass (Figure 5-66)

Will: 2 match. Zones over the tailback. Will be alert for a checkdown.

Mike: 3 match. Collisions and runs with the tight end on a drag.

Sam: 2 match. Takes the fullback in the flat. Runs the stripe.

Strong safety: Zones the quarter.

Free safety: Zones the quarter.

Corners: #1 man

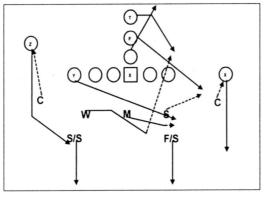

Figure 5-66. Flood pass

Waggle (Figure 5-67)

Will: 2 match. Zones over the tailback.
Mike: 3 match. Collisions and runs with the tight end on a drag.
Sam: 2 match. Takes the fullback in the flat. Runs the stripe.
Strong safety: Zones the quarter.
Free safety: Zones the quarter.
Corners: #1 man

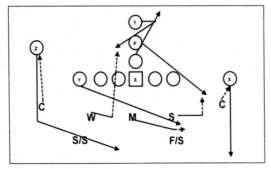

Figure 5-67. Waggle

Sprint Passes (Figures 5-68 through 5-70)

Corner: #1 man
Onside linebacker: Plasters #2 (takes him man-to-man).
Mike: 3 match with a possible recage on the quarterback
Offside linebacker: 2 match. Looks for screen or crosser.
Onside safety: Zones the quarter.
Offside safety: Zones the quarter.

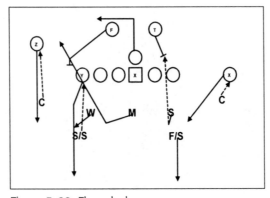

Figure 5-68. Flow dash

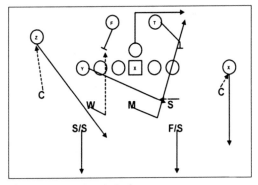

Figure 5-69. Flood dash

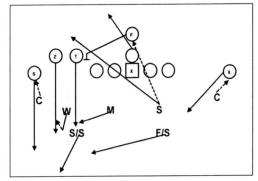

Figure 5-70. Sprint pass

Cover 8 Motion Adjustments
(Figures 5-71 through 5-78)

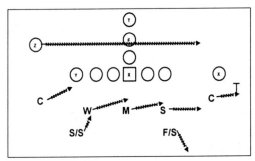

Figure 5-71. Pro to slot—dead call

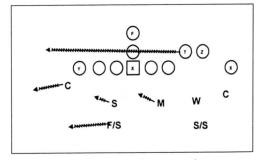

Figure 5-72. Trips closed to spread

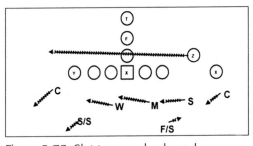

Figure 5-73. Slot to pro—check read

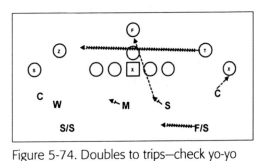

Figure 5-74. Doubles to trips—check yo-yo

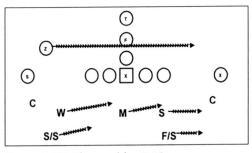

Figure 5-75. Three wides ZAC

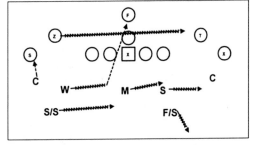

Figure 5-76. Doubles to trips—check yo-yo

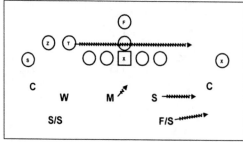

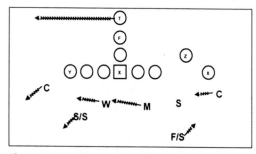

Figure 5-77. Trips open to doubles—check read   Figure 5-78. Slot to spread

Cover 8 Coaching Points—Linebackers

Linebackers must read receiver distribution. The outside linebackers Will and Sam are 2 match players, which means they zone over the #2 receiver. Mike is a 3 match player. He will zone over #3. Linebackers, like other defenders, have a five-yard no-cover rule. Receivers under five yards will not be covered in cover 8. Linebackers leverage routes deep to short and inside-out. They get reroutes or make the receiver avoid linebackers, which takes speed off their route. Versus a displaced #2, outside linebackers will play halfway between #2 and the end man on the line of scrimmage (EMLOS). Versus 3x1 sets, outside linebackers will give a bump trips call and split #2 and #3. Trips adjustments will be covered later in this chapter. Mike is a 3 match player. He has #3 on a go route out of the backfield. Mike will open to #3's release, which can be a strong or weak turn. If #2 and #3 close together, Mike will give a banjo call, which alerts defenders that #2 and #3 can cross on their distributions.

Outside Linebacker's 2 Match Technique

#2 Vertical (Figure 5-79)

The outside linebacker will reroute and carry #2 to 10 yards and level. As he carries #2, the outside linebacker will vision #1 for the smash route. If #1 is on a short route and the corner gives a smash call, the outside linebacker will drive inside-out on #1.

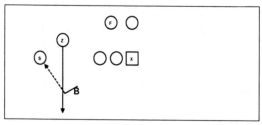

Figure 5-79. #2 vertical

#2 In or Drag (Figure 5-80)

The outside linebacker will squeeze #2, looking for a new #2 coming inside-out. He will give an in call to the Mike. If no #2 shows from inside-out, he may be coming from the other side.

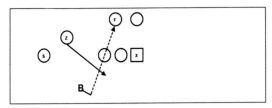

Figure 5-80. #2 in or drag

#2 Pass Blocks (Figure 5-81)

The outside linebacker will gain a depth of 8 to 10 yards and hang with peripheral vision on the quarterback. The outside linebacker observes the five-yard no-cover rule, but will drive on checkdowns, delays, screens, or quarterback scrambles.

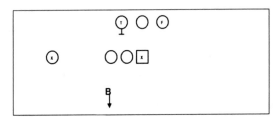

Figure 5-81. #2 pass blocks

#2 Flat Route (Figure 5-82)

The outside linebacker runs the stripe and is responsible for the wheel route. The backer peeks at the #1 for a pick play. If #1 is a threat, he will go over the top of #1.

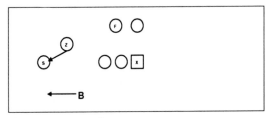

Figure 5-82. #2 flat route

#2 Flare Route (Figure 5-83)

The flare is played like the flat route. The backer will run the stripe.

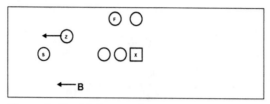

Figure 5-83. #2 flare route

#2 Goes Away (Figure 5-84)

The outside linebacker gains depth looking for a new #2. He will get his vision on the quarterback.

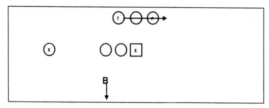

Figure 5-84. #2 goes away

Mike's 3 Match Technique

#3 Blocks (Figure 5-85)

Mike gains a depth of 8 to 10 yards with vision on the quarterback. He will drive on delays, screens, checkdowns, and quarterback scrambles.

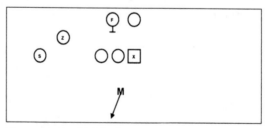

Figure 5-85. #3 blocks

#3 Flare Route (Figure 5-86)

Mike gains width and depth, looking for a new #3. He will give an out call and anticipate an in call from the outside linebacker.

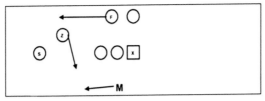

Figure 5-86. #3 flare route

#3 Vertical (Figure 5-87)

Mike reroutes #3 and carry to the safety. With #2 and #3 close together, he will give a banjo call.

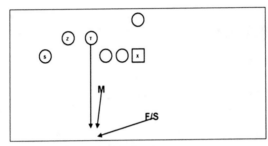

Figure 5-87. #3 vertical

#3 In (Figure 5-88)

Mike squeezes and plays from deep to short, looking for a new #3. He will give an in call.

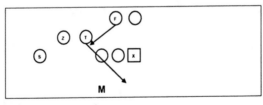

Figure 5-88. #3 in

#3 Out (Figure 5-89)

Mike expands, looking for a new #3.

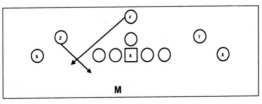

Figure 5-89. #3 out

#3 Flare (Figure 5-90)

Mike expands, looking for a new #3.

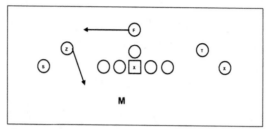

Figure 5-90. #3 flare

Cover 8 Coaching Points—Secondary

Safety Coaching Points

The strong safety and free safety positions in cover 8 are mirrored positions. Alignment is nine yards deep at the edge of the box with no displaced #2. With a displaced #2, the safety will line up nine yards deep with inside leverage on #2. The free safety backside of a 3x1 formation will line up 10 yards deep in the B gap. This formation is referred to as a B-10 alignment. The safeties will read the triangle. The triangle is the near side offensive line to the near back. The safeties will look for high or low helmets, which signify either pass or run. The safeties will bounce step as they read #2. Following are rules for the safety as he reads #2:

- *#2 Run Blocks* (Figure 5-91): The safety will stack with the end.
- *#2 Pass Blocks* (Figure 5-92): The safety will zone the quarter.

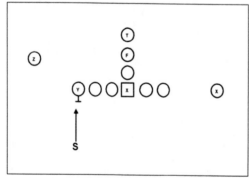

Figure 5-91. #2 run blocks

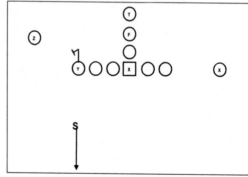

Figure 5-92. #2 pass blocks

- *#2 Vertical* (Figure 5-93): The safety will take #2 man-to-man inside-out on a vertical route. Vertical is defined as passing the linebacker who will collision and carry the receiver 10 yards from the line of scrimmage.
- *#2 Inside* (Figure 5-94): The safety will zone the quarter. As he zones the quarter, he will read the quarterback's eyes.
- *#2 Flat* (Figure 5-95): With #2 on a flat route, the safety will rob or double #1.
- *#2 Flare* (Figure 5-96): The safety will drive inside-out on #2 for the bubble or belly flip.

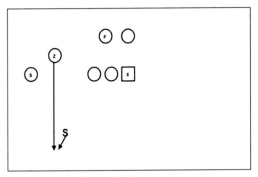

Figure 5-93. #2 vertical

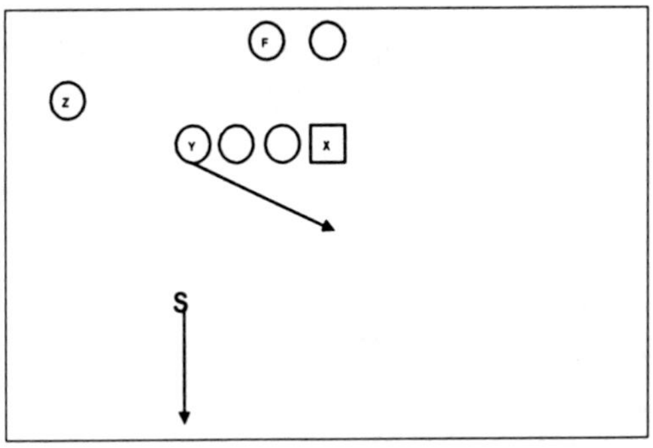

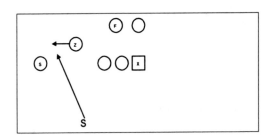

Figure 5-94. #2 inside

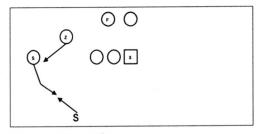

Figure 5-95. #2 flat

Figure 5-96. #2 flare

Corner Coaching Points

Corners, as a basic rule, align 1x7 inside on #1 with their outside foot forward. The corner has #1 man-to-man on any route over five yards deep. The corners, like the linebackers, have a five-yard no-cover rule. However, the corners will drive on a three-step pass. The corner will key the three-step drop as he backpedals. As the quarterback clears the three-step, the corner will get his eyes back on the receiver. Any route over five yards results in the corner taking the receiver man-to-man. Corners must always keep inside leverage on #1. Depending on what #2 does, the corner may or may not have safety help. The corner must never assume he will have post help. The corner must never respect an outside fake by the receiver. Following are corner reactions:

- *#1 Post* (Figure 5-97): The corner must never give up the post. Chances are the corner will have no post help.
- *#1 Go Route* (Figure 5-98): The corner has #1 man. He will man-turn and keep inside leverage.
- *#1 Quick Route* (Figure 5-99): The corner will drive outside-in.
- *Quick Screen* (Figure 5-100): The corner plays this reaction just like a three-step drop. He will drive outside-in.
- *#1 Drag* (Figure 5-101): With no displaced #2, the corner will turn this play over to the safety, who will drive on it. The corner will squeeze with depth, looking for work.
- *Smash* (Figure 5-102): With #1 on a route under five yards, the corner will midpoint the receivers, yell "Smash," and point to #1.

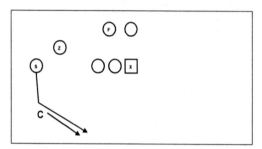

Figure 5-97. #1 post

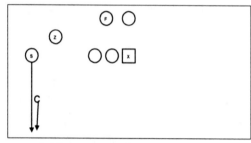

Figure 5-98. #1 go route

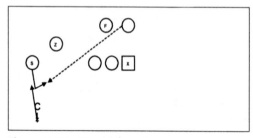

Figure 5-99. #1 quick route

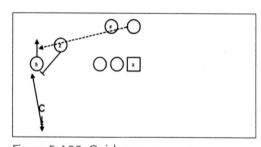

Figure 5-100. Quick screen

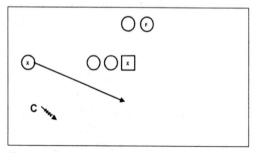

Figure 5-101. #1 drag

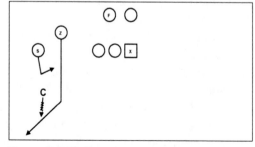

Figure 5-102. Smash

Cover 8 Variations

A number of variations or change-ups are available in cover 8. These variations give the offense a different look, give individual players some protection, and are sound adjustments to particular formations.

Zorro

Zorro is used when #1 and #2 are aligned close and a wheel route is likely. As a basic rule, the outside linebacker has the wheel route by #2 man-to-man. Some quarters coverage schemes will check to a soft cover 2 look to that side. In doing so, the defense would lose the safety in the run fit. This defense prefers not to do that. In order to keep the safety in the run fit, a Zorro call is made. The Zorro adjustment has the onside corner pressing #1 with the outside linebacker lining up deeper so he can get over the top of #1 on an inside or pick route. The safety still has his run fit, but versus a pass will automatically zone the quarter. He will supply deep help for the backer if #2 runs the wheel. The corner presses and takes #1 man-to-man.

Yo-Yo (Figure 5-103)

Any 3x1 formation forces cover 8 to make an adjustment. To keep the offense from taking advantage of a predictable response, the defense must have more than one adjustment. Following are some possibilities. The defense should make these adjustments as late as possible to force the offense to adapt after the snap.

Yo-yo is the base way to play a 3x1 formation. With a yo-yo call, Mike and Sam make a bump trips call, which moves them to 30 alignments. Will, frontside corner, and the strong safety play a normal read technique. Sam has the back man-to-man. The backside corner has the weakside receiver man-to-man with a slant technique. The free safety moves to a B-10 alignment late and cross keys to #3. The free safety will take the #3 man if he goes vertical. If #3 doesn't go vertical, he looks to help Sam on any deep route by the back.

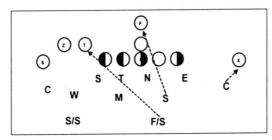

Figure 5-103. Yo-yo

Squeeze (Figure 5-104)

As stated earlier, a predictable response to a 3x1 set gives the offense a distinct advantage. If a yo-yo adjustment is the norm, the offense can scheme to get Sam or the backside corner on an island. A second adjustment to a 3x1 is called squeeze. With a squeeze call, the strong corner takes #1 man-to-man. Will moves late to outside leverage on #2, with Mike leveraging #3 inside. The strong safety will top #2 and #3. The strong safety will play equal distance between #2 and #3, supplying deep help. He is not concerned with #1 because the corner has him man-to-man. To the weakside, the defense is in a cover 2 look. This provides protection for the weak corner and Sam. Squeeze is also a good way to defend an empty set.

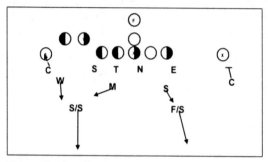

Figure 5-104. Squeeze

Steeler (Figure 5-105)

The strong corner tops #1 with the strong safety topping #2, and #3. Will jumps #1, Mike jumps #2, and the free safety jumps #3. Sam takes the back man-to-man with the weak corner taking #1 man.

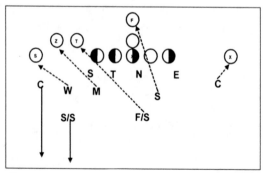

Figure 5-105. Steeler

Quads (Figure 5-106)

The strong corner, Will, and the strong safety play normal yo-yo rules. Sam takes #2 from weakside man-to-man with the free safety on #3 strong man-to-man. The weakside corner takes #1 man. Another way to play quads is to check Tampa. Tampa is a cover 2 check.

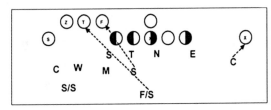

Figure 5-106. Quads

Flat

A flat call enables the defense to keep the linebackers close to the box, which enhances their ability to play the run. A flat call also allows the defense to play the bubble screen more aggressively. On a flat call, the corner and safety read the release of #2. The corner will press bail #1 while keying #2. If #2 goes vertical or drags, the corner will take #1 man-to-man. If #2 flares or runs a flat route, the corner will take him man-to-man. With #2 vertical, the safety will take him man-to-man. Should #2 run a flare or flat, the safety will take #1 man-to-man. The backer plays closer to the box, which enables him to be involved more in the run game. The backer will drop to the hash and is responsible for #3 to the flat. If no #3 shows, the backer will zone up and find work. Mike is normal. Figure 5-107 shows a bubble route with a flat call, and Figure 5-108 illustrates a double vertical route.

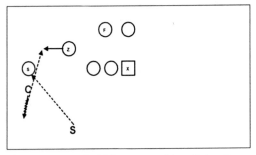

Figure 5-107. Bubble route with a flat call

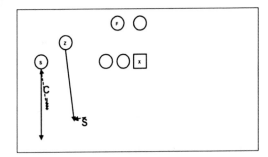

Figure 5-108. Double vertical route

Cloud

The corner will check cloud whenever #1 is aligned tight. The force changes from safety to corner force. The shell to the cloud side is a cover 2 shell. Versus a pass, the corner has the flat, and the safety has deep half. Each side is independent from the other. The corner replaces the safety on a run away run fit. The safety is responsible for reverse. Figure 5-109 shows a cloud call versus a wing I formation. The weakside still has a cover 8 read concept. Figure 5-110 shows a cloud call versus a flanker set. The strongside still has a cover 8 read scheme.

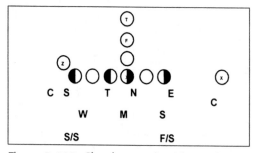

Figure 5-109. Cloud vs. a wing I formation

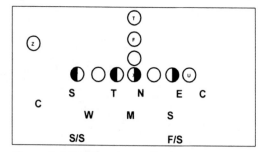

Figure 5-110. Cloud vs. a flanker set

Cover 8 Match

Cover 8 match can be used against 21 personnel, which likes to align in slot, motion to slot, or motion from slot to pro sets. Cover 8 match tells the corners to match up with the wideouts. Figure 5-111 shows defensive reaction to a slot set. With a slot set, the linebackers will have trio coverage on the backs with the strong safety man on the tight end. Figure 5-112 shows defensive reaction to pro to slot motion. If the offense lines up in pro or motions to pro from slot, the defense plays normal cover 8 read techniques (Figure 5-113).

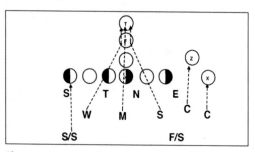

Figure 5-111. Defensive reaction to a slot set

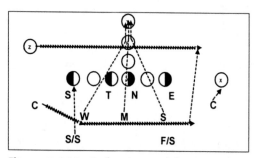

Figure 5-112. Defensive reaction to pro to slot motion

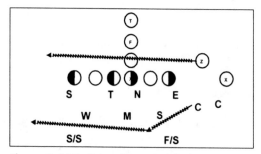

Figure 5-113. Cover 8 read techniques

Cover 3

No two-high safety defensive system would be complete without a three-deep concept change-up. Included in this chapter is a three-deep strong rotation called cover 3Y and a weak rotation called cover 3X.

Strengths of Cover 3

- It is an eight-men-in-the-box zone defense.
- 3Y looks like cover black and 3X mimics cover China. Man routes tailored for black and China would be ineffective against a three-deep look.
- It is a four-under, three-deep zone with a four-man rush.
- It is effective versus any formation.
- It starts from a two-deep shell.
- There will always be a post defender. Route concepts designed to split a two-high shell will find a deep hole player.

Weaknesses of Cover 3

- Quick game versus deep-third defenders
- Seam concepts using 2x2 formations
- Four verticals against three deep

Additional Information

- A bail call can be used (cover 3 bail).
- A dead call is given versus slot sets.
- The drop safety will dive and the hole safety will spin on the snap. They hold the cover 8 shell as long as possible.
- As a base rule, in 3Y Will is the curl-flat player and the strong safety is the hook-curl defender. With a flip call, Will is the hook-curl defender and the strong safety becomes the curl-flat player. The same thing applies in 3X. As a base rule, Sam has curl-flat and the free safety is the hook-curl defender. With a flip call, they switch zones.
- A check cloud call can be used versus Z or X close formations.
- A Mabel call is used against 3x1 formations

Alignments for Formations in Cover 3Y
(Figures 5-114 through 5-125)

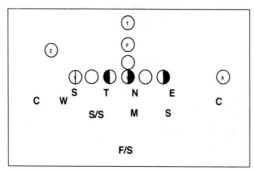

Figure 5-114. Pro

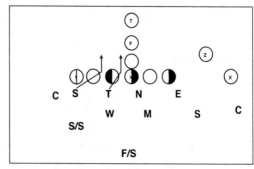

Figure 5-115. Slot—check cloud, check dead

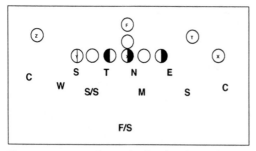

Figure 5-116. Spread—check alert danger (four verticals)

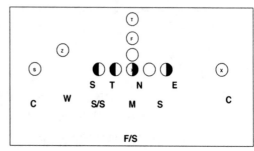

Figure 5-117. Three wides

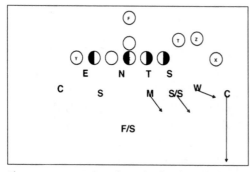

Figure 5-118. Trips closed—check Mabel

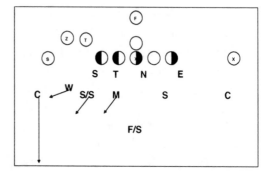

Figure 5-119. Trips open—check Mabel

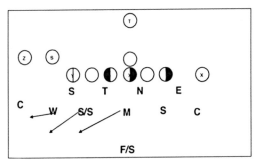

Figure 5-120. Trey—check Mabel

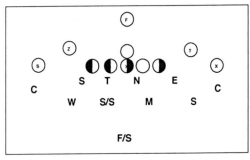

Figure 5-121. Doubles—check alert danger (four verticals)

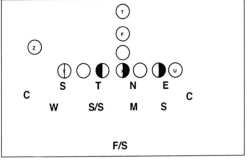

Figure 5-122. Flanker

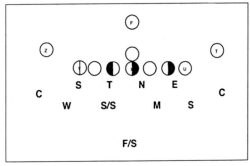

Figure 5-123. Tech—check alert danger (four verticals)

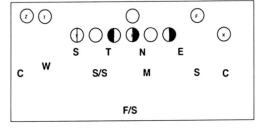

Figure 5-124. Empty trey

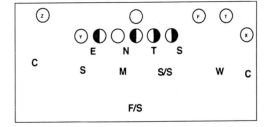

Figure 5-125. Empty spread

Mabel Call

Mabel is used against 3x1 formations. Will, the strong safety, and Mike work over one zone. Will has the flat, the strong safety has the curl, and Mike works to the hook area.

Run Fits for Cover 3Y

Flow Run (Figure 5-126)

Will: D+; force
Strong safety: Over the top
Mike: A+ to over the top
Sam: Cutback B–
Free safety: Alley
Onside corner: Secondary contain
Offside corner: Cutback to cutoff

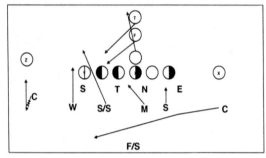

Figure 5-126. Flow run

Flood Run (Figure 5-127)

Will: D+; BCR (bootleg, counter, reverse)
Strong safety: A+
Mike: Quick to B–
Sam: B–. Spills.
Free safety: Alley
Outside corner: Secondary contain
Offside corner: Cutback to cutoff

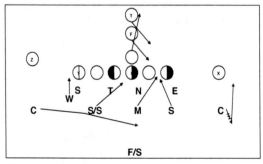

Figure 5-127. Flood run

Divide Run (Figure 5-128)

Will: D+; force
Strong safety: Over the top to A+
Mike: A+ to B–
Sam: B– to C–
Free safety: Alley
Onside corner: Secondary contain
Offside corner: Cutback to cutoff

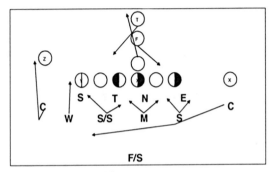

Figure 5-128. Divide run

Cover 3Y vs. Play-Action, Dash, and Sprint Passes

Fire Pass (Figure 5-129)

Will: Curl-flat; fullback
Strong safety: Hook-curl; tailback checkdown
Mike: Weak hook-curl; X dig
Sam: Curl-flat; tight end drag
Free safety: Hole
Corners: Deep third

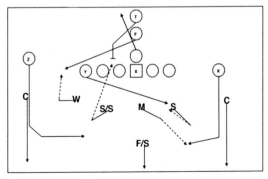

Figure 5-129. Fire passes

Flow Pass (Figure 5-130)

Will: Curl-flat; fullback
Strong safety: Hook-curl. Carries the tight end.
Mike: Hook-curl; tailback checkdown
Sam: Curl-flat; X dig
Free Safety: Hole
Corners: Deep third

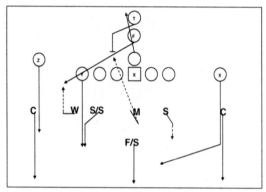

Figure 5-130. Flow pass

Flood Pass (Figure 5-131)

Will: Curl-flat; Z dig
Strong safety: Hook-curl; tailback checkdown
Mike: Hook-curl; tight end
Sam: Curl-flat; fullback
Free safety: Hole
Corners: Deep third

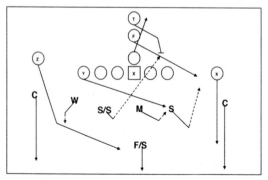

Figure 5-131. Flood pass

Waggle (Figure 5-132)

Will: Curl-flat; Z dig
Strong safety: Hook-curl; tailback checkdown or screen
Mike: Hook-curl; tight end drag
Sam: Curl-flat; fullback
Free safety: Hole
Corners: Deep third

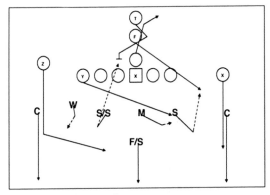

Figure 5-132. Waggle

Sprint Passes (Figures 5-133 through 5-135)

Note: Underneath defenders sling, or work over, one zone to the sprint side.

Onside corner: Deep third
Will: Curl-flat. Flat buzzes #1. Takes away the deep out or comeback route.
Strong safety: Hook-curl. Drives inside-out on #2 in the curl.
Mike: Offside hook-curl. Works to frontside hook and relate to #3. Possible recage on the quarterback.
Sam: Offside curl-flat. Stays in hook, looking for crossers or screen.
Free safety: Hole. Checks for throwback post to X.
Offside corner: Squeezes #1 for throwback. Looks for #2.

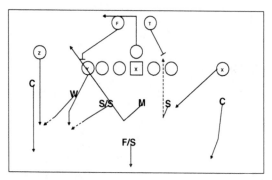
Figure 5-133. Flow dash

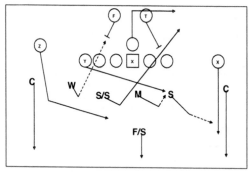
Figure 5-134. Flood dash

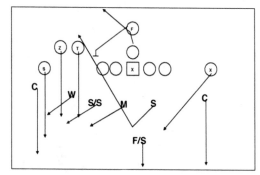
Figure 5-135. Sprint pass

Cover 3Y Motion Adjustments

Motions will be handled by the four underneath players. These players will slide to motion and play their assigned zones.

Flip Call

As mentioned earlier, the base rule in cover 3Y has Will playing the curl-flat, and the strong safety is assigned the hook-curl area. Figure 5-136 shows the base way of playing doubles. Figure 5-137 illustrates cover 3Y flip against the same set.

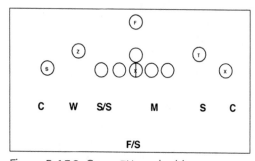
Figure 5-136. Cover 3Y vs. doubles

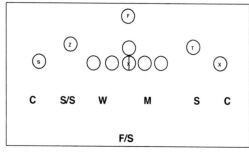
Figure 5-137. Cover 3Y flip vs. doubles

Cover 3X

As previously discussed, cover 3X involves weakside rotation. The free safety becomes the drop down safety. Back in the day, Bob Sanders of the Indianapolis Colts would drop down in 3X like he was shot out of a cannon. He made it look like he was on a stunt. When he did this, he was unaccounted for and made an untold number of tackles. As a base rule, the free safety is a curl-flat player against two-back formations. Against a displaced #2, the free safety is a hook-curl player unless a flip call is made. In this case, he is a curl-flat defender, and Sam is the hook-curl player.

One thing a coach must really contemplate when using cover 3X is how to handle 3x1 formations. Should a coach drop down the free safety backside of a 3x1 formation, he cannot Mabel frontside and with good offensive spacing may be outnumbered to the strongside. Should the defensive coach choose to dive the free safety backside a 3x1 set, he will still have a four-under, three-deep shell. As an alternative, the coach may choose to dive the strong safety and Mabel to the overload. This concept ties in with the Linda and Rita calls developed in Chapter 6, which are used with the eight-men-in-the-box coverage package. Linda and Rita is a simple way to get the safety down to the offensive strength. The following cover 3X alignment section will show the free safety dropped regardless of the formation. Also, the Oregon front will be used.

Alignments for Formations in Cover 3X
(Figures 5-138 through 5-149)

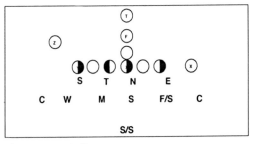

Figure 5-138. Pro

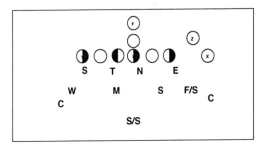

Figure 5-139. Slot

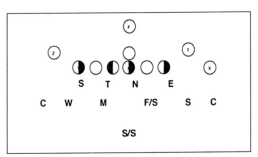

Figure 5-140. Spread—check alert danger (four verticals)

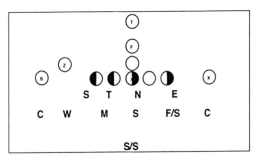

Figure 5-141. Three wides

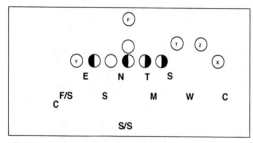

Figure 5-142. Trips closed

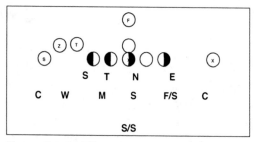

Figure 5-143. Trips open

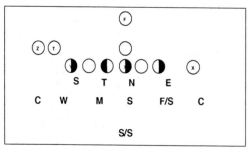

Figure 5-144. Trey—check alert danger (four verticals)

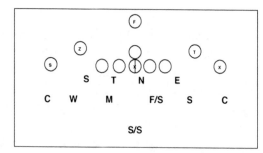

Figure 5-145. Doubles—check alert danger (four verticals)

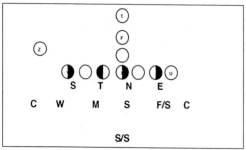

Figure 5-146. Flanker

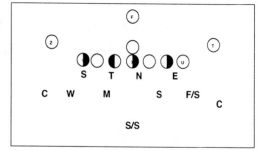

Figure 5-147. Tech—check alert danger (four verticals)

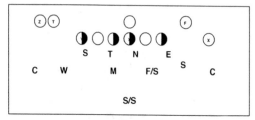

Figure 5-148. Empty trey

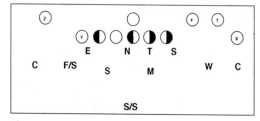

Figure 5-149. Empty spread

Run Fits for Cover 3X

Flow Run (Figure 5-150)

Will: D+; force
Mike: A+ to over the top. Spills.
Sam: A+
Free safety: Cutback B–
Strong safety: Alley
Onside corner: Secondary contain
Offside corner: Cutback to cutoff

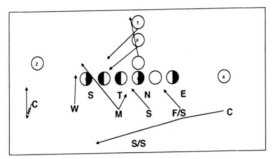

Figure 5-150. Flow run

Flood Run: (Figure 5-151)

Will: Cutback D+; BCR and tight end delay
Mike: A+
Sam: B–. Spills.
Free safety: B–. Turns in.
Strong safety: Alley
Onside corner: Secondary contain
Offside corner: Cutback to cutoff

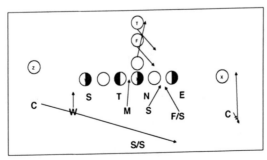

Figure 5-151. Flood run

Divide Run: (Figure 5-152)

Will: D+
Mike: Over the top to A+
Sam: A+ to B–
Free safety: B– to C–
Strong safety: Alley
Onside corner: Secondary contain
Offside corner: Cutback to cutoff

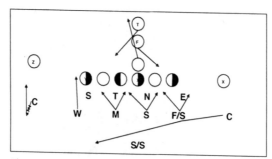

Figure 5-152. Divide run

Cover 3X vs. Play-Action, Dash, and Sprint Passes

Fire Pass (Figure 5-153)

Will: Curl-flat; fullback
Mike: Hook-curl; tailback checkdown
Sam: Hook-curl; tight end
Free safety: Curl-flat; first crosser to dig
Strong safety: Hole
Corners: Deep third

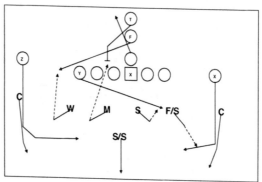

Figure 5-153. Fire pass

Flow Pass (Figure 5-154)

Will: Curl-flat; fullback
Mike: Hook-curl. Carries tight end.
Sam: Hook-curl; tailback checkdown
Free safety: Curl-flat; first crosser to dig
Strong safety: Hole
Corners: Deep third

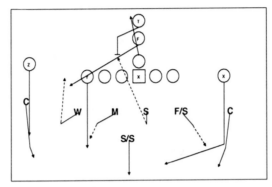

Figure 5-154. Flow pass

Flood Pass (Figure 5-155)

Will: Curl-flat; Z dig
Mike: Hook-curl; tailback checkdown
Sam: Hook-curl; tight end
Free safety: Curl-flat; fullback
Strong safety: Hole
Corners: Deep third

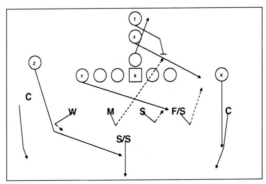

Figure 5-155. Flood pass

Waggle (Figure 5-156)

Will: Curl-flat; Z dig
Mike: Hook-curl; tailback checkdown or screen
Sam: Hook-curl; tight end
Free safety: Curl-flat; fullback

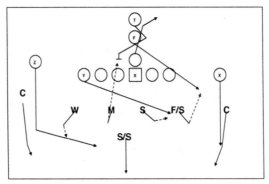

Figure 5-156. Waggle

Sprint Passes (Figures 5-157 through 5-159)

Note: Underneath defenders sling, or move, one zone to the sprint side.

Onside corner: Deep third
Will: Curl-flat. Flat buzzes #1. Takes away the deep out or comeback route.
Mike: Hook-curl. Drives inside-out on #2 in the curl.
Sam: Offside hook-curl. Works to frontside hook and relates to #3. Possible recage on quarterback.
Free safety: Offside curl-flat. Stays in hook, looking for crossers or screen.
Strong safety: Hole. Checks for throwback post to X.
Offside corner: Squeezes #1 for throwback. Looks for #2.

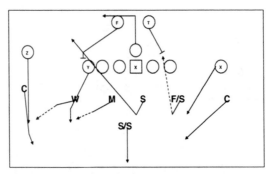

Figure 5-157. Flow dash

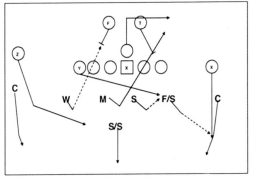

Figure 5-158. Flood dash

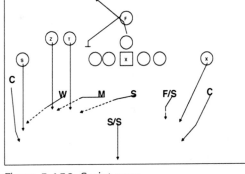

Figure 5-159. Sprint pass

Cover 3X Motion Adjustments

Motion will be handled by the four underneath players. These players will slide to motion and play their assigned zones.

Cover 3Y and 3X Coaching Points

Zones

Three-deep coverages have 11 areas to cover. The area from the line of scrimmage to a depth of five yards on the defensive side of the ball is designated as the no-cover zone. Following are the 11 areas to cover:

- *Flats:* 12 to 14 yards deep from the widest eligible receiver to the sideline
- *Curl:* 12 to 14 yards deep between the flat and hook zone
- *Hook:* 12 to 14 yards deep from the head of the center to the outside shoulder of a normally spaced third man
- *Seams:* Areas overlapping the inside of the curl to the hook area
- *Deep third:* A third of the field starting 14 yards deep

Corner's Deep Third Technique

- Keys the quarterback through the three-step drop.
- Plants and drives on the three-step drop unless he has multiple receivers to his side.
- Sees #1 and #2 on drop.
- If #1 is short or intermediate, looks for #2 to threaten deep.
- Plays post and goes routes first. Plays the post unless #2 is on a wheel. If the corner reads the wheel, he should split the two deep routes.
- Never comes off a post route unless #2 is on a wheel.
- Versus waggle, plays the post route.
- Versus dig routes, gains depth for the post corner.

- Remains aware of the divider rule.
- Versus running plays, has secondary contain on run to and cutback to cutoff or runs away. Never commits to the line of scrimmage until the ball crosses the line unless on a crack replace. Against a crack block, forces at a 45-degree angle.
- Escapes stalk blocks to the outside using hands and feet.

Corner's Divider Rule

A divider rule is instituted to get the corner in the middle of his deep third zone versus multiple receivers. This rule is referred to as the 511 rule. With the ball on the far hash with multiple receivers, the corner aligns five yards above the numbers, which places him 14 yards from the sideline (Figure 5-160). Figure 5-161 shows the corner's alignment with the ball in the middle of the field. The corner is one yard above the numbers, which places him 10 yards from the sideline. Should the ball be on the near hash, the corner aligns one yard below the numbers, which places him six yards from the sideline (Figure 5-162).

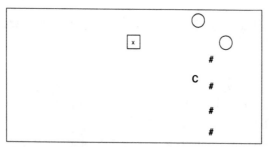

Figure 5-160. Corner's alignment with the ball on the far hash

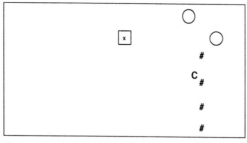

Figure 5-161. Corner's alignment with the ball in the middle of the field

Figure 5-162. Corner's alignment with the ball on the near hash

Deep Safety's Hole Rule

Depending upon the coverage, one safety will dive and the other safety will spin to the hole. The hole safety tries to split the distance between the widest receivers. He keys the uncovered lineman to the quarterback. He reads run slowly but is very aggressive when he reads run. He is an alley player versus running plays. Should he read #2 on a wheel route, he gains depth looking to play #1 on the post.

Underneath Zone Techniques

As illustrated earlier, there are six underneath zones. On either side of the ball, there are hook, curl, and flat zones.

Hook-Curl Technique

The hook-curl zone is usually from the football to the outside shoulder of a normally spaced third receiver. To the one-receiver side, the defender reads from #2 to #1. To the two-receiver side, the defender reads from #3 to #2. If the closest receiver goes out, the defender should expect the next receiver to come in. The defender should listen for an in call. If a receiver crosses the face of a hook-curl defender, he should give a drag call. The defender should attack checkdowns inside-out.

Curl-Flat Technique

This defender starts to drop to a point 12 yards deep. He should pattern read as he goes. He will open his hips and drive to the aim point. He crosses over and gains depth quickly. He should look up #2. Should #2 be on a seam, the defender must reroute him to the outside while eyeballing #1 for a seam-in or a smash route. As the curl-flat defender drops, he should peripherally vision the quarterback for a three-step drop and draw. Versus a three-step concept, he should get under control and react to the slant if the quarterback is looking his way. Against a draw, he should plant his outside foot and retrace, maintaining an outside-in position on the ball. Should the quarterback clear the three-step area, the curl-flat defender continues to drop, reading #2. He must never react to anything in front of him until he sees the ball thrown. If #2 crosses his face, he must give an in call. If #2 goes outside, he should look up #1. He never chases #2. The defender should attack checkdowns outside-in.

Slant Technique

Backside of a 3x1 set, the corner lines up inside the receiver to defend the slant.

6

Eight-Men-in-the-Box
Man Coverages

This chapter will examine coverages black, China, and white. These coverages involve an eighth-men-in-the-box concept. Black and white involve strong rotation. China is a weak rotation. The following will be included for each coverage:

- An overview with strengths and weaknesses
- Alignments, techniques, and keys
- Run and pass responsibilities
- Run fits
- Motion adjustments
- Coverage variations
- Coaching points

Cover Black

Cover black is an eight-men-in-the-box with strong or tight end rotation. The strong safety is the eighth man down. The corners have match coverage on the wideouts. The coverage will always have a low hole plugger and a deep hole player. Cover black supplies a four-man rush element.

Strengths of Cover Black

- Eight men in the box
- Corners in match coverage, which places the defense's best cover men on the wideouts
- Plugger available for crossing routes and misdirection passes
- Great for short yardage and play-action passes. The defense gets a body on a body. There is no guarding grass.

Weaknesses of Cover Black

- Slant route versus an off corner
- Only a base four-man rush

Additional Information

- The defense checks to special versus one-back formations. The safety to the side of the displaced #2 has him man-to-man with the other safety in the hole.
- Corners are responsible for reverse off Zarc motion.
- The strong safety has a 2x2 landmark on the tight end. The strong safety will rock down as the free safety spins to the hole. The defense should show a cover 8 shell as long as possible.
- Trio coverage is used on two backs.
- Reggie coverage is used on one back.
- With a special call, the Will has the tight end man-to-man.
- Ohio or Oregon front is used to give the strong safety outside leverage on the tight end. Also, with the Stud inside, the strong safety gets a great pass or run read on the tight end.

Alignments for Formations in Cover Black
(Figures 6-1 through 6-12)

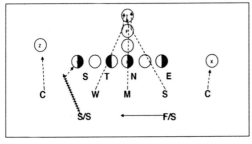

Figure 6-1. Pro

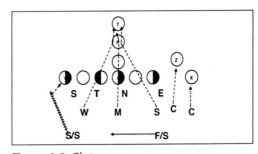

Figure 6-2. Slot

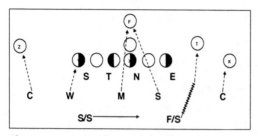
Figure 6-3. Spread—special call

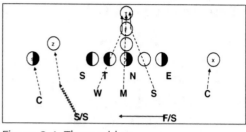
Figure 6-4. Three wides

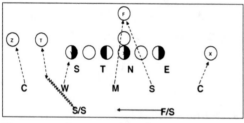
Figure 6-5. Trips closed—special call

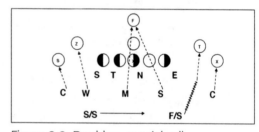
Figure 6-6. Trips open—special call

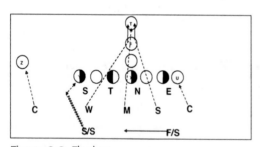
Figure 6-7. Trey—special call

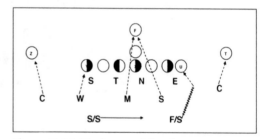
Figure 6-8. Doubles—special call

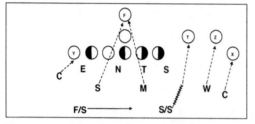
Figure 6-9. Flanker

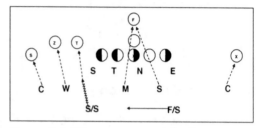
Figure 6-10. Tech—special call

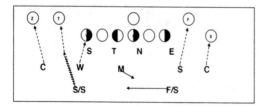
Figure 6-11. Empty trey—special call

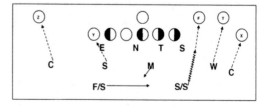
Figure 6-12. Empty spread—special call

Run Fits for Cover Black

Flow Run (Figure 6-13)

Will: Over the top. Spills all blocks.

Mike: A+

Sam: Cutback B−. With a spike call, Sam can go over the top because the tackle would play a cutback.

Strong safety: D+; force

Free safety: Alley

Onside corner: Secondary contain

Offside corner: Cutback to cutoff

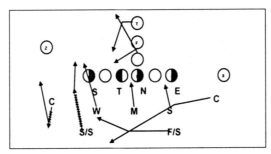

Figure 6-13. Flow run

Flood Run (Figure 6-14)

Will: A+

Mike: Quick to B−

Sam: B−. Spills all blocks.

Strong safety: D+. Will be alert for a tight end delay.

Free safety: Alley

Onside corner: Secondary contain

Offside corner: Cutback to cutoff

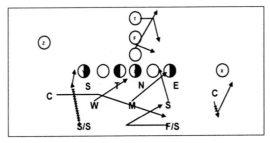

Figure 6-14. Flood run

Divide Run (Figure 6-15)

Will: Over the top to A+
Mike: A+ to over the top
Sam: B– to C–
Strong safety: D+
Free safety: Alley
Onside corner: Secondary contain
Offside corner: Cutback to cutoff

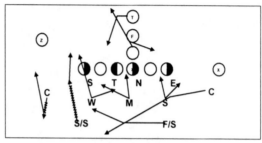

Figure 6-15. Divide run

Cover Black vs. Play-Action, Dash, and Sprint Passes

Fire Pass (Figure 6-16)

Will: Trio coverage. Linebackers have the two backs, depending upon their distribution. The free linebacker is the plugger. He will drop 8 to 10 yards over the ball, looking for crossers. Versus a fire pass, Will has the fullback.
Mike: Tailback
Sam: Plugger. Helps on the tight end.
Strong safety: Tight end
Free safety: Hole
Corners: #1

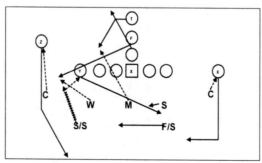

Figure 6-16. Fire pass

Flow Pass (Figure 6-17)

Will: Fullback
Mike: Tailback
Sam: Plugger. Drops 8 to 10 yards over the ball, looking for crossers.
Strong safety: Tight end
Free safety: Hole
Corners: #1

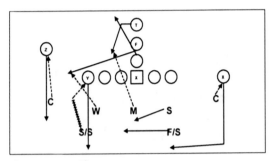

Figure 6-17. Flow pass

Flood Pass (Figure 6-18)

Will: Plugger
Mike: Tailback
Sam: Fullback
Strong safety: Tight end
Free safety: Hole
Corners: #1

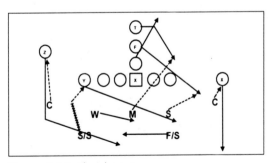

Figure 6-18. Flood pass

Waggle (Figure 6-19)

Will: Tailback
Mike: Plugger with a possible recage on the quarterback
Sam: Fullback
Strong safety: Tight end
Free safety: Hole
Corner: #1

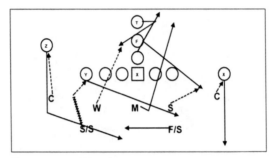

Figure 6-19. Waggle

Sprint Passes (Figures 6-20 through 6-22)

Coverage is man-to-man. If the assigned man pass blocks, the defender will hug the blocker. Hug means go get the assigned man. The defender on a blocker will recage the quarterback. If, on a sprint pass, the offense likes to use the blocker as a checkdown receiver, the plugger can be used as the recage defender.

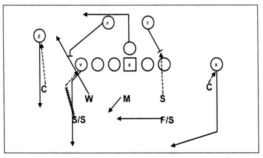

Figure 6-20. Flow dash

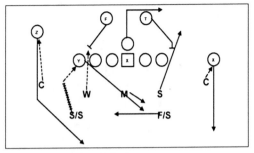

Figure 6-21. Flood dash

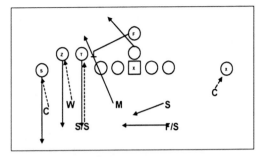

Figure 6-22. Sprint pass

Cover Black Motion Adjustments

The man assigned the motion man will adjust. Figure 6-23 shows Z motion. Motion from the backfield is covered by the outside linebacker to that side (Figures 6-24 and 6-25). If the offense is trying to get a mismatch on the linebacker, the defense can make a special call and have the safeties adjust (Figures 6-26 and 6-27).

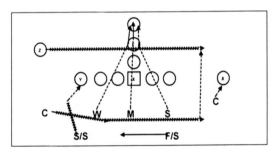

Figure 6-23. Z motion

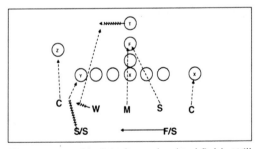

Figure 6-24. Motion from the backfield—Will takes fly motion

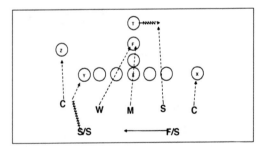

Figure 6-25. Motion from the backfield—Sam takes peel motion

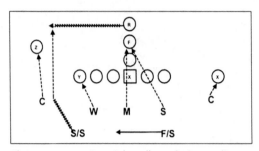

Figure 6-26. Special call, safeties adjust—strong safety takes strong motion that leaves the backfield

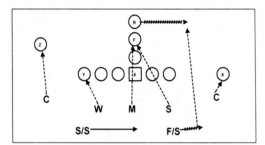

Figure 6-27. Special call, safeties adjust—free safety takes weak motion that leaves the backfield

Cover Black Coaching Points

Trio Coverage

Versus a two-back set, the three linebackers will take the backs man-to-man, depending upon their distribution. The linebacker with no back becomes a plugger. He will drop 8 to 10 yards over the ball, keying the quarterback and looking for crossers.

Reggie

Whenever the offense has only one back, the defense will make a special call. A special call places the safety to the side of the displaced #2 on him man-to-man. The Will linebacker assumes responsibility for the tight end. Mike and Sam now have the remaining back, depending upon his distribution (Reggie). The linebacker to the side of the back's release has him man-to-man. The free linebacker becomes the plugger.

Cover Black Variations

The following variations are plugger change-ups. As a base rule, the plugger will drop 8 to 10 yards, looking for crossers. However, he can do other things:

- *Russian* (Figure 6-28): The plugger can free rush the quarterback. He will find a gap and go.
- *Cut* (Figure 6-29): The plugger doubles a designated receiver.
- *Spy* (Figure 6-30): Versus an athletic quarterback, the plugger can be assigned as a spy on him.

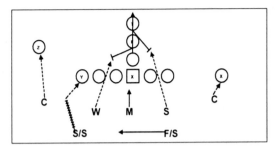
Figure 6-28. Russian

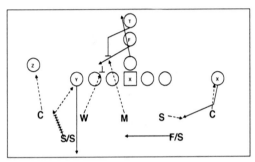
Figure 6-29. Cut

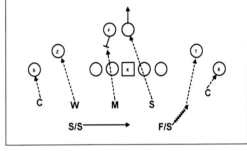
Figure 6-30. Spy

Cover China

China is similar to black in that it is an eight-men-in-the-box coverage. Like black, it involves man coverage. Unlike black, China is a weakside rotation with the free safety as the eighth man. Many of the same concepts used in black are also used in China. Many of the same advantages and disadvantages are present in both coverages. There is a carryover on many of the calls and adjustments. China can be run out of the over front, but the prevalent front used is under.

Alignments for Formations in Cover China (Figures 6-31 through 6-42)

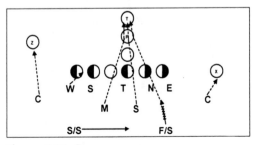
Figure 6-31. Pro

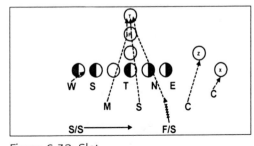
Figure 6-32. Slot

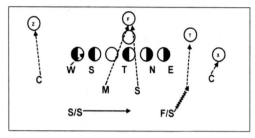

Figure 6-33. Spread—special call

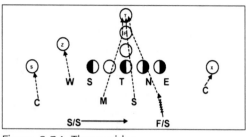

Figure 6-34. Three wides

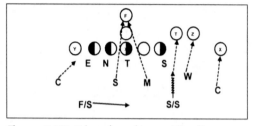

Figure 6-35. Trips closed—special call

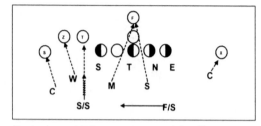

Figure 6-36. Trips open—special call

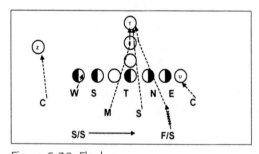

Figure 6-37. Trey—special call

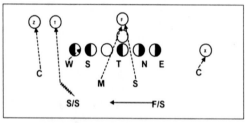

Figure 6-38. Doubles—special call

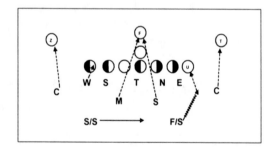

Figure 6-39. Flanker

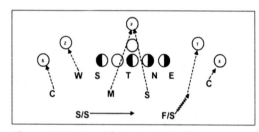

Figure 6-40. Tech—special call

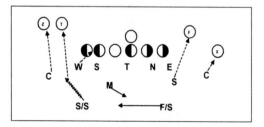

Figure 6-41. Empty trey—special call

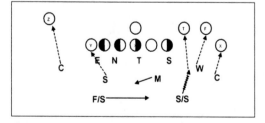

Figure 6-42. Empty spread—special call

Run Fits for Cover China

Flow Run (Figure 6-43)

Will: Box
Mike: B+. Spills all blocks.
Sam: Quick to B+
Strong safety: Alley
Free safety: Cutback A–
Onside corner: Secondary contain
Offside corner: Cutback to cutoff

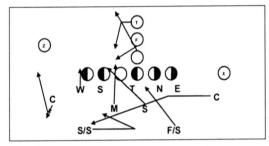

Figure 6-43. Flow run

Flood Run (Figure 6-44)

Will: Chase. Will be alert for a tight end delay.
Mike: Cutback B+
Sam: A–. Spills all blocks.
Strong safety: Alley
Free safety: A–. Spills all blocks.
Onside corner: Secondary contain
Offside corner: Cutback to cutoff

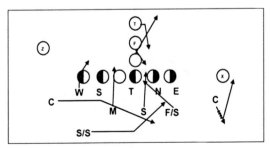

Figure 6-44. Flood run

Divide Run (Figure 6-45)

Will: D+
Mike: B+
Sam: A+
Strong safety: Alley
Free safety: C–
Onside corner: Secondary contain
Offside corner: Cutback to cutoff

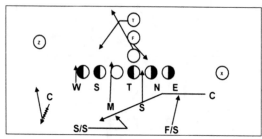

Figure 6-45. Divide run

Cover China vs. Play-Action, Dash, and Sprint Passes

Fire Pass (Figure 6-46)

Will: Tight end man. The free safety will help on a drag.
Mike: Trio coverage. Mike, Sam, and the free safety have the two backs, depending upon their distribution. Versus a fire pass, Mike takes the fullback.
Sam: Tailback
Strong safety: Hole
Free safety: Plugger. Helps on the tight end.
Corners: #1 man

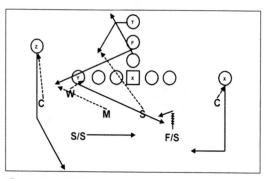

Figure 6-46. Fire pass

Flow Pass (Figure 6-47)

Will: Tight end
Mike: Fullback
Sam: Tailback
Strong safety: Hole
Free safety: Plugger. Drops 8 to 10 yards over the ball, looking for crossers.
Corners: #1 man

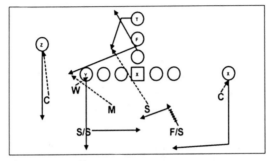

Figure 6-47. Flow pass

Flood Pass (Figure 6-48)

Will: Tight end
Mike: Plugger
Sam: Tailback
Strong safety: Hole
Free safety: Fullback
Corners: #1 man

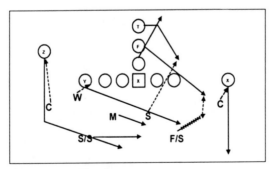

Figure 6-48. Flood pass

Waggle (Figure 6-49)

Will: Tight end
Mike: Tailback
Sam: Plugger
Strong safety: Hole
Free safety: Fullback
Corners: #1

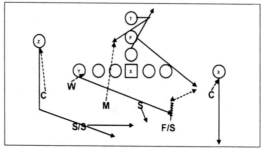

Figure 6-49. Waggle

Sprint Passes (Figures 6-50 through 6-52)

Coverage is man-to-man. If the assigned man pass blocks, the defender will hug (go get) him. The defender on a blocker will recage the quarterback on a sprint pass. If the offense likes to use the blocker as a checkdown receiver, the plugger can be used as the recage defender.

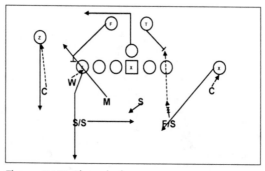

Figure 6-50. Flow dash

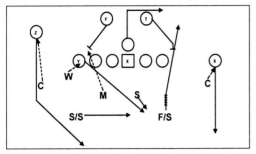

Figure 6-51. Flood dash

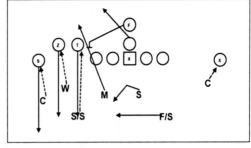

Figure 6-52. Sprint pass

Cover China Motion Adjustments

The man on the motion man will adjust. Figure 6-53 shows Z motion from a slot set. Motion from the backfield will be covered by the free safety. Mike and Sam will then Reggie the remaining back.

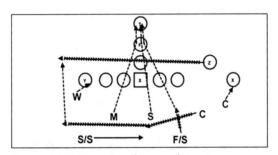

Figure 6-53. Z motion from a slot set

Cover China Coaching Points

Will Backer's 9 Technique

For Will to play on the line in a 9 technique, he must develop a new skill set since he usually plays off the line.

Base Block

Will must turn the tight end's shoulders inside, which is the same steer technique used by the defensive line. He must keep his hips and feet back and lock out. He must be ready for a bounce out.

Hook Block

Will must turn the tight end's shoulders outside by steering while keeping his hips and feet back. He will try to get to a spot 4x1 upfield.

Down Block and Kickout

Will uses a box technique. He should close with the down block while getting his eyes to the pull lane. He must get to the depth of the blocker and take him on with an inside forearm and force the ball inside.

Tight End and Wing

The tight end and wing is called a pair. Will plays all blocks as if a wing were not there. If the wing blocks down on him, the Will must fight into him. Will cannot be caved. He does not attempt to fight outside and crossface the wing. He must keep his head in the crack and fight upfield.

Chase Technique

The chase technique is used on flood runs. Versus a down block, Will should close to the ball on the offensive side of the line of scrimmage. Will has bootleg, counter, and reverse (BCR) responsibilities. Versus a base or high wall block, he must steer and fold.

Cover China Variations

Many of the same calls and adjustments in black and China are similar. Included are plugger change-ups. Russian, cut, and spy wrinkles can also be used in cover China.

Cover White

Cover white is similar to cover black in that white involves strong rotation. However, unlike black, which uses strong eagle fronts (e.g., Ohio or Oregon), white uses the under front. White, like black and China, is an eight-men-in-the-box coverage with man coverage. Many of the same coverage concepts used in black and China are incorporated in cover white. There is a carryover on many of the calls and adjustments involved in the other eight-men-in-the-box coverages.

Alignments for Formations in Cover White
(Figures 6-54 through 6-65)

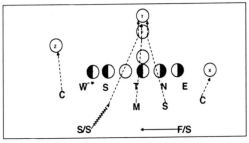

Figure 6-54. Pro

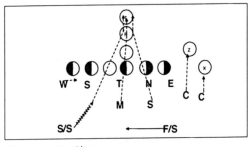

Figure 6-55. Slot

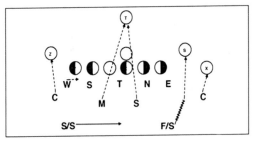

Figure 6-56. Spread—special call

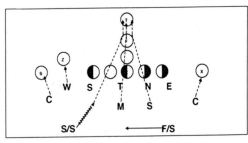

Figure 6-57. Three wides

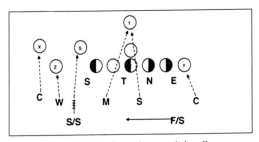

Figure 6-58. Trips closed—special call

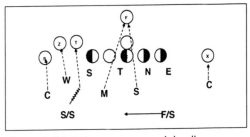

Figure 6-59. Trips open—special call

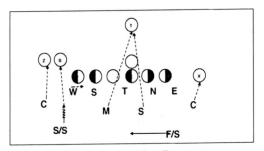

Figure 6-60. Trey—special call

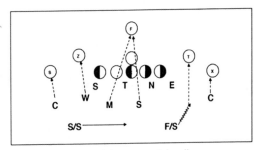

Figure 6-61. Doubles—special call

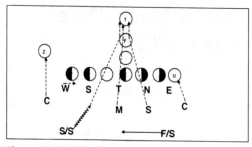

Figure 6-62. Flanker

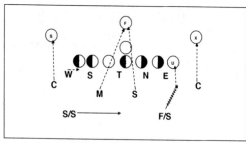

Figure 6-63. Tech—special call

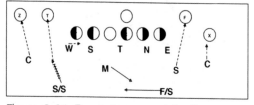

Figure 6-64. Empty trey—special call

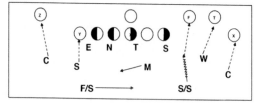

Figure 6-65. Empty spread—special call

Run Fits for Cover White

Flow Run (Figure 6-66)

Will: D+; box
Mike: B+. Spills all blocks.
Sam: Cutback A–
Strong safety: B+. Turns into over the top.
Free safety: Alley
Onside corner: Secondary contain
Offside corner: Cutback to cutoff

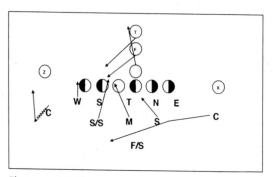

Figure 6-66. Flow run

Flood Run (Figure 6-67)

Will: Chase. Will be alert for tight end delay.
Mike: Quick to A–
Sam: A–. Spills all blocks.
Strong safety: Cutback B+
Free safety: Alley
Onside corner: Secondary contain
Offside corner: Cutback to cutoff

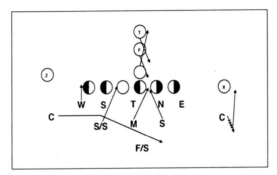

Figure 6-67. Flood run

Divide Run (Figure 6-68)

Will: D+; box
Mike: B+ to A–
Sam: A– to C–
Strong safety: Over the top to B+
Free safety: Alley
Onside corner: Secondary contain
Offside corner: Cutback to cutoff

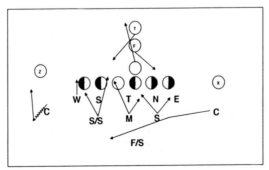

Figure 6-68. Divide run

Cover White vs. Play-Action, Dash, and Sprint Passes

Fire Pass (Figure 6-69)

Will: Tight end man. Sam will help on a drag.

Mike: Trio coverage. The Mike, strong safety, and Sam have the two backs, depending upon their distribution. The strong safety has the first back strong, with Sam taking the first back weak. Mike has the second back to either side. If the backs divide, Mike becomes the plugger. Versus a fire pass, Mike has the tailback.

Sam: Plugger. Helps on a tight end drag.

Strong safety: Fullback

Free safety: Hole

Corners: #1 man

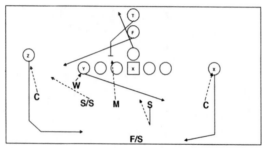

Figure 6-69. Fire pass

Flow Pass (Figure 6-70)

Will: Tight end

Mike: Tailback

Sam: Plugger

Strong safety: Fullback

Free safety: Hole

Corners: #1

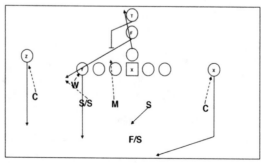

Figure 6-70. Flow pass

Flood Pass (Figure 6-71)

Will: Tight end
Mike: Tailback
Sam: Fullback
Strong safety: Plugger
Free safety: Hole
Corners: #1

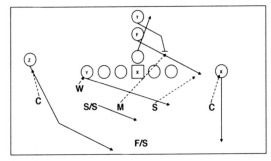

Figure 6-71. Flood pass

Waggle (Figure 6-72)

Will: Tight end
Mike: Plugger. Will recage the quarterback.
Sam: Fullback
Strong safety: Tailback
Free safety: Hole
Corners: #1

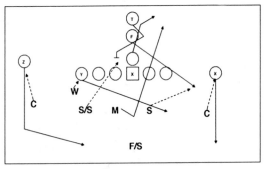

Figure 6-72. Waggle

Sprint Passes (Figures 6-73 through 6-75)

Coverage is man-to-man. If man on pass blocks, the assigned defender will hug the back. The defender will go and get the receiver. On a block, the defender will recage the quarterback on a sprint pass. If the offense likes to use the blocker as a checkdown receiver, the plugger can be used as the recage defender.

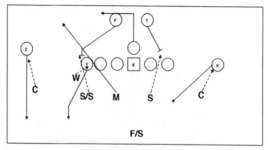

Figure 6-73. Flow dash

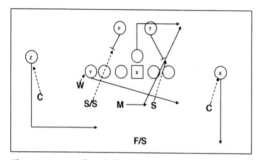

Figure 6-74. Flood dash

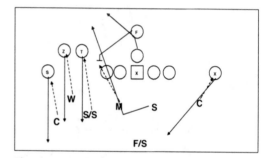

Figure 6-75. Sprint pass

Cover White Motion Adjustments

The man on the motion man will adjust. Figure 6-76 shows Z motion from a pro set. Motion from the backfield will be covered by the strong safety. Mike and Sam will Reggie the remaining back.

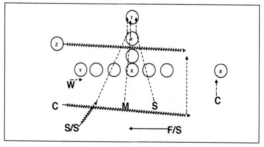

Figure 6-76. Z motion from a pro set

Cover White Variations

Many of the same calls and adjustments in covers black, China, and white are similar. Included are plugger change-ups. Russian, cut, and spy wrinkles can also be used in cover white.

Rita/Linda Calls
(Figures 6-77 through 6-79)

Versus tilt or offset backfields, it is advantageous to drop down the safety to the overloaded side, regardless of whether a strong or weak rotation was called. If the safety to the right drops down, he makes a Rita call followed by an "I'm here" call to let the linebackers know that he has dropped down. A Linda call informs the linebackers that a safety has dropped down to the left. With a Rita or Linda call, Mike and Sam will Reggie the tailback.

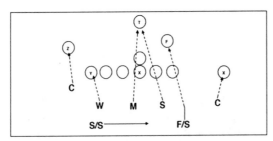

Figure 6-77. Black adjustment—Rita

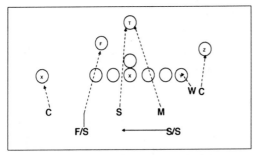

Figure 6-78. White adjustment—Linda

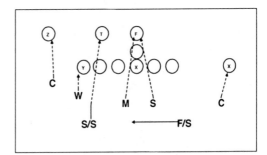

Figure 6-79. China adjustment—Linda

7

Stunt Coverages

Chapter 7 explores cover 4 and cover 0. Cover 4 involves five-man pressures. Cover 4 is equally effective versus passes or runs. These stunts can be considered run stunts or pass pressures. All back seven defenders have a stunt package. This flexibility doesn't allow the offense to lock in on one or two likely blitzers; rather, they must be prepared for any linebacker or secondary player to the stunt threat. Cover 4 concepts are used not only in the five-man stunt game, but are also applicable to the peel blitz and mustang (3-3-5) packages. A variety of line games are used within the cover 4 package. All stunts will start from a cover 8 shell. The quarterback should see the same defensive shell pre-snap. The defense must recognize one-back or two-back formations to get into the cover scheme. This isn't very difficult when players understand formation possibilities inherent in offensive personnel packages. For example, in a 10 personnel grouping, the offense will normally line up in a trips, doubles, or empty formation. In the cover 4 package, the strong safety will cover up for Will, Mike, and the strong corner. The free safety will cover up for the weak corner and Sam.

Two-Back Rules

Defenders will close to the tight end. If there is no tight end, they close to the numbers. They should always close to a three-receiver side.

Will on the Stunt

Corners: Match coverage. The corners lock on to the wideouts and take them man-to-man.
Strong safety: Takes the tight end man-to-man or #2 man if no tight end is present.
Mike and Sam: Duo the backs. Duo means two defenders have the two backs man-to-man, depending upon the backs' distribution.
Free safety: Spins to the hole.

If Will is on a stunt and the offense comes out in a 3x1 formation, Mike will assume the stunt with Will taking #3. This helps with disguise, and the defense gets a better match-up. This adjustment is called flip-flop.

Mike on the Stunt

Corners: Match coverage. Take the wideouts man-to-man.
Will: Man on the tight end. If no tight end, takes #2.
Strong safety and Sam: Duo the two backs.
Free safety: Spins to the hole.

Sam on the Stunt

Corners: Match coverage.
Will: Man on the tight end
Mike and the free safety: Duo the backs.
Strong safety: Spins to the hole.

Anytime Sam is on a stunt this triggers a "special alert." Special alert means that any 3x1 formation places the strong safety on #3 instead of Mike. It is a better defensive match-up if Mike stays in the box on the back instead of Mike on #3 and the free safety on the back. This call will be illustrated later in the chapter.

Strong Safety on the Stunt

Corners: Match coverage.
Will: Man on the tight end
Mike and Sam: Duo the backs.
Free safety: Spins to the hole.

Free Safety on the Stunt

Corners: Match coverage.
Will: Man on the tight end
Mike and Sam: Duo the backs.
Strong safety: Spins to the hole.

Strong Corner on the Stunt (Viper)

Defenders will always close to the numbers whenever a corner stunt is called.

Will: #2 man
Mike and Sam: Duo the backs.
Strong safety: #1 to stunt corner side man-to-man
Free safety: Spins to the hole.
Weak corner: #1 man

Weak Corner on the Stunt (Cobra)

Defenders will always close to the numbers whenever a corner stunt is called.

Will: Tight end man
Mike and Sam: Duo the backs.
Free safety: #1 to the stunt corner
Strong safety: Spins to the hole.
Strong corner: #1 man

One-Back Rules

Defenders will close to the numbers.

Will on the Stunt

Corners: #1 man
Strong safety: #2 man
Mike: #3 man
Sam: #2 man
Free safety: Spins to the hole.

A flip-flop alert is in place on any Will stunt.

Mike on the Stunt

Corners: #1 man
Will: #2 man
Strong safety: #3 man
Free safety: Spins to the hole.

Sam on the Stunt

Corners: #1 man
Will: #2 man
Mike: #3 man
Free safety: #2 man
Strong safety: Spins to the hole.

A special alert is in effect anytime Sam is on a stunt.

Strong Safety on the Stunt

Corners: #1 man
Will: #2 man
Mike: #3 man
Sam: #2 man
Free safety: Spins to the hole.

Free Safety on the Stunt

Corners: #1 man
Will: #2 man
Mike: #3 man
Sam: #2 man
Strong safety: Spins to the hole.

Strong Corner on the Stunt (Viper)

Defenders will close to the numbers.

Will: #2 man
Mike: #3 man
Sam: #2 man
Strong safety: #1 man to the stunt corner side
Free safety: Spins to the hole.
Weak corner: #1 man

Weak Corner on the Stunt (Cobra)

Defenders will close to the numbers.

Strong corner: #1 man
Will: #2 man
Mike: #3 man
Sam: #2 man
Strong safety: Spins to the hole.
Free safety: #1 man to the stunt corner

Line Games

As discussed earlier, a variety of line games can be used in conjunction with cover 4. These games can be used in most cases regardless of the linebacker or defensive back stunting. Most line games can be used against tight end or open sets. However, some games may be better suited for open sets. Figures 7-1 through 7-7 illustrate some of the most commonly used games in the cover 4 stunt package.

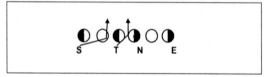

Figure 7-1. Pirate

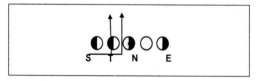

Figure 7-2. Robber

Figure 7-3. Pistol

Figure 7-4. Spike

Figure 7-5. Taco Bell

Figure 7-6. Switch

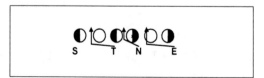

Figure 7-7. Slant

Selected Cover 4 Stunts

Depending on which of the back seven players is on the stunt these games can be run out of over or under fronts. Because of space constraints, all games with each possible stunter will not be drawn up. Instead, each stunter will be shown on a pirate stunt. The reader will get the idea on how he can marry the other line games with any one of the possible seven stunters in the cover 4 stunt package. Included will be a pro set, a slot set, and a one-back doubles set to give the reader an idea of defensive adjustments for each stunt.

Over Will Pirate 4 (Figures 7-8 through 7-10)

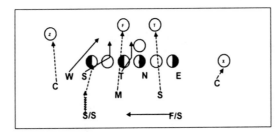

Figure 7-8. Pro set

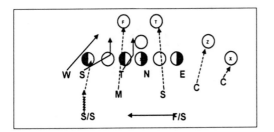

Figure 7-9. Slot set

Figure 7-10. Doubles

Under Sam Pirate 4 (Figures 7-11 through 7-13)

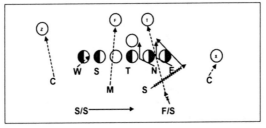

Figure 7-11. Pro set

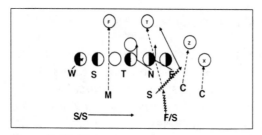

Figure 7-12. Slot set

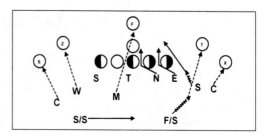

Figure 7-13. Doubles

Over Strong Safety Pirate (Figures 7-14 through 7-16)

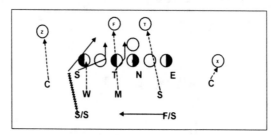

Figure 7-14. Pro set

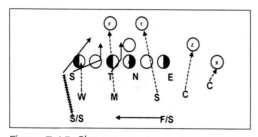

Figure 7-15. Slot set

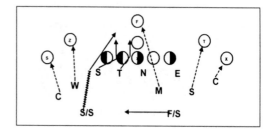

Figure 7-16. Doubles

Under Free Safety Pirate 4 (Figures 7-17 through 7-19)

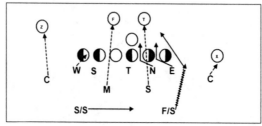

Figure 7-17. Pro set

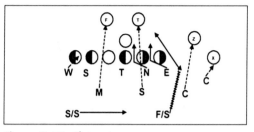

Figure 7-18. Slot set

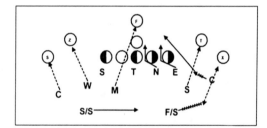

Figure 7-19. Doubles

Under Cobra Pirate 4 (Figure 7-20 through 7-22)

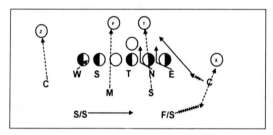

Figure 7-20. Pro set

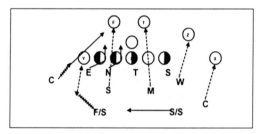

Figure 7-21. Slot set

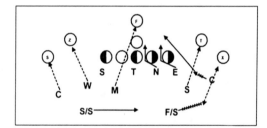

Figure 7-22. Doubles

Over Viper Pirate 4 (Figures 7-23 through 7-25)

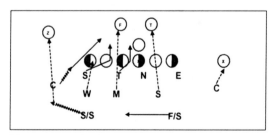

Figure 7-23. Pro set

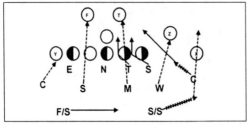

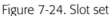

Figure 7-24. Slot set

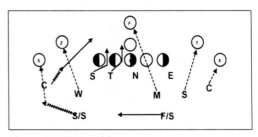

Figure 7-25. Doubles

Mike Stunts (Figures 7-26 through 7-29)

Because of Mike's position at the center of the defense, he has more stunt lanes to exploit. He can run the pirate plus the following stunts.

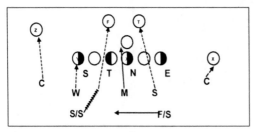

Figure 7-26. Oregon Mike go 4

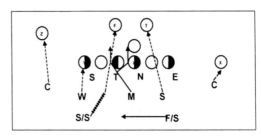

Figure 7-27. Oregon Mike spike 4

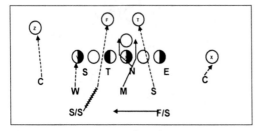

Figure 7-28. Oregon Mike olay 4

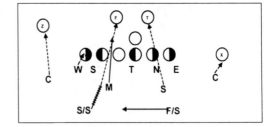

Figure 7-29. Under Mike fire 4

Cover 4 Adjustments

How the defense adjusts to offensive maneuvers such as sprint passes, tight end trades, and motion are discussed in this section.

Play-Action Pass

Versus play-action passes, defenders will cover their assigned man. If a defender's assigned man blocks, he will insert with a hug technique. Figure 7-30 shows Mike and Sam hugging their back on a flow pass. The hug helps when defending screen passes. Also, if the back is a pass blocker, the defender is free to rush the quarterback on a pass play, which is referred to as a green dog.

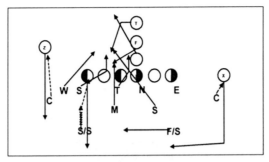

Figure 7-30. Hug technique

Sprint Pass

Figure 7-31 shows Sam on a run-through on a sprint pass with an over strong safety switch 4 call.

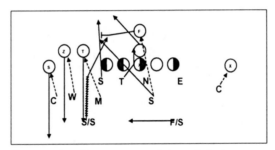

Figure 7-31. Over strong safety switch 4

Tight End Trade

The defender assigned to the tight end will follow him on a trade. The defense can Omaha the trade and realign the front, or they can freeze with no movement of the front. Figure 7-32 illustrates defensive adjustment on an over Mike go 4 stunt with a freeze concept.

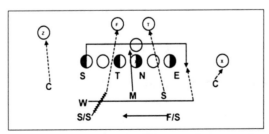

Figure 7-32. Defensive adjustment for over Mike go 4 stunt with a freeze concept

Motion

The defense adjusts to motion by having the defender assigned to the motion man follow him when he motions. The Defense should not attempt to bump or realign the front. Figure 7-33 shows defensive adjustment to Zac motion on under cobra pirate 4.

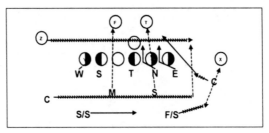

Figure 7-33. Under cobra pirate 4

Cover 4 Trap

This wrinkle attempts to take advantage of the offensive philosophy of throwing to the stunt side when they read a blitz. Cover 4 trap tells the hole player to roll and play half field to the blitz side instead of playing the hole. This technique allows defenders to the stunt side to squat on their assigned man because they have deep help. The offside must understand that they will not have hole help. The backside corner must play a hard David shade. David is an inside alignment on a receiver. Over strong safety robber 4 trap is illustrated in Figure 7-34 against a doubles set.

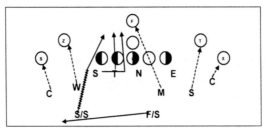

Figure 7-34. Over strong safety robber 4 trap

Cover 0

Cover 0 can be a six-man pressure with Will and Sam in the rush, or a seven-man pressure in the bullets look with Will, Sam, and Mike on the blitz. Cover 0 is great for short-yardage and three-back sets. The major weakness of cover 0, obviously, is the corners will be on an island. However, on pass plays, the ball must come out quickly. The defense will close to the numbers. The six-man pressure is called storm 0. In storm 0, Will and Sam run dog stunts. The dog angle is at the quarterback. The defense uses two ways to get into storm. A stem storm 0 call gives the offense an over 8 pre-snap look. Individual defenders, on their own, will move to their assigned areas. A straight storm 0 call tells the defense to line up in assigned areas. The storm 0 call is beneficial if the defense is expecting an offensive quick snap. Figure 7-35 illustrates a stem storm 0 call. A storm 0 call is shown in Figure 7-36.

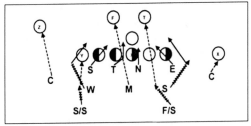

Figure 7-35. Stem storm 0

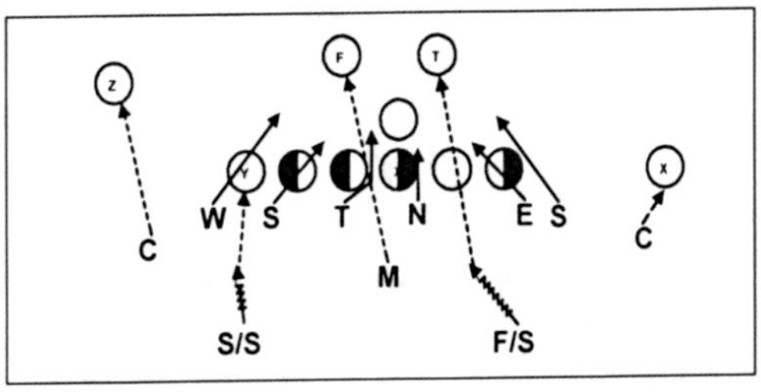

Figure 7-36. Storm 0

Storm 0

Will and Sam: Take dog angle to the quarterback.

Mike: Takes a single back man-to-man. Against an I set, takes the tailback. Against split backs, takes the strong back. Versus empty sets, Mike will take #3 strong.

Corners: #1 man

Strong safety: #2 to closed side man

Free safety: Takes #3 man, counting from the closed side. Does not count the back in a one-back set. Versus two backs, does not count the strong back in split backs. Versus an I formation, takes the fullback. Versus empty, takes #2 weak. Versus two-back motion, the free safety will take the motion man, and Mike will take the remaining back.

Ends: Execute an end it. An end it is an inside charge through the V of the neck of the offensive tackle. The ends will close on a down block and go underneath on a base or pass set. They will redirect on a reach block.

Tackle: Executes a spike. He too will close on a down block and go under a base block or a pass set. Like the end, he will redirect on a reach block.

Nose: Plays a normal 1 technique.

Figures 7-37 through 7-40 show storm 0 against a variety of formations.

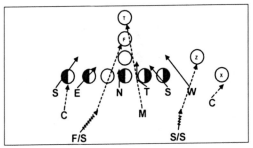

Figure 7-37. Slot

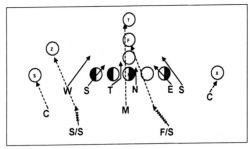

Figure 7-38. Three wides

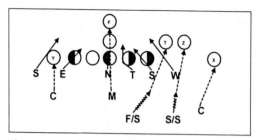

Figure 7-39. Trips closed

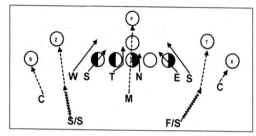

Figure 7-40. Doubles

Storm 0 Variations (Figures 7-41 through 7-45)

Storm is normally run out of the over front; however, it can be run out of other fronts and with a mix of line lane exchanges. Following are other ways to run storm 0. Even though these are variations of fronts and lane exchanges, the coverage aspect does not change.

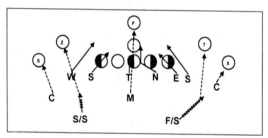

Figure 7-41. Under storm 0

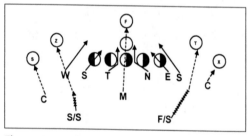

Figure 7-42. Green storm 0

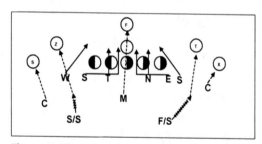

Figure 7-43. Green storm robber 0

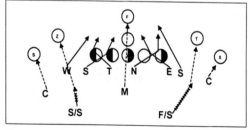

Figure 7-44. Storm pick 0

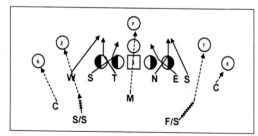

Figure 7-45. Green storm pop 0

Green storm robber, storm pick, and green storm pop are effective pass rush change-ups. Figure 7-46 shows 22 storm 0. This call is used on third-and-one, or fourth-and-one situations, when a quarterback sneak is a distinct possibility. With two A gap defenders, the quarterback must work out to the B gap on a sneak attempt.

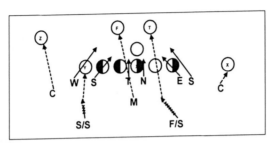

Figure 7-46. 22 storm 0

Hurricane 0

This call is used on short-yardage and goal-line situations. Both tackles align in A gaps with the ends moving to B gap. All linemen will tough charge their assigned gap. Will and Sam execute their dog stunt. Should they have a tight end, they will line up in the C gap and tough charge. The secondary and Mike follow cover 0 rules. Figure 7-47 illustrates hurricane 0 against a flanker set.

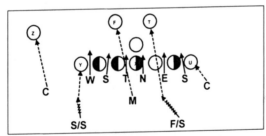

Figure 7-47. Hurricane 0 against a flanker set

Hurricane Sell the Farm

This call, obviously, is a last-gasp effort to keep the offense out of the end zone or stopping the offense on a crucial fourth-down attempt. The defensive line and linebackers follow hurricane rules. The secondary follows cover 0 rules. If their assigned man is a tight end or is aligned in the backfield, they will run an onside back angle stunt. Figure 7-48 illustrates hurricane sell the farm against a pro set. Figure 7-49 has the offense in a mirror set.

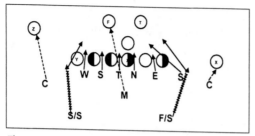

Figure 7-48. Hurricane sell the farm against a pro set

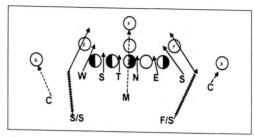

Figure 7-49. Mirror set

Blizzard 0 (Figure 7-50)

To keep the offense off-balance and not give away a six-man pressure when Will and Mike walk up on the line of scrimmage, blizzard 0 can be used to give the illusion of six-man pressure. Blizzard 0 is storm 0 to everyone except Will and Sam. They will bluff a dog and play from the line of scrimmage. They will take the quarterback on option plays and will take the flats on pass plays. They help the corners on slant passes and in cuts.

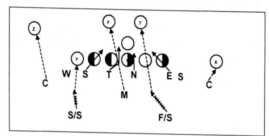

Figure 7-50. Blizzard 0

Storm 0 Coaching Points

- With a stem storm 0 call, the defense will show a cover 8 shell, and individually move to the assigned alignment.
- With a storm 0 call, defenders will immediately line up in their assigned alignments.
- Will and Sam will split the pair against wing sets. Figure 7-51 shows Will and Sam splitting the pair.
- When a defensive back's assigned man blocks, he must immediately shoot the gun, which means to immediately fit where needed. Figure 7-52 shows the corner and strong safety fitting when Will is blocked on a splitting the pair technique against a wing-T set.

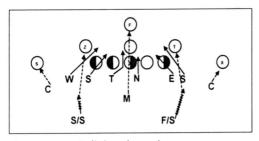

Figure 7-51. Splitting the pair

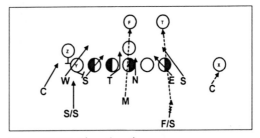

Figure 7-52. Shooting the gun

Bullets 0 (Figures 7-53 through 7-55)

Bullets is a seven-man pressure. All three linebackers stunt their home gap. The end man on the line of scrimmage will peel the single back in one-back sets, the strong back in split backs, and the tailback in the I formation. The secondary follows cover 0 rules. Mike must read out and take #3 versus empty sets.

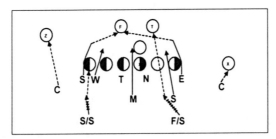

Figure 7-53. Over bullets

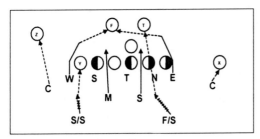

Figure 7-54. Under bullets

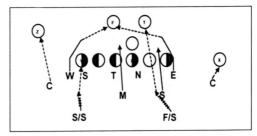

Figure 7-55. Oregon bullets

8

Peel Blitzes

Peel blitzes in this playbook are tailored after zone blitz concepts. Originally, the author ran the typical five-man pressures with a three-deep and three-under concept. However, it became obvious that practice time was insufficient to master all the adjustments and nuances involved. For example, not all ends were athletic enough to drop into coverage, nor were all tackles nimble enough to be cage players. Corners had to master a divider rule with multiple receivers on his side, yet cover a single receiver basically man. Fire zone schemes also must be able to adjust to wing, switch, stack, and high-low receiver releases. A displaced #2 and motion require complex adjustments. Figure 8-1 shows the typical NCAA blitz against a pro set. The same blitz is shown in Figure 8-2 against a doubles set. The reader can easily notice the change in assignments required.

NCAA Blitz Assignments Against a Pro Set
Stud: Long stick
Tackle: Stick the center
Nose: Stick to cage
End: Deuce player. Drops over #2. Stays alert for a gut call. With a gut call, the end will trade responsibilities with Sam and become a final 3 player. Also, the end should be aware that he must not be beaten to the flat by #2, and he must take #2 on a flat and up route.
Will: Blitz
Mike: Key blitz

Sam: Final 3 player. With a displaced #2, gives a gut call and becomes a deuce player.

Strong safety: Deuce player

Free safety: Spins to the hole.

Corners: Deep third. If the corner has only one receiver, he will basically cover him man-to-man. With multiple receivers, the corner must follow a divider rule to split the receivers so he can cover his deep third. The corner must be as deep as the deepest receiver.

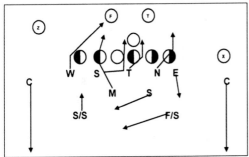

Figure 8-1. NCAA blitz against a pro set

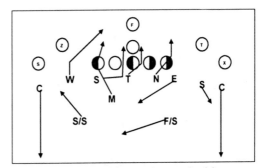

Figure 8-2. NCAA blitz against a doubles set

This playbook has married the cover 4 concepts in Chapter 7 with zone blitz concepts to create the peel package. Now the defense doesn't have to worry about all the adjustments involved in a true zone blitz scheme. Motion, trades, and multiple formations are easily handled using cover 4 rules. Following are peel blitzes and assigned duties. Also included are variations of each blitz. As with any defensive call in the playbook, the cover 8 shell is shown pre-snap. The quarterback should see the same pre-snap look each play.

Under Will Buccaneer 4 (Figure 8-3)

Will and end: Peel the back. Peel means the widest rushers will take the assigned back should he flare. Mike will point out the back which will be peeled. The peel rule says peel a single back, peel the strong back in a split backfield, or peel the tailback in an I formation.

Mike: Key blitz. Key blitz technique involves reading the offensive tackle as he blitzes. If the offensive tackle blocks out, the Mike will stunt inside. If the offensive tackle blocks inside, the Mike will work outside him. Mike will read out of the stunt and take #3 versus an empty set. Will still stunts, but Mike is no longer on the stunt.

Sam: #2 man. The triple rule puts him on #3 against a 3x1 set.

Strong safety: #2 man

Free safety: Spins to the hole.

Corners: #1 man

Defensive line: Cop the back. Cop the back involves defensive linemen covering the assigned back should he show up in their gap.

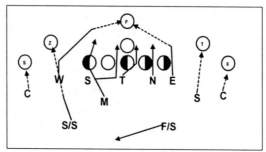

Figure 8-3. Under Will buccaneer 4

This peel blitz can be run with the following variations:

- *Mug Under Will Buccaneer 4* (Figure 8-4): This variation has Mike lined up in the B gap.
- *Under Will Buccaneer Bracket 4* (Figure 8-5): Stud will jet with both Will and Mike stunting inside. Mike will read the guard, and Will stunts the B gap.
- *Under Will Buccaneer X 4* (Figure 8-6): Will goes under any block because Mike will assume cage responsibilities.

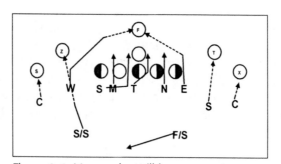

Figure 8-4. Mug under Will buccaneer 4

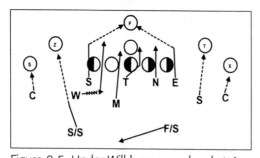

Figure 8-5. Under Will buccaneer bracket 4

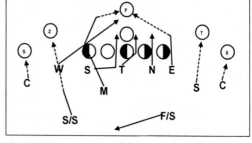

Figure 8-6. Under Will buccaneer X 4

Under Strong Safety Shark 4 (Figure 8-7)

Will: #2 man
End: Peels the back.
Mike: Key blitz

Sam: #2 man

Strong safety: Blitz. Peels the back.

Free safety: Spins to the hole.

Corners: #1 man

Defensive line: Cop the back.

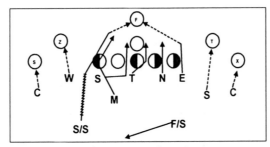

Figure 8-7. Under strong safety shark 4

This peel blitz can be run with the following variations:

- *Mug Under Strong Safety Shark 4* (Figure 8-8): This variation has Mike lined up in the B gap.
- *Under Strong Safety Shark Bracket 4* (Figure 8-9): Stud will jet with Mike and the strong safety stunting inside. Mike will read the guard.
- *Under Strong Safety Shark X 4* (Figure 8-10): The strong safety will go under any block because Mike will assume cage responsibilities.

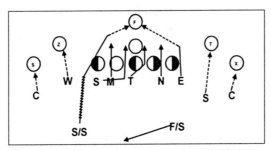

Figure 8-8. Mug under strong safety shark 4

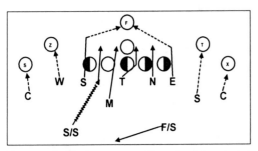

Figure 8-9. Under strong safety shark bracket 4

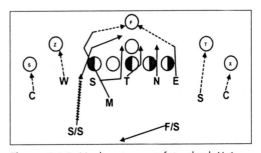

Figure 8-10. Under strong safety shark X 4

Over Sam Blackbeard 4 (Figure 8-11)

Will: #2 man

Stud and Sam: Peel the back. Anytime Sam is on a stunt there is a special alert. As explained in Chapter 7, a special alert puts the strong safety on #3 and the free safety in the hole on a 3x1 formation.

Mike: Key blitz

Strong safety: Spins to the hole.

Free safety: #2 man. Alert for special call.

Corners: #1 man

Defensive line: Cop the back.

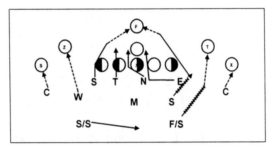

Figure 8-11. Over Sam blackbeard 4

This peel blitz can be run with the following variations:

- *Mug Over Sam Blackbeard 4* (Figure 8-12): Mike lines up in the B gap.
- *Over Sam Blackbeard Bracket 4* (Figure 8-13): The end will jet with Mike and Sam stunting inside. Mike reads the guard.
- *Over Sam Blackbeard X 4* (Figure 8-14): Sam goes under any block because Mike assumes cage responsibilities.

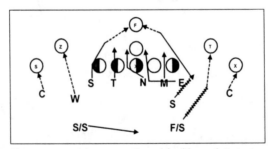

Figure 8-12. Mug over Sam blackbeard 4

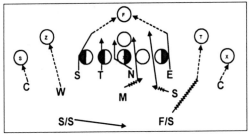

Figure 8-13. Over Sam blackbeard bracket 4

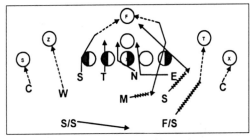

Figure 8-14. Over Sam blackbeard X 4

Over Free Safety Dolphin 4 (Figure 8-15)

Will: #2 man

Stud and the free safety: Peel the back.

Mike: Key blitz

Sam: #2 man

Strong safety: Spins to the hole.

Corners: #1 man

Defensive line: Cop the back

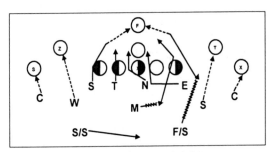

Figure 8-15. Over free safety dolphin 4

This peel blitz can be run with the following variations:

- *Mug Over Free Safety Dolphin 4* (Figure 8-16): Mike lines up in the B gap.

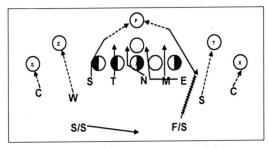

Figure 8-16. Mug over free safety dolphin 4

- *Over Free Safety Dolphin Bracket 4* (Figure 8-17): Stud is on a jet with Mike and the free safety stunting inside. Mike will read the guard.
- *Over Free Safety Dolphin X 4* (Figure 8-18): The free safety will go under any block because Mike will assume cage responsibilities.

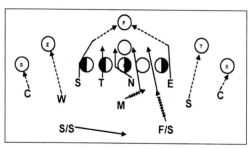

Figure 8-17. Over free safety dolphin bracket 4

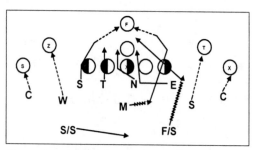

Figure 8-18. Over free safety dolphin X 4

Over Cat (Figure 8-19)

Will: #2 man
Stud and the weak corner: Peel the back.
Mike: Key blitz
Sam: #2 man. Alert triple call.
Strong safety: Spins to the hole.
Free safety: #1 man to the weak corner's side
Strong corner: #1 man
Defensive line: Cop the back.

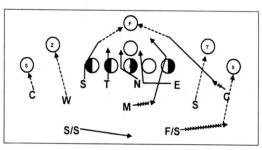

Figure 8-19. Over cat

This peel blitz can be run with the following variations:
- *Mug Over Cat* (Figure 8-20): Mike will line up in the B gap.
- *Over Cat Bracket* (Figure 8-21): The end will jet with the corner and Mike stunting inside.
- *Over Cat X 4* (Figure 8-22): The corner will go under any block because Sam has cage responsibilities.

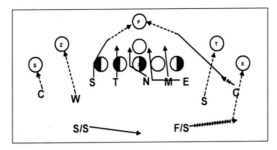

Figure 8-20. Mug over cat

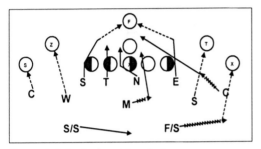

Figure 8-21. Over cat bracket

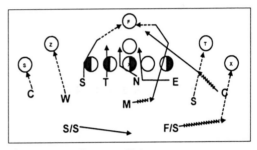

Figure 8-22. Over cat X 4

Green Sam Maroon 4 (Figure 8-23)

Will: #2 man
Stud and end: Peel the back.
Mike: Blitz A+ gap
Sam: Blitz A– gap
Strong safety: Spins to the hole.
Free safety: #2 man
Corners: #1 man
Defensive line: Cop the back.

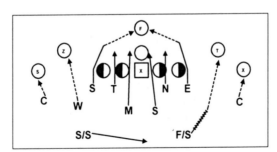

Figure 8-23. Green Sam maroon 4

This peel blitz can be run with the following variations:
- *Green Sam cross 4* (Figure 8-24): Mike goes first.
- *Over Sam cross 4* (Figure 8-25)

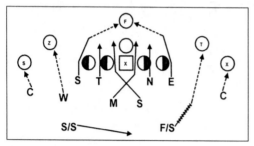

Figure 8-24. Green Sam cross 4

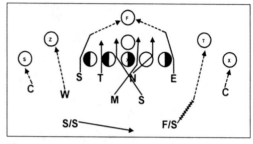

Figure 8-25. Over Sam cross 4

Under Sam Gallows 4 (Figure 8-26)

Will: #2 man
Mike: Blitz A+ gap. Mike goes first.
Sam: Blitz B+ gap. Sam goes second.
Stud and end: Peel the back.
Strong safety: Spins to the hole.
Free safety: #2 man
Corners: #1 man
Defensive line: Cop the back.

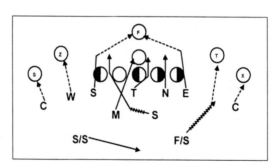

Figure 8-26. Under Sam gallows 4

Note: Under Sam Gallows 4 does not have any variations as the other peel blitzes do. It can be run only as illustrated in Figure 8-26.

9

Red Zone and Goal Line Defense

This chapter deals with red zone calls, which are used from the −20 to the −10-yard line, and the 6-2 defensive configuration, which is used against 22, 23, 32, and 31 personnel groups from the −10-yard line to the goal line.

Red Zone Coverages

Cover 8, the base coverage, is great anywhere on the field. From the −20 on in, cover 8 up is an excellent call. With less field to defend, the safeties align at seven yards depth. Figure 9-1 shows a cover 8 up call versus a pro set. Also, individual line charges may get an unblocked defender at the handoff point. For example, over spike and over end are good calls. Over pirate is another excellent call. Against teams that like to use play-action and bootleg action, Oregon pirate black (Figure 9-2) and under China (Figure 9-3) are effective. Cover China is a great antidote to doubles and trips open sets because the defense can keep six in the box (Figure 9-4). The cover 4 package has been great in red zone situations. Versus pro set teams that are run-oriented, Oregon cram lighting 4 is a good call (Figure 9-5). Over 2 middle with normal personnel (Figure 9-6), mustang 2 middle (Figure 9-7), and over pirate 2 loose (Figure 9-8) are effective against teams that need a touchdown late in the game. Marrying the green package to these red zone coverages is a good option. Some spread teams never get into a true goal line set. For those teams, the storm package is the answer if defenses want to press the issue. Storm cover 0 is also a great antidote to three-back sets. Figure 9-9 shows storm 0 against a power I set.

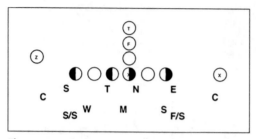

Figure 9-1. Cover 8 up call versus a pro set

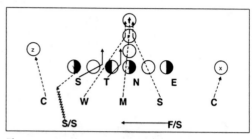

Figure 9-2. Oregon pirate black

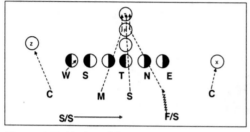

Figure 9-3. Under China

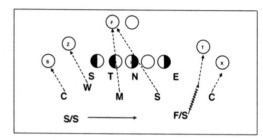

Figure 9-4. Cover China

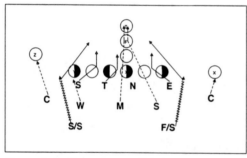

Figure 9-5. Oregon cram lighting 4

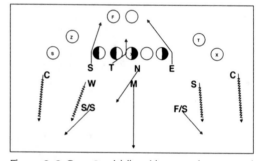

Figure 9-6. Over 2 middle with normal personnel

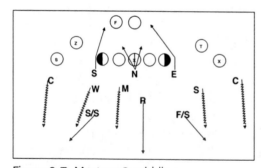

Figure 9-7. Mustang 2 middle

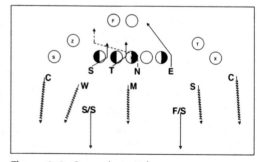

Figure 9-8. Over pirate 2 loose

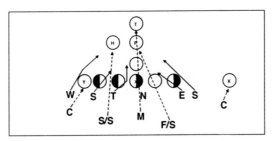

Figure 9-9. Storm 0 against a power I set

Goal Line Defense

As a basic rule, the goal line package is used mainly against power sets in 22, 23, 32, and 31 personnel groups. Goal line is a 6-2 alignment.

Goal Line Personnel

- Two guards
- Two tackles
- Two ends
- Mike
- Sam
- Two corners
- One strong safety

Goal Line vs. Run

Following are possible calls used in the goal line package.

Base (Figure 9-10)

Guards: A gap. Penetrate. They must never be reached by the center.
Strong tackle: 5 technique
Weak tackle: B gap penetration
Ends: Tight 9 techniques
Mike: B+
Sam: B–
Closed corner: 2xLOS off the wing. Cloud force.
Weak corner: Stacks with the end.
Strong safety: Head-up on the wing three yards deep.

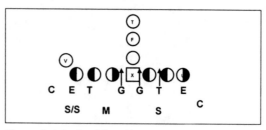

Figure 9-10. Goal line base

Flow Run Fit (Figure 9-11)

Guards: A gaps
Strong tackle: C gap
Weak tackle: B gap
Strong end: D gap
Weak end: Chase
Mike: Spills B+. Causes a train wreck.
Sam: Quick to B+.
Closed corner: Force. Spills the play.
Weak corner: Reads off the end. If the end closes, the corner has the D– gap. If the end is base blocked, the corner fits to C– gap. Whether the corner has C– or D–, he is responsible for a quarterback naked, reverse, drag, delay, or throw back to the quarterback.
Strong safety: Stacks with the end.

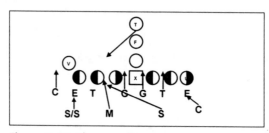

Figure 9-11. Flow run fits

Flood Run Fit (Figure 9-12)

Guards: A gaps
Strong tackle: C gap
Weak tackle: B gap
Strong end: Chases.
Weak end: D gap
Mike: Over the top

Sam: C– spill

Closed corner: E+. He is responsible for quarterback naked, reverse, drag, delay, or throwback to the quarterback.

Weak corner: Reads off the end.

Strong safety: Cutback B+.

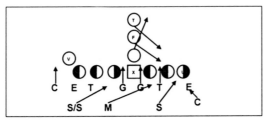

Figure 9-12. Flood run fit

Divide Run Fit (Figure 9-13)

Treat this fit as a flow run. Sam is quick to B+, but must fall back if needed.

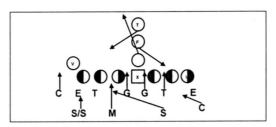

Figure 9-13. Divide run fit

Goal Line vs. Pass

The field is divided into fifths (Figure 9-14). Those areas include the following:
- *Flat:* The area from the end man on the line of scrimmage (EMLOS) to the sideline on both sides
- *Track:* The area over the end man on the line of scrimmage on both sides
- *Ball:* The area over the box from a tight end or ghost tight end to the other tight end or ghost tight end

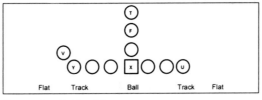

Figure 9-14. Goal line pass zones

Level 3 Pass (Figure 9-15)

Corners: Flat
Strong safety: Outside track
Mike: Inside track
Sam: Track

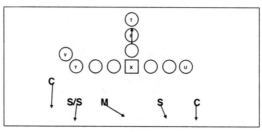

Figure 9-15. Level 3 pass

Flow Pass (Figure 9-16)

Closed corner: Flat
Strong safety: Outside track
Mike: Inside track
Sam: Ball
Weakside corner: Track to flat. Stays alert for a quarterback throwback.

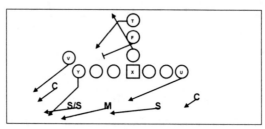

Figure 9-16. Flow pass

Fire Pass (Figure 9-17)

Closed corner: Flat
Strong safety: Outside track
Mike: Inside track
Sam: Ball. Collisions Y or V.
Weakside corner: Flat

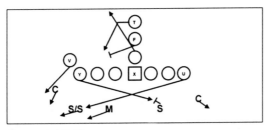

Figure 9-17. Fire pass

Flood Pass (Figure 9-18)

Closed corner: Flat. Stays alert for a quarterback throwback.
Strong safety: Track
Mike: Ball
Sam: Track
Weakside corner: Flat

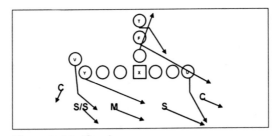

Figure 9-18. Flood pass

Goal Line Change-Ups

In addition to base, other calls can be used in the goal line package.

Double Easy (Figure 9-19)

This call places the strong tackle in B+. The only change from base is that Mike and Sam are over the top on any running play to either side.

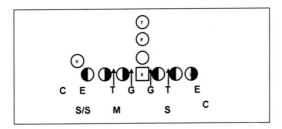

Figure 9-19. Double easy

Pinch (Figure 9-20)

Guards: Base rules
Tackles: Double easy rules
Ends: 9 technique stick
Mike and Sam: Play over the top on flow or flood runs. Base pass drop rules apply.
Closed corner and the strong safety: Base rules versus runs or passes
Weakside corner: D– on flood runs. D– on flow runs. Base rules against passes

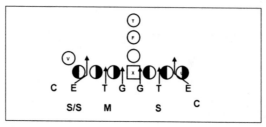

Figure 9-20. Pinch

Rebel (Figure 9-21)

Rebel is used as a sell-out defense when the situation calls for it. The defense gives up the tight ends should the offense call a pass play. This defense is used on the –1-yard line.

Guards: Double easy rules but with a tough charge.
Ends: Pre-snap move to the C gap. Use a tough charge.
Mike and Sam: Double easy rules with a sell the farm technique. A sell the farm technique has the linebackers launching over the line on the snap.
Corners: Blitz unless #1 is detached. If #1 is detached, the corners play the flat.
Strong safety: Base rules. If the #1 is detached, the safety blitzes in place of the corner.

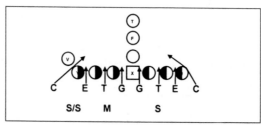

Figure 9-21. Rebel

Rifle (Figure 9-22)

Guards: Rebel rules

Tackles: Rebel rules

Ends: Align in a 6 technique. They take the tight end man-to-man. They must not allow the tight end to release inside.

Mike and Sam: Rebel rules

Corners: Rebel rules

Strong safety: Rebel rules

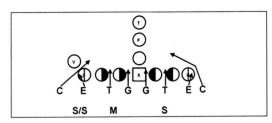

Figure 9-22. Rifle

Pittsburgh Check (Figures 9-23 through 9-26)

In case the offense breaks the formation, the defense must have an answer. Pittsburgh is that answer.

Defensive line: Double easy rules

Corners: #1 man-to-man

Strong safety: #2 man-to-man

Mike: #3 man-to-man

Sam: #2 man-to-man

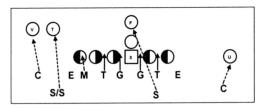

Figure 9-23. Trey

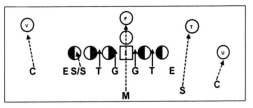

Figure 9-24. Spread

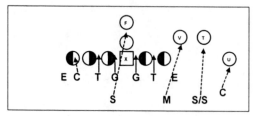

Figure 9-25. Trips closed

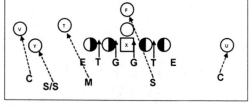

Figure 9-26. Trips open

Versus an opponent with a lot of back motion, Pittsburgh can be automatic in the game plan that week (Figure 9-27). Assign the corners #1, the strong safety #2, and the linebacker man-to-man on the offset or motion back.

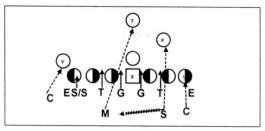

Figure 9-27. Game plan Pittsburgh call

Goal Line Adjustments

Defenses must be prepared should the offense play games with the formation.

Unbalanced With the Pair to the Overload Side (Figure 9-28)

If the pair is to the overload side, the defensive line moves to the center man in the formation. Declare the front to the unbalanced side. The strong safety goes to the two-receiver side.

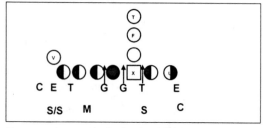

Figure 9-28. Unbalanced with the pair to the overload side

Unbalanced With the Pair Away From the Overload Side (Figure 9-29)

With the pair away from the overload side, the defensive line moves to the center man in the formation. Declare the defense to the unbalanced side. The strong safety goes to the two-receiver side.

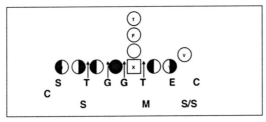

Figure 9-29. Unbalanced with the pair away from the overload side

Four-Man Surface (Figures 9-30 and 9-31)

Corners: Align outside #1.
Closed end: Aligns in an outside shade on #2.
Closed tackle: Aligns in an inside shade on #3.

Everyone else is normal.

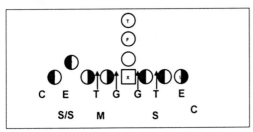

Figure 9-30. Four-man surface—Y off

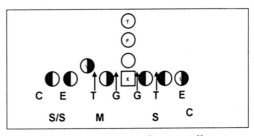

Figure 9-31. Four-man surface—V off

10

Mustang Package (3-3-5 Defense)

Most successful defenses have an effective change-up to their base defense. Odd fronts have an even look as a change of pace. Even front defenses need an odd look as a counter. The odd look detailed in this chapter is a 3-3-5 scheme. This change-up is accomplished by taking out a lineman and inserting a defensive back. Figure 10-1 illustrates the mustang package.

Positions and Base Alignments
Stud: Closed side end
Nose: Only tackle in the game
End: Openside end
Will: Closed side outside linebacker
Mike: Middle linebacker
Sam: Openside outside linebacker
Strong safety: Closed side safety
Free safety: Openside safety
Corners: Left and right side corners
Rover: The Rover (denoted with an R in the diagrams) is a wild card. He has the freedom to line up in various places.

As the reader can readily see, there are 10 holdover players. The secondary still shows the cover 8 shell. Within the mustang package, the defense has the capability of sending three, four, or five men.

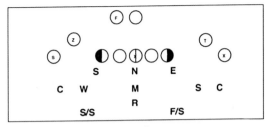

Figure 10-1. Mustang package

Three-Man Pressures

Figure 10-2 shows the base mustang front. In the base front, the nose two-gaps the center with both ends in tight 5 techniques. From the base look, a variety of line games are available. As the base rule, all stunts originate from the base look. Three-man pressures are illustrated as follows:

- *Plus* (Figure 10-3): A plus call tells the nose to stick to the strength. The ends play normal.
- *Minus* (Figure 10-4): A minus call has the nose sticking weak. Again, the ends play 5 techniques.
- *Sun* (Figure 10-5): Sun means Stud under the nose. The end is normal.
- *Eon* (Figure 10-6): Eon means end under the nose. The Stud is normal. Sun and eon can be used as lane exchanges in a three-man rush or incorporated as part of blitz package.
- *Sun or Eon 2 Middle* (Figure 10-7): Cover 2 middle is used late in the half or at the end of the game. Rover is placed deep between the safeties in a cover 2 look, which allows the safeties to widen and be more of a factor in the hole area.
- *Sun or Eon 2 Spy* (Figure 10-8): The defense executes the called line exchange with a cover 2 look. Rover is a spy on the quarterback.
- *Sun or Eon 2 Man Spy* (Figure 10-9): The defense executes cover 2 man with the Rover spying the quarterback.
- *Sun or Eon 8 Spy* (Figure 10-10): Cover 8 is executed with Rover again assigned to the quarterback.

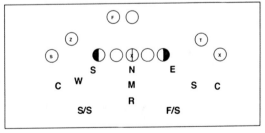

Figure 10-2. Base mustang

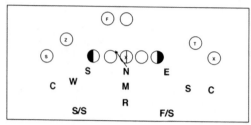

Figure 10-3. Plus

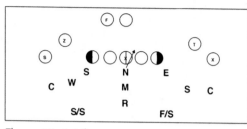

Figure 10-4. Minus

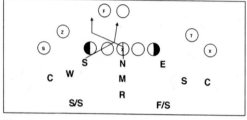

Figure 10-5. Sun

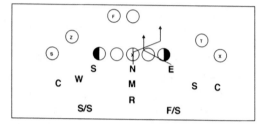

Figure 10-6. Eon

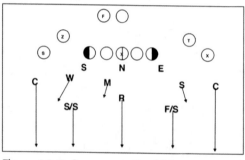

Figure 10-7. Sun or eon 2 middle

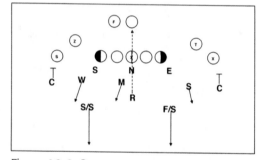

Figure 10-8. Sun or eon 2 spy

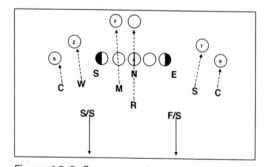

Figure 10-9. Sun or eon 2 man spy

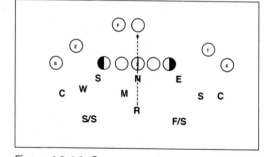

Figure 10-10. Sun or eon 8 spy

Four-Man Pressures

As previously discussed, Rover is used in a variety of ways. He is used as the fourth rusher in the four-man pressure package. In the four-man pressure scheme, the line will slant or post stick. Figure 10-11 shows the defensive line slanting weak. Figure 10-12 shows a strong slant. Post stick means that instead of slanting to the called side, defensive linemen will slide pre-snap to the called side. Figure 10-13 shows a weak post stick alignment, and a strong post stick is shown in Figure 10-14. Rover's rule is to blitz opposite the slant. For example, on a weak slant, Rover stunts from the strongside. Conversely, a strong slant has the Rover coming from the weakside. Weak 8 is shown in Figure 10-15. As previously stated, a sun or eon exchange can be used in packages other than the three-man pressure concept. Figure 10-16 shows a weak eon 8 call. Figure 10-17 illustrates a strong sun 8 call.

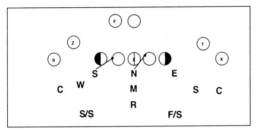

Figure 10-11. Weak slant

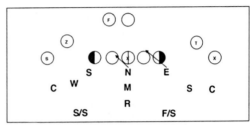

Figure 10-12. Strong slant

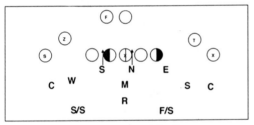

Figure 10-13. Weak post stick alignment

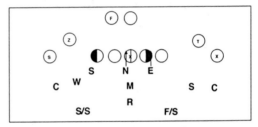

Figure 10-14. Strong post stick alignment

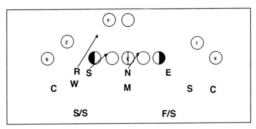

Figure 10-15. Weak 8

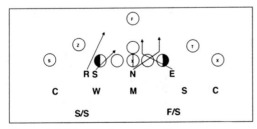

Figure 10-16. Weak eon 8 call

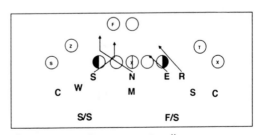

Figure 10-17. Strong sun 8 call

Five-Man Pressures

The same peel blitzes described in Chapter 8 are available in the mustang package (Figures 10-18 through 10-39). As a matter of fact, it may be more effective in the 3-3-5 package. Cover 4 rules are in place for everyone except Rover. Rover will take #3 man-to-man. Remember, Rover has the availability to move around and feint a blitz. The only stipulation is that he be in position to execute his assigned duties. Linemen do not cop the back, nor do the edge rushers peel the back. Also, Mike does not have to read out and cover #3 in an empty set. No special check has to be used on Sam stunts. Sun and eon stunts can be added to the back end of the blitz.

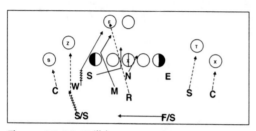

Figure 10-18. Will buccaneer 4

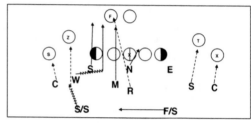

Figure 10-19. Will buccaneer bracket 4

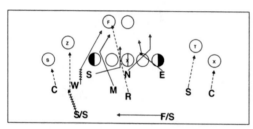

Figure 10-20. Will buccaneer eon 4

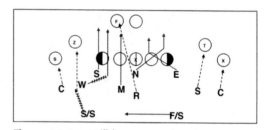

Figure 10-21. Will buccaneer bracket eon 4

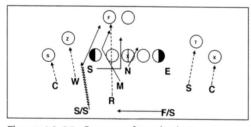

Figure 10-22. Strong safety shark 4

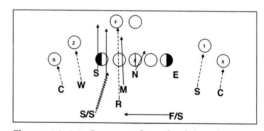

Figure 10-23. Strong safety shark bracket 4

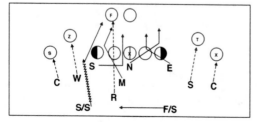

Figure 10-24. Strong safety shark eon 4

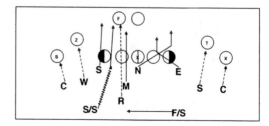

Figure 10-25. Strong safety shark bracket eon

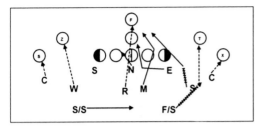

Figure 10-26. Sam blackbeard 4

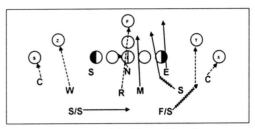

Figure 10-27. Sam blackbeard bracket 4

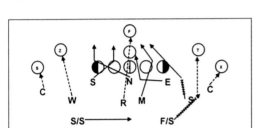

Figure 10-28. Sam blackbeard Sun

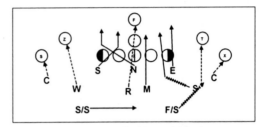

Figure 10-29. Sam blackbeard bracket sun 4

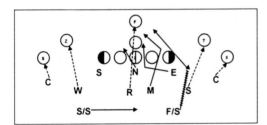

Figure 10-30. Free safety dolphin 4

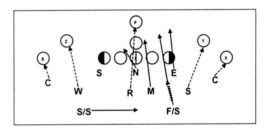

Figure 10-31. Free safety dolphin bracket 4

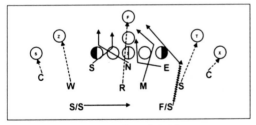

Figure 10-32. Free safety dolphin sun 4

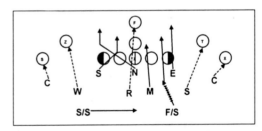

Figure 10-33. Free safety dolphin bracket sun 4

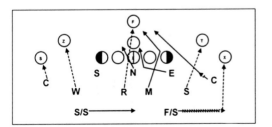

Figure 10-34. Cobra 4

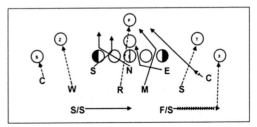

Figure 10-35. Cobra sun 4

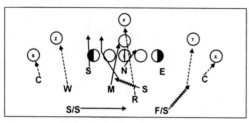

Figure 10-36. Sam gallows 4

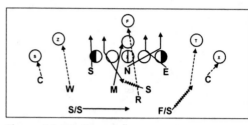

Figure 10-37. Sam gallows eon 4

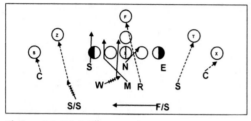

Figure 10-38. Will swap 4

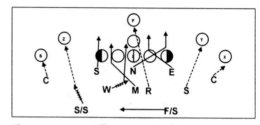

Figure 10-39. Will swap eon 4

Another group of five-man pressures are available by stunting Will and Sam (Figures 10-40 through 10-42). In this group of blitzes, cover 1 is used.

Cover 1 Rules
Will and Sam: On the stunt
Strong safety: #2 strong man
Mike: #3 man. If #3 is wide, takes the back.
Rover: #2 weak man. If #2 weak is a back, takes #3 strong.
Free safety: Hole
Corners: #1 man

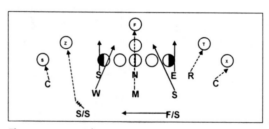

Figure 10-40. Blast 1

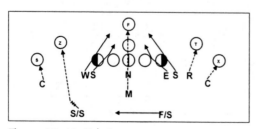

Figure 10-41. Tab 1

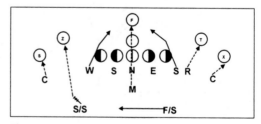

Figure 10-42. Bear 1

11

Special Situations

This chapter covers situational defensive football, which includes time-affiliated situations, kick safe defenses, surprise formations, special situations, alerts, and defending trick plays. All defenses—no matter the structure or philosophy—should have an antidote or plan for these situations.

Time-Affiliated Situations

- Four-minute defense
- Two-minute defense
- Quarter change
- Big Ben defense
- Armageddon (kneel-down defense)
- Defensive time-out protocol

Kick Safe Defenses

- Punt safe
- Field goal safe

Surprise Formations

- Swinging gate
- Loco
- Unbalanced
- Emory & Henry

Special Situations and Alerts

- Quarterback scramble rules
- Receiver double-move alert
- Defensive alerts
- Interception return responsibilities
- Fumble recovery

Trick Plays

- Halfback pass
- Flea flicker
- Reverse
- Reverse pass
- Fake reverse
- Hitch-and-pitch
- Throwback to the quarterback
- Watch call

Time-Affiliated Situations

Four-Minute Defense

When the opponent has the lead near the end of the game, they will try to run as much time off the clock as possible. In a four-minute situation, a well-coached defense will do the following:

- Have saved time-outs just for this situation. When calling time-out, do it aggressively. Call time-out as the runner is going down.
- Force turnovers. Strip the ball. The first man should ensure the tackle while others strip the ball.
- Force three-and-out. Don't allow a first down.
- Force runners out-of-bounds to stop the clock.
- Treat each play as a short-yardage play. Force the issue.

- Use attacking aggressive fronts and charges. Hopefully, a minus-yardage play or a defender at the handoff spot may cause a fumble.
- Make use of run blitzes. Load the box.
- Unpile quickly. Get off the runner, and allow the officials to quickly spot the ball. If the ball is loose after the play, pick it up and hand it to the official.

Notes:
- Coach defenders where officials will be at the end of a particular play so defenders can quickly find them and get a time-out called quickly. One or two seconds saved can make a big difference at the end of the game.
- Practice clock time-out situations. Players should be schooled on what stops the clock so the defense will not stop the clock on plays that kill the clock.

Two-Minute Defense

The two-minute situation is the antithesis of the four-minute scenario. In this situation, the defense wants the clock to run. The defensive team has the lead with very little time left on the clock. The main objective is to keep the clock running while keeping the offense from scoring. Obviously, defensive reactions are influenced by the number of points the offense needs. Do they need to score a touchdown or a field goal? Regardless, the defense should execute the following basics:
- Gang tackle.
- Unpile slowly, but be onside for the next play. Get the next defensive call quickly.
- Take time getting on the ball on a completed pass, but be onside when the referee declares the ball ready for play.
- Don't allow the ballcarrier to run out-of-bounds and stop the clock.
- Don't stop the clock with a defensive penalty.
- Call a time-out only when instructed to do so by the sideline.
- Understand that the offense will usually go on quick counts if the clock is running. Defensive linemen can use this to get a great jump on the snap. However, defenders should be careful if the clock has stopped or the offense needs five yards or less for a first down.
- Be aware the offense may be in a four-down mode.
- Don't scoop-and-score on fumbles. Treat a fumble as a victory fumble. Fall on and possess the ball.
- Be alert for double moves (e.g., out-and-up, quick-and-go, slant-and-up etc.).
- Be alert for the watch play, where the quarterback feigns a spike and throws a forward pass.
- If a field goal is blocked, fall on the ball. Possession is the objective.

In addition, coaches should have the field-goal block team alerted, especially if the offense doesn't have a time-out available.

Quarter Change

The quarter change is a great time to communicate with the defense, especially if the offense is mounting a drive. While the defense jogs to the other end of the field, players should work down the hash closest to the defensive bench and look to the sideline for instructions from position coaches. Mike will come to the sideline for any instructions and get the next defensive call.

Big Ben Defense

This call is used for the last play or two near the end of the game when the defense has the lead and the offense will be throwing Hail Mary passes.

Big Ben Team Coaching Points

- Defenders should commit no penalties. They should not give the offense another play.
- Defenders should not allow the receiver to get out-of-bounds on a short completion.
- Defenders should knock the ball down or intercept. They should not tip the ball!
- On an interception, defenders should get down immediately. The game is over (victory interception).

Big Ben Line Coaching Points

- Defenders should contain the quarterback, and force a bad throw. They should not allow the quarterback to break contain. This would allow extra time for receivers to get downfield.
- The nose, with the ball on a hash, shades the center to the wideside of the field. If the ball is in the middle of the field, he should shade to the quarterback's throwing arm side.

Big Ben Underneath Defenders Coaching Points

- Corners align in an outside shade at five yards and jam the receivers. After jamming, they run to the spot. The spot is the area where the Hail Mary pass will come down. The strong corner is a late out route player.
- The corner to a one-receiver side aligns in an inside shade. He jams the receiver then does a zone turn and runs to the spot. He should be alert for throwbacks and a hitch-and-pitch pass.
- Outside linebackers align in an inside shade at five yards. They jam and run to the spot. Outside linebackers are jumpers. Jumpers get involved where the ball comes down. Jumpers try to high point the ball.
- Mike aligns over #3 at 10 yards and runs to the spot. Mike is a front catcher. Mike looks for a ball tipped back toward the line of scrimmage.

Big Ben Deep Three Coaching Points

- Defenders should align at 30 yards depth, but no deeper than one yard in the end zone. The ballside defender and the middle defender are jumpers.
- The offside defender works behind the jumpers for the tip. *He does not get involved in the jump ball!*

Figures 11-1 through 11-4 show the Big Ben defense against four likely formations.

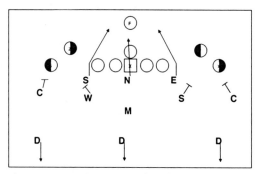

Figure 11-1. Big Ben vs. doubles

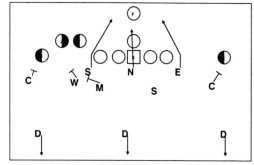

Figure 11-2. Big Ben vs. trips

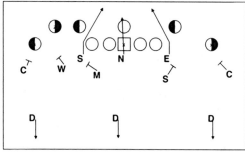

Figure 11-3. Big Ben vs. empty

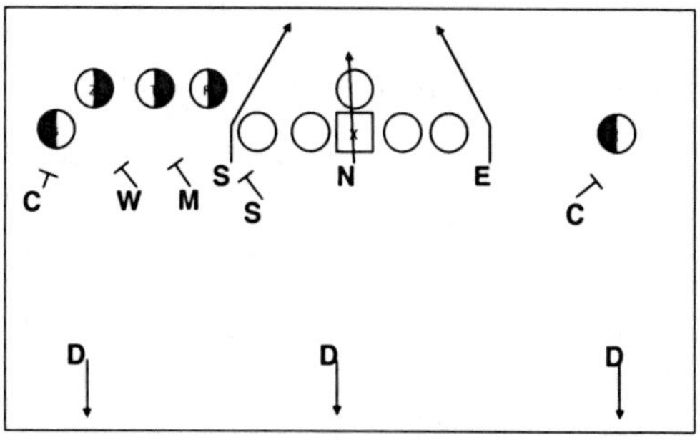

Figure 11-4. Big Ben vs. quads

Armageddon (Figure 11-5)

Armageddon is a defense when the offense is kneeling the ball in a victory formation. With all due respect to Tom Coughlin, miracles do happen. The game isn't over until the final horn.

Ends: Align head-up on the offensive tackles and drive them outside.

Tackles: Align head-up on the offensive guards and drive them outside.

Mike: Aligns head-up on the center in a four-point stance and drives through his legs. Causes a fumbled snap. Anticipates the snap. A five-yard penalty at this point is irrelevant.

Will: Aligns in a three-point stance and drive through the A+ gap.

Sam: Aligns in a three-point stance and drive through the A– gap.

Strong safety: Aligns in a three-point stance and crash through the tight end's outside hip. If he gets a "here" call from the corner, he moves to C+.

Corners: Move out with a wide #1. If there are multiple receivers, split the distance and zone off. If #1 is tight, give the strong safety a "here" call and come hard off the edge and drive to the quarterback.

Free safety: Hole player

Coaching points: Interior men should fall on a loose ball and treat a fumble as a city fumble. Outside players should scoop and score and treat a fumble as a country fumble.

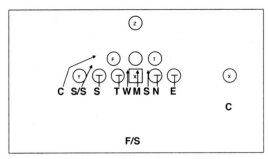

Figure 11-5. Armageddon

Defensive Time-Out Protocol

This particular time-out is used in a four-minute scenario when the opponent has the ball. This time-out is to be called after the next offensive play if the clock is still running. Time-out protocol should be taught in fall camp. Periodically, the system needs to be reviewed. Time-out mechanics should be covered every Thursday during the season. Following is a blueprint for time-outs:

- The signal will be the coach placing his right hand upward and making a circular motion.
- Time-outs will be signaled from the sideline or as instructed by the defensive coordinator or head coach (i.e., clock time-out).
- Mike or the free safety may call a time-out if the defense doesn't have the proper number or right combination of players on the field. Mike controls the front while the free safety controls the secondary.
- On all time-outs Mike and the free safety come to the sideline. In some situations, the entire defense may be called to the sideline.
- During an official time-out, when the teams have to stay on the field, the defense may be called to the hash.

Kick Safe Defenses

Whenever there is an increased possibility of a fake kick, the defense will stay on the field. Also, a safe call can be called if the defensive team has the lead and the coach is content just to get the ball. If the kicking team is close to a first down and the coach fears a defender might jump and give the offense a first down, a cushion call can be added. This call tells the linemen to back off the ball one yard. This allows for a margin of error should a defender flinch or jump pre-snap. Two schemes are used. A single return man is called safe single. Should weather conditions warrant, a double safety setup can be used, which is called safe double.

Safe Single (Figure 11-6)

Tackles: Penetrate the A gap.

Ends: Penetrate the C gap.

Linemen: Force the kick. They penetrate and go full-speed to the personal protector. Should a fumbled or errant snap occur, linemen keep going and play football. If the punter has it clean, they should pull up.

Corners: Man on #1

Strong safety: Man on #2 strong

Will: Man on #3 strong

Mike: Man on #3 weak

Sam: Man on #2 weak

Free safety: May return the punt, or a substitute may be inserted for the free safety. The returner should not take a hit. If in doubt, he should fair catch the ball.

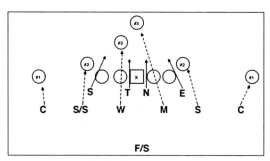

Figure 11-6. Safe single

Safe Double (Figure 11-7)

Safe double is used to expand the coverage area by using two returners. The free safety is in charge as to who catches the ball.

Linemen: Same as safe single.

Corners: Man on #1

Strong safety: Becomes the second returner, or a substitute may be inserted.

Will: Man on #2 strong

Mike: Responsible for both the personal protector and the punter.

Sam: Man on #2 weak

Free safety: Is in charge. Gives you-me calls as to who catches the ball.

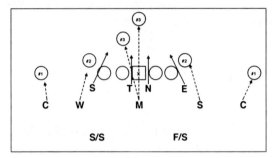

Figure 11-7. Safe double

Field Goal Safe (Figure 11-8)

This scheme is used whenever the defense feels there is a good chance of a fake field goal.

Tackles: Penetrate the A gap, and block the kick.

Ends: Penetrate the C gap, and block the kick.

Corners: Man on #1

Strong safety: Man on #2 strong

Free safety: Man on #2 weak

Mike: Responsible for both the holder and the kicker.

Will and Sam: Contain rush outside the wings. Turn in all fakes. Scoop and score on any loose balls.

Figure 11-9 shows field goal safe against an unbalanced field goal formation. Linemen move over one man to center up the formation. From there linemen follow normal rules. The free safety will take #3 man-to-man while everyone else follows base safe rules.

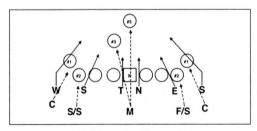

Figure 11-8. Field goal safe

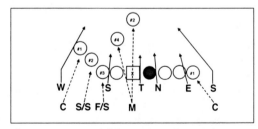

Figure 11-9. Field goal safe against an unbalanced field goal formation

Pigtail Adjustment

Should the coach think the kick will be short, he can take out Mike and sub in a return man. Everyone else follows safe rules. This is a great opportunity to get a return because kick coverage will be poor.

Surprise Formations

This section deals with bastard or trick formations, which most offensive teams have in their playbook. The formations serve to disorient and confuse defenses. Covered will be the swinging gate, group formations (Loco), unbalanced line, and Emory & Henry.

Swinging Gate (Figures 11-10 through 11-12)

The defense will follow punt safe rules. Mike declares strength to the ball. If the center is the widest player, he is considered #1.

Left tackle: Lines up over the ball. If the center has an eligible number, gets a hold up on him.

Right tackle: Finds the middle of the detached formation and penetrates.

Ends: The end closest to the ball becomes the shooter. The shooter lines up near the end man and bursts across the line of scrimmage. He should pick off any throw in that direction. The other end aligns head-up on the end man on the line of scrimmage and holds him up. This is called a butch technique.

Corners: Man on #1

Strong safety: Man on #2 strong

Will: Man on #3 strong

Mike: Man on #3 weak

Sam: Man on #2 weak

Free safety: Hole

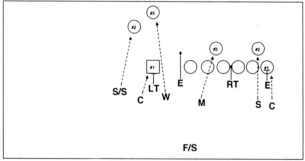

Figure 11-10. Swinging gate base formation

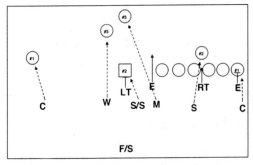

Figure 11-11. Swinging gate formation #1

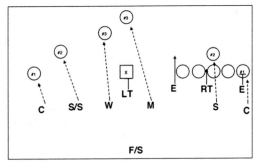

Figure 11-12. Swinging gate formation #2

Loco (Figures 11-13 and 11-14)

A group formation is any wide formation that includes one interior lineman. When the defense gets such a set, it makes a Loco call.

Loco Rules

- Outside linebackers keying the offensive tackles in the huddle should alert the defense.
- Cover 3 cloud to the side of the group is automatic.
- Will and Sam align in the seam.
- The end to the side of the group becomes the shooter.
- The remaining linemen adjust to a three-man line and balance it up. The tackle over the center will two-gap the center.
- Mike will declare to the numbers.

Figure 11-13 illustrates a group formation and the defensive adjustment in base defense with a left call. Figure 11-14 shows mustang adjustments. In the mustang package, the Rover will go to the call and become the shooter. Mustang linemen stay in the box. All other defenders follow normal rules.

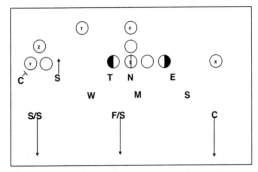

Figure 11-13. Group formation and the defensive adjustment in base defense with a left call

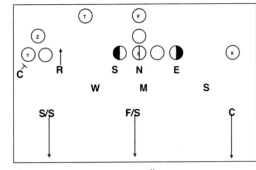

Figure 11-14. Mustang adjustments

Unbalanced (Figures 11-15 and 11-16)

Some offenses will align both offensive tackles to the same side of the formation. With outside linebackers keying the offensive tackle to their side in the huddle, the defense should not be fooled.

Unbalanced Rules

- The outside linebacker will give a tackle over call if his offensive tackle crosses to the other side of the line of scrimmage.
- If the unbalanced side is away from the tight end and the tight end is to the shortside, the defender will give a right or left, unbalanced slide right or left call. The defense will move one man away from the tight end (Figure 11-15).
- If the unbalanced side is to the tight end, the defender will give a strength right or left unbalanced, slide right or left call. The defense will move one man to the tight end (Figure 11-16).
- These rules apply no matter the defensive calls. If a blitz has been called, blitz paths must reflect the change in defensive linemen alignment.

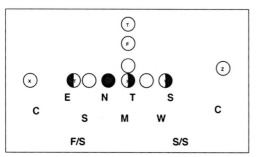

Figure 11-15. Defense moves one man away from the tight end

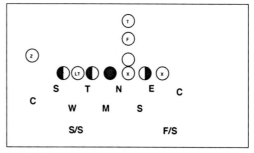

Figure 11-16. Defense moves one man to the tight end

Emory & Henry (Figures 11-17 through 11-20)

The Emory & Henry formation (Figure 11-17) was popularized by Steve Spurrier, when he was coaching at the University of Florida.

Tackles: Charge the A gap.

Ends: With the quarterback under center, play a tight 5 technique. Must be ready to take the dive on a dive option play. If the quarterback is in the gun or there are no backs, get wide and go.

Will and Sam: Shooters

Mike: Aligns over the ball. Takes the quarterback on an option play. Versus pass, takes the back man-to-man.

Strong safety and free safety: Man on #2 to their side

Corners: Man on #1

Figure 11-18 illustrates that if two receivers are off the line of scrimmage on one side they all are eligible to that side. Versus empty sets, Mike is the adjuster while all the other defenders follow base rules (Figure 11-19). If the defense is in mustang, everyone follows base rules except the nose, who will two-gap the center, and Rover, who will play the hole (Figure 11-20).

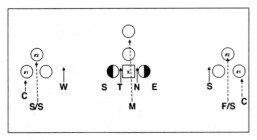

Figure 11-17. Base Emory & Henry

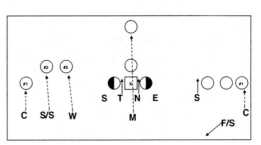

Figure 11-18. Trips left

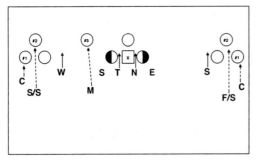

Figure 11-19. Empty set

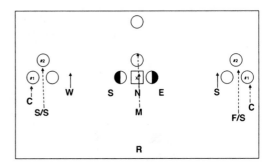

Figure 11-20. Base vs. mustang package

Special Situations and Alerts

Following are unusual or special situations that arise during games. Included are scramble rules, double-move alerts, defensive alerts, interception return responsibilities, and fumble recoveries.

Scramble Rules

Whenever the quarterback is flushed from the pocket, the defense should use the following rules:
- Defenders should plaster frontside zones. They should get all over potential receivers.
- Defenders should carry the receivers through the zone.
- Deep players should never come out of the deep zones.
- Short zone players should not leave coverage until the quarterback crosses the line of scrimmage.
- The backside flat player maintains backside leverage at all times.

Receiver Double-Move Alert

Late in the half or game, especially in a two-minute situation, the defense should expect a double move from receivers (e.g., hitch-and-go, out-and-up, slant-and-up, etc.). They should give up the short route, keeping horizontal and vertical leverage. They should make the sure tackle and keep the clock running.

Defensive Alerts

Following are some post-snap communication terms:
- *Pass:* When anyone recognizes that the play is a pass.
- *Ball:* When anyone recognizes the quarterback has thrown the ball. This alert is especially valuable in man coverage when some defenders will have their back turned to the quarterback.
- *Run:* When anyone recognizes the play is a run. Again, this alert is crucial in man coverage.
- *Crack:* When wideouts block inside.
- *In or out:* Calls to and by linebackers to alert that receivers are entering or leaving their area.
- *Reverse:* Whenever a receiver is going against the grain on a running play.
- *Stay:* A reminder for defensive backs when a quarterback starts to scramble.

Interception Return Responsibilities

Everyone has responsibilities whenever a pass has been intercepted. Those defensive responsibilities follow.

Rush Element

- Peel to the near numbers, and sprint to the interceptor. Spread out. Don't follow the same number.
- The rusher opposite the throw will block the quarterback.
- Communicate.

Interceptor

- Return to the nearest sideline.
- Avoid cutting back. It might look good in there, but "there" is where most of their people are. Also, an interceptor opens himself to a blindside hit and possible fumble.

Coverage Element

- The closest defender to the intended receiver blocks him.
- Others turn and work toward the near sideline and block the first opposite-colored jersey.

Interception Coaching Points

- Block someone. Don't be a spectator.
- Block above the waist and in front.
- If the ball is out in front, don't block! However, defenders may be able to shield someone.
- Interceptor must give an Oskie call. Secure the ball. Don't give it back. Get the ball in the outside arm, and chin the ball.
- If the defensive team is ahead in a two-minute situation, don't take a hit. Fall on the ball (victory interception).

Fumble Recovery

In addition to using good technique on fumble recoveries, players must know the situation. If the defense is ahead late in the game, possession of the ball is the goal. They should fall on the ball, which is called a victory fumble. In other situations, there are two types of fumbles: country or city. A country fumble is a fumble where not a lot of people are around. In this case, the defense should scoop and score. However, players only get one shot. If defensive players don't get the ball cleanly on the first attempt, they must fall on the ball unless there is absolutely no one in the area. A city fumble is a fumble that occurs in a crowd. In this case, defenders immediately fall on the ball. On a country fumble, defenders should get their knuckles on the ground and scoop the ball off to the side so they don't accidentally kick the ball. Defenders should cover the tip of the ball and chin the ball. Chinning the ball means the defender will hold the ball high and tight with the forward tip under his chin. The fall-on technique has the defender covering the tips of the ball and getting his top leg over the top.

Trick Plays

All offensive systems have tricks or specials. These plays seek to take advantage of surprise or poor defensive technique. Playing good disciplined defense is the best way to combat trick plays. Fundamentally sound defenses are hard to trick or fool. Simply following built-in rules will nullify most trick plays. In this section, the following special plays are covered and the antidote discussed:

- Halfback pass
- Flea flicker
- Reverse
- Reverse pass
- Fake reverse

- Hitch-and-pitch
- Throwback to the quarterback
- Watch call

Halfback Pass (Figure 11-21)

The corner, on secondary contain, should never come up until the ball crosses the line of scrimmage.

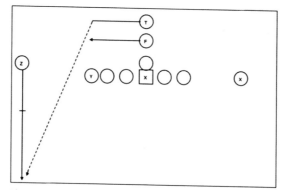

Figure 11-21. Halfback pass

Flea Flicker (Figure 11-22)

Secondary contain does not come up until the ball crosses the line of scrimmage. The hole player keys the uncovered linemen and does not run the alley until he sees offensive linemen downfield. On the flea flicker, the hole player should read high helmets.

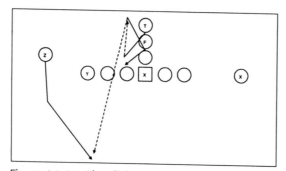

Figure 11-22. Flea flicker

Reverse (Figure 11-23)

Tip-offs include a reduced split by the receiver and fast flow action. The corner should give an ORCA (out, reverse, crack, away) call versus a reduced split. He should yell reverse whenever the receiver goes away on the snap. He should then play the fake reverse. Backside defenders should be alert for a reverse call. The backside end should get upfield to turn the play inside.

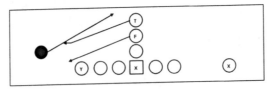

Figure 11-23. Reverse

Reverse Pass (Figure 11-24)

The frontside corner will not come up until the ball crosses the line of scrimmage. The corner has secondary contain.

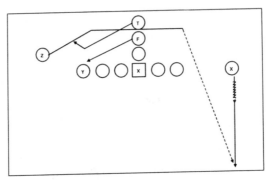

Figure 11-24. Reverse pass

Fake Reverse (Figure 11-25)

The frontside corner should search the running back to make sure the ball is given before he plays cutback to cutoff.

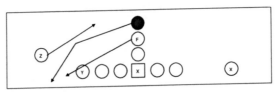

Figure 11-25. Fake reverse

Hitch-and-Pitch (Figure 11-26)

This play will come off a three-step drop and a #2 at or near the edge of the box. The corner must be aware of #2, especially in zone coverage. This play will usually be run late in the game with the offensive team behind on the scoreboard.

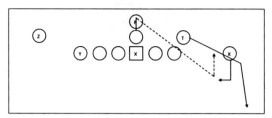

Figure 11-26. Hitch-and-pitch

Throwback to the Quarterback (Figure 11-27)

Tape study will show what the quarterback usually does after he hands the ball off or tosses the ball on a fast flow play. If he is sprinting out the back door, this play should be expected. As a basic rule, backside defenders should search the quarterback especially on the goal line.

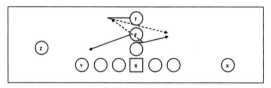

Figure 11-27. Throwback to the quarterback

Watch Call (Figure 11-28)

The watch call is a trick play off the spike or clock play. Instead of spiking the ball in a hurry-up situation, the quarterback will fake a spike and throw to a receiver. The defense should run the called defense full-speed, even if it appears the spike is coming. The watch play should be expected in a hurry-up scenario. Defenders must not relax!

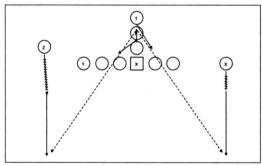

Figure 11-28. Watch call

12

Line Play

This chapter will explore the mental and physical qualifications needed to successfully implement and execute the line schemes and techniques covered in this playbook. Emphasis must be placed on the following areas to be a great defensive line:

- *Discipline:* Players must follow the instructions of the coach. Discipline keeps a player from acquiring bad habits that will hurt him and his team.
- *Mental discipline:* One mental mistake by one player can lead to a touchdown, field goal, keep a drive alive, give field position, or extend the time of possession for an opponent. Mental mistakes usually result from lack of concentration in meetings, not studying handouts, or when a player is fatigued. Knowing assignments eliminates confusion and allows a player to react correctly and play aggressively.
- *Physical discipline:* Physical discipline allows a player to push himself through the whole practice. When players get tired, they don't concentrate, hustle, and are not as intense. An edge can be gained on defense when defenders outhustle the opponent. Most games are won or lost in the fourth quarter. The fourth quarter must belong to the defense. The great competitors know the difference between pain and injury.
- *Consistency:* An athlete can't be a great player if he is an up-and-down player from day to day or week to week. Defensive linemen should discipline themselves to be consistent every day. A player who works hard to improve will be better than consistent, he will be consistently better. "You play like you practice" is the old saying. Linemen must develop good practice habits.
- *Team concepts:* Personal sacrifice instead of personal glorification, what a player can give not what a player can receive, should be the mentality.

Techniques and Fundamentals

These basic areas must be worked on and improved each day to benefit the team and help the individual player develop his craft.

Attack-Read Stance

From this stance, the player will attack first and read second. He will play run first and react to passes. A stance should allow a player to get into a relaxed and comfortable position that will enable him to uncoil for maximum explosion and quick movement. The shaded foot should be back, and the shaded hand should be down. The free hand will hang about a foot off the ground in front of the assigned gap. Feet are armpit-width apart or slightly wider, with the heels out. One foot is staggered, heel-to-toe, to allow the defender to uncoil with power, hitting the opponent hard enough to force him away from the defender's body. Weight is distributed between the balls of the feet and the fingertips of the hand on the ground. The down hand is four to six inches in front of the defender's head. Weight will be forward with 60 percent on the down hand and 40 percent on the feet. The off hand will be in position for a hand shiver. Eyes are up, and linemen should look through their eyebrows with peripheral view on everything. Toes are slightly pointed inside with the knees and shoulders pointed straight ahead. The neck is bulled, and knees are flexed with the tail slightly higher than the head and shoulders. Defenders are ready and in a cocked position with a Z in the knee. From this stance, the defensive lineman will Superman on the snap.

Jet Stance

The jet is a sprinter's stance utilized for pass rush. This stance will be used in passing situations. Defenders play pass first and react to runs. Linemen will elongate their stance with 10 percent of weight on the feet and 90 percent on the down hand.

Alignment (Vertical and Horizontal)

No matter the stance, care must be taken to ensure correct vertical and lateral alignment. Tips include crowding the ball by aligning on the near tip of the ball, which is called the credit card rule. If the center tips the ball upward, defenders should crowd the ball more. Defenders don't align on the opponent; they align on the ball. Base alignment has the defender placing his shaded foot on the opponent's crotch. A wide shade has the defender's shaded foot even with the offensive man's foot. A jet stance has the defender's foot outside the offensive man's foot. The defensive lineman's visual key is the helmet of the offensive lineman with peripheral vision on the ball. More specifically, the visual key is the screw on the helmet to the side of the defender's shade. In a passing situation or on a jet charge, linemen key the tip of the football.

Takeoff

First and foremost, quickness off the ball is an attitude. Linemen should be ready to move off the offensive man with peripheral vision on the ball. They should have a hair trigger, and beat the opponent to the punch. Defensive linemen get off as the ball starts to move. Players should visualize a string tied from the tip of the ball to their nose. On any movement, they go. The defender must get his feet into the neutral zone while creating a new line of scrimmage. However, coming out of the stance requires a zero step. A zero step means the hands attack before the feet even move. This fosters a Superman takeoff. The ball usually moves first; however, the quarterback's foot or butt may move first. Defenders should find out what moves first and use that as the movement key. Defensive linemen should fall out of their stance and lead with their hands, nose, and head. They should visualize throwing the body forward attacking the V of the neck of the offensive lineman. The first step replaces the down hand with a 6-8 step, which is called the power step. The second step should get on the ground quickly with the defensive lineman clawing the grass while keeping his numbers over the toes, staying low. Hands shoot for the breastplate, stabbing and grabbing the blocker, and gaining control of the blocker with hands. Hands are the fastest part of the body and are the defensive lineman's best friend. Defenders should attack with the hard part of the hands while keeping the hands inside the blocker. The defender should keep his thumbs at 12:00 with the elbows tucked inward. This posture gets the muscles of the upper back involved. All hand movement is forward with no windup or hitch. Defensive linemen should not try to step and strike at the same time, which only serves to slow down the hands. The strength of the blow comes from the quickness of the blow. As the defender attacks, he should roll his hips to get under the opponent, thinking facemask under his facemask. He can get the opponent on his heels by attacking through the man unless on a jet charge. On contact, he should patter the feet while staying square to the line of scrimmage. Defenders react to the blocker's movement or the ball, not sound. They should allow no gifts or errors on the cadence. Defenders shouldn't listen to the quarterback; movement is the stimulus. Players should have cotton in their ears. Coaches can help foster the movement stimulus by using movement keys in defensive drills instead of sound. Do not start defensive drills using sound; use movement. Coaches should also vary voice inflection in get-off drills.

Running

Running is one of the most important fundamentals in football. From correct running form, a player gets improved movement, balance, and quickness. Football is a game of movement, and running technique can be improved. Improving running form can help anyone become a better athlete. Players should run with good form in all their work, even when they jog and loosen up. Correct technique includes keeping the thumbs up and using the arms while running on the inside balls of the feet, working for good balance and keeping the shoulders over the feet. Defensive linemen should be in a good fundamental position so they can react and drive off either foot. This technique will help with balance, quickness, and body control.

Pursuit

A major part of team pride is getting everyone to the ball. Players should stay in their lane, never allowing the defense to be split. Defensive linemen must work through the blocker by fighting pressure and not running around the blocker while steering the block. They must work to gain separation and never stay blocked. Defensive linemen should take the appropriate angle to the ballcarrier and never follow the same colored jersey to the ball. Desire is the number-one requirement to get there. There is always some way to get to the ballcarrier.

Tackle

Each player must have the desire to make the tackle himself. Defenders must never assume someone else will make the play. Tackling is 10 percent technique and 90 percent desire. Vince Lombardi equated tackling to a situation where someone is running down the street with everything you own, and you are going to stop him. That is motivation!

Defensive Line Progression of Responsibility

Following is the natural progression of defensive line play from the huddle to the culmination of the play:

- Maintain proper alignment in the hanging huddle.
- Listen intently for the defensive call. Mike will give the call, but all defenders should recognize the sideline signal as well.
- Maintain proper post-huddle alignment.
- Listen for the strength declaration, and get aligned in the proper defense quickly. Mike will make a right call for strong right and a left call for strong left. Mike will then call the backfield set. Example: I, strong, weak, or ace.
- Listen for any checks or alerts from the linebackers.
- Be alert for any pre-snap reads. Examples: Offensive linemen splits or stance for run-pass key. Use flying or land animal code words to alert teammates to the nature of the upcoming play. For example, use rabbit for a run alert or hawk for a pass read.
- Position in a good defensive line stance with proper weight distribution.
- Focus on the key.
- Move on offensive movement; be explosive.
- Take the proper step, and deliver a blow.
- Maintain proper reaction to keys.
- Get to the ball with the proper pursuit angle with 100 percent effort.
- If knocked down, get off the ground and get to the ball. The ground is a hot stove.
- Make a sure and punishing tackle.

Pre-Snap Observation

An astute observer can decode a lot of plays by observing the offensive line at the line of scrimmag pre-snap. Observation and film study can give a defensive lineman a huge advantage. Following are some pre-snap keys defensive linemen should observe.

Offensive Line Stances

Offensive linemen high in their stance with little weight on the down hand and leaning backward indicates pass (bird call). Offensive linemen getting down in a stance with a lot of weight on the down hand and leaning forward indicates a run (rabbit call). Offensive linemen leaning right or left indicates a pull. Defenders should look for stance combinations. For example, the center giving a definite run look while the guard is setting light might indicate a trap play.

Line Splits

Tight splits usually indicate a pass or outside runs. Wide splits indicate inside runs (e.g., midline, dive option, and traps). A built-in split rule allows a defender to move head-up on his assignment if the offensive man aligns in a wide split (over four feet). An outside shade defender is allowed to move to an inside shade if the split is over four feet. He must give a sink call to the linebacker. In effect, the defensive lineman and the linebacker exchange gap responsibility pre-snap.

Basic Pre-Snap Reads

How to Identify Running Plays

- Offensive linemen with weight forward
- Big line splits
- Running backs leaning or pointing
- Offensive backfield set (game plan)
- Down-and-distance (game plan)

How to Identify Passes

- Lineman light in his stance
- Lineman in a two-point stance, staring at the defensive lineman across from him
- Quarterback mannerisms (e.g., licking his fingers, walking to the line looking at the receivers)
- Tight line splits
- Backfield sets (game plan)
- Game situation

How to Identify a Draw Play

- Offensive linemen inviting the rusher upfield
- Linemen popping up and pushing or clubbing defensive linemen upfield
- Running back crow hopping to the quarterback

How to Identify Screens

- Offensive tackle cutting a defender after a pass set
- Quarterback taking an excessively deep drop
- Offensive linemen slipping out under the rush
- Running back flashing across the defender's face after he sets up

Alignments and Shades (Figure 12-1)

This playbook illustrates a variety of defensive line alignments. These numbers give the defender his alignment, assignment, and responsibility. The keys to playing sound gap control include attacking half man in the assigned gap, getting great extension with the arms while keeping a flat back with the feet behind the butt, and keeping a good base with the hips and shoulders square to the line of scrimmage. Vertically the defender will crowd the ball while horizontal alignments will be adjusted for ability levels and/or game situations. Even though a wide variety of alignments are used, few techniques are needed to execute the defense. Outside and inside techniques are used mainly. Two head-up techniques are used: a 0 on the center, and a 6 technique on the tight end.

Figure 12-1. Alignments and shades

Outside Shades

1: Shade on the center (If to the tight end it is referred to as a plus 1 shade. If weak on the center, it is referred to as a minus 1 shade.)
3: Outside eye on the guard
5: Outside eye on the tackle
9: Outside eye on the Y

Inside Shades

2: Inside eye of the guard
4: Inside eye of the tackle
7: Inside eye of the tight end

Any defensive call can be tagged with a gap call, which places the defensive lineman in the gap to the shade call. For example, a 3 technique will basically line up in the B gap with a gap call.

Outside Shades (1, 3, 5, 9 Techniques)

The defender aligns with the inside foot on the offensive lineman's crotch with tight alignment on the ball. The stance is a three-point base with the inside foot back with a toe-to-heel stagger and the shaded hand down. From this base stance, the defensive lineman will take a six-inch power step. The defender will concentrate on the screw on the opponent's helmet. The shaded hand is the trail hand, with the free hand tabbed as the power hand.

Outside Shade Responsibilities

- Protect gap responsibility.
- Never be reached.
- Close on all down blocks. Protect the linebacker by getting hands on the blocker.
- Pursue all plays away, which is called a collapse technique. Squeeze flat to prevent cutbacks. No team wins without great effort backside. Once the ball crosses the line of scrimmage, take a deep angle to the ball.
- Avoid running around the tail of the blocker.
- Never, ever be passive. Attack at all costs.
- Rush the passer through the prescribed rush lane.

Outside Shade 1-on-1 Blocks

This section will explore the basic 1-on-1 blocks for each shade and defensive reactions. The basic blocks include base, down, reach, and pass. The points of emphasis for defensive linemen, whether in an inside or outside shade, include the following:

- Stance
- Get-off
- Keys
- Eyes
- Hand and helmet placement (stab and grab)
- Attack
- Gap control
- Lockout
- Separation
- Pursuit
- Tackle

Base (Figure 12-2)

The base is the number-one block a defensive lineman must defeat. Who is the better man? The defender should keep his shoulders square to the line of scrimmage while steering the blocker inside and constricting the running lane by pushing the blocker's outside breast and pulling his outside arm to turn the blockers shoulders to the inside. This is called a steer technique. Hand placement, on the blocker, should be above the defender's own eyes. The defender must keep his outside shoulder and leg free for a bounce out. If the defender feels no pressure, he is running around the block. Defensive linemen should always fight pressure. When the ballcarrier commits, the lineman must disengage and pursue.

Figure 12-2. Base

Down (Figure 12-3)

The defender should avoid running around the tail of a down block. He must get a piece of the blocker and close through the blocker's hip. If the outside shade can get his off hand on the blocker, the ability to play trap or take dive is enhanced. The defensive lineman attacks the first thing that shows off the down block. He should wrong-arm and spill any inside-out block. If the scheme is a jump through, the lineman should work down the line of scrimmage, looking for cutbacks (collapse). When the ball crosses the line of scrimmage, the linemen should take a proper pursuit angle. They should never follow the same color.

Figure 12-3. Down

Reach (Figure 12-4)

The total defensive scheme is in jeopardy if an outside shade is reached. The three basic types of reach blocks include a tight reach, wide reach, and an arc reach. Tackles facing a reach block should try to get a spot outside the blocker. The spot is one yard outside the offensive lineman and two yards deep. Ends facing a reach block should get to the spot of 4x1. Defensive linemen should take their eyes to the spot and find the ball when they get there. The defender should end up in the same alignment as he started, which was an outside shade on the offensive lineman. He must keep his outside shoulder free and work upfield and outside to the spot. He should work at a

45-degree angle, but not fly out. Defenders should keep their feet back and get great extension, steering as they go. A defender should keep his inside foot outside the blocker's outside foot. He should long-arm/short-arm the blocker at a 45-degree angle by pushing with his outside arm and pulling with his inside arm. If the defender feels he is getting reached, he should throw his hips outside. The hips are the key. They must stay outside the blocker. He should keep separation and not expose the chest. He must never allow the blocker to get his head outside and squared up.

Figure 12-4. Reach

Pass Set (Figure 12-5)

As a base rule, the defender should rush through his assigned gap. Tackles should collapse the pocket by aiming for the quarterback's near number. The 3 technique has a two-way go on the guard unless a stunt has been called. The ends should force the quarterback to step up into the pocket by targeting the quarterback's upfield shoulder. The called scheme dictates whether defensive linemen have the option of exchanging rush lanes. Example: Hot calls.

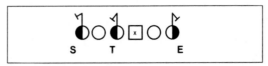

Figure 12-5. Pass set

Outside Shade Combo Blocks

Power Scoop (Figure 12-6)

Defensive linemen must keep their shoulders square to the line of scrimmage. Defenders should not allow the blocker off inside on the linebacker. They should grab and turn the blocker with the inside hand so he cannot work to the second level. Defenders should fight to stay in the crease. The defender must keep his head in the crack, staying low and working. He should play down the line, thinking cutback to a good pursuit angle. The defender must not be knocked off the line. He should keep his playside shoulder and leg free. The defender must never allow the tackle's head to cross in front. He should never be two-hatted! Blockers will usually tip off this scheme by their split. The split will normally be tight, and the tackle will usually be a little deeper than the guard.

Figure 12-6. Power scoop

Zone (Figure 12-7)

Defenders should treat the zone as a reach and press upfield. They should get to the spot. Defenders should not allow the ballcarrier to stretch the play. They should make him make a decision.

Figure 12-7. Zone

Double-Team (Figure 12-8)

A pre-snap tip-off might be a reduced split with the drive man closer to the line. The defender must beat the post block first while seeing the drive block through peripheral vision. As the defender feels outside pressure, he should turn his shoulders perpendicular to the line, keeping his head in the crack and turning his shoulders toward the ball. He should not allow the drive blocker to leverage the outside shoulder. The defender should try to get the blockers on different levels. He can hold on to the post blocker and twist the hips to the drive blocker. He should not be driven off the line into the linebackers. As a last resort, he should collapse.

Figure 12-8. Double-team

Inside Shades (2, 4, 7)

The defender aligns the outside foot to the crotch of the offensive lineman tight to the ball. The stance is a three-point stance with the outside foot back with a toe-to-heel stagger and the shaded hand down. The shaded hand is the trail hand with the free hand tabbed as the power hand. From the base stance, the defender will take a six-inch power step. The defensive lineman will concentrate on the screw on the front of the opponent's helmet.

Inside Shade Responsibilities

- Protect gap responsibility.
- Keep inside leverage.
- Never get shoeshined.
- Close if a blocker doesn't immediately block on (influence trap).
- Never get scooped by the next lineman inside.
- After defeating a shoeshine block, squeeze flat to prevent cutback lanes. No team wins without great effort backside.
- Rush in the prescribed rush lane.

Inside Shade 1-on-1 Blocks

Base (Figure 12-9)

The base is the number-one block to defeat. Who is the better man? The defender should keep his shoulders square while steering the blocker outside and constricting the running lane by pushing the blocker's inside breast and pulling the blocker's inside arm to turn his shoulders to the outside using the steer technique. The defender must hold the point. Hand placement should be above the defender's own eyes. The defender must keep his inside shoulder and leg free until the ball is no longer a cutback threat. If the defensive lineman feels no pressure, he is running around a block. When the runner commits, the defender must disengage and pursue.

Figure 12-9. Base

Shoeshine (Figure 12-10)

The defender thinks fumbled center snap to cutback. He has a great shot at recovering a fumbled snap. The defender should flatten down the line of scrimmage with no penetration unless the ball is in the area and he can ensure the tackle. He should run away from this block while playing from the ground up, keeping his legs and hips back.

Figure 12-10. Shoeshine

Outside Release (Figure 12-11)

The defender should recognize the outside release on his first step. If he is not immediately blocked, he should get inside immediately. He must turn inside and spill the ball versus a trap. The next offensive lineman inside will be the key for trap, dive, or zone. With an outside release, tackles think trap while the ends think dive.

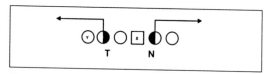

Figure 12-11. Outside release

Pass Set (Figure 12-12)

Defenders rush the passer in the prescribed rush lane. Defenders must not allow outside offensive linemen to block him 1-on-1 without help. Inside defensive shades are in a direct line to the quarterback on a level-three drop.

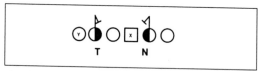

Figure 12-12. Pass set

Inside Shade Combo Blocks

Zone (Figure 12-13)

The defender should attack and squeeze the blocker outside while extending hands and pushing the offensive tackle outside, hindering him as he seeks to work to the second level. He should twist the hips toward the offensive tackle. This scheme ends up as a reach block by the guard. The defender should never allow the guard's head to cross in front. The defender must never be two-hatted! He should force the guard to climb to the linebacker.

Figure 12-13. Zone

Fan Block (Figure 12-14)

The defender should stay square with outside leverage on the guard by locking out the arms. Defenders keep the inside gap squeezed down, but keep outside leverage on the guard.

Figure 12-14. Fan block

6 Technique

The 6 technique is used in the Ohio front or with a butch call. Alignment is head-up foot-to-foot with the tight end should he take a normal split of four feet. The 6 technique must never be oversplit. If the tight end splits over four feet, the 6 will move inside to a 7 technique. The 6 must dominate the tight end. The 6 must control the C gap and get a hold up if the tight end tries to pass release.

6 Technique Blocks

Base (Figure 12-15)

The defender should explode and whip the end, playing pad under pad. He should take any threat in the C gap. The defender should only crossface the end when the ball is definitely inside. He should keep the tight end's shoulders square and not allow the end to gain inside or outside leverage.

Figure 12-15. Base

Reach (Figure 12-16)

The defender should press the tight end inside-out and anchor the C gap, looking for the ball to cut back. The 6 technique will only crossface when the ball crosses his face. He must not get knocked back, which would cut off level-two pursuit.

Figure 12-16. Reach

Co-Op Block (Figure 12-17)

The tight end will reach the 6 and then slip off to the second level with the offensive tackle cleaning up. The 6 must explode into the tight end. The tackle must never reach the 6 technique.

Figure 12-17. Co-op block

Cutoff Block (Figure 12-18)

The tight end's head will be in the C gap. This block will look similar to a down block. The defender must never allow the end to cut off and high wall. The 6 has C gap responsibility. The 6 should close down the line, looking for cutbacks. He must not get knocked off the line of scrimmage.

Figure 12-18. Cutoff block

Out-Out (Figure 12-19)

Once the tight end declares his block on the level-two player, the 6 technique must get his eyes back inside on the offensive tackle. He should attack the tackle outside-in. The 6 should use a push-pull move to work back square to the line of scrimmage, keeping his shoulders square to the line looking for the ball to bounce out. He must not run upfield. He should squeeze the C gap with his outside leg back while staying pad under pad.

Figure 12-19. Out-out block

Tight End Outside Release With a Near Back or Guard Kickout Block (Figure 12-20)

The progression should be eyes inside, to the pull lane, to the onside back. When the 6 technique recognizes a kickout block, he will wrong-arm and spill the block. He must get his head into the C gap and avoid running upfield.

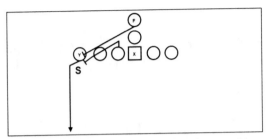

Figure 12-20. Tight end outside release with a near back or guard kickout block

Tight End Outside Release and an Option Play (Figure 12-21)

When the 6 reads an outside release, he takes his eyes to the pull lane. When he reads the ball down the line, he will close and take the first threat.

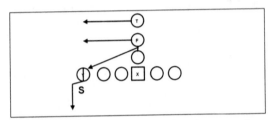

Figure 12-21. Tight end outside release and an option play

Tight End Pass Release (Figure 12-22)

When the defender's eyes go back inside to the pull lane, the 6 will see a pass set by the offensive tackle. He then rushes the passer using a pass-rush technique. The 6 has cage responsibility.

Figure 12-22. Tight end pass release

Sprint Pass (Figure 12-23)

The offensive tackle will turn back or reach-punch and turn back. The 6 must see the difference between a kickout block and a pin block by the near back. The 6 must get to the deepest back, which will be the tailback in an I formation. The 6 should feel the fullback, but see the tailback. He must protect his legs and stay up, never getting cut. He must never allow the quarterback outside. He must pull up the quarterback as soon as possible.

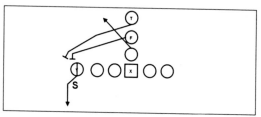

Figure 12-23. Sprint pass

Steer Technique

The steer technique is used by defensive linemen to turn and control the blocker's shoulders. The defensive lineman will use good hand placement and turn the blocker's shoulders toward the point of attack. This tactic is called a long-arm/short-arm technique.

Steer by an Inside Shade Defensive Player

If the ball comes to the defender but stays inside the tackle box outside of his gap responsibility and the threat of cutback is present, the defender will steer the blocker and constrict and squeeze the running seam by pushing the blocker's outside breast up and away while pulling the blocker's inside arm to turn the blocker's shoulders to the sideline. The defender will squeeze the next gap outside and will be ready for a cutback. If the ball comes to the defender and goes outside the tackle box and no cutback threat is present, he steers the blocker by pushing his outside breast up and away while pulling his inside arm to turn his shoulders to the sideline. After turning the blocker's shoulders, he will give ground and rip, swim, or crossface wipe as the defender steps across the blocker's face and pursues the ball. As a last resort, the defender can backdoor the block. If the ball goes away from a defender and stays in the tackle box and cutback threat is present, or if the ball goes outside the tackle box, he should steer the blocker by pushing his outside breast and pulling his inside arm to turn his shoulders to the sideline. He should power rip under, then squeeze to the ball flat down the line or trail deep if he is a contain player.

Steer by an Outside Shade Player

If the ball comes to the defender and stays inside the tackle box and inside of his gap responsibility, he should steer the blocker inside to constrict the running seam to try to make the ball bounce outside. He can steer by pushing the blocker's inside breast up and away while pulling the blocker's outside arm to turn his shoulders to the inside. He should constrict the inside running seam. If the ball comes to the defender and goes inside the tackle box, he can steer the blocker by pushing his inside breast up and away and pulling his outside shoulder to turn his shoulders inside. He should power rip or crossface wipe, come off the block, and make the play. If the ball goes away and stays in the tackle box and cutback threat is present, or if the ball goes outside the tackle box, he can steer and squeeze the blocker by pushing his inside breast up and pulling his outside arm to turn his shoulders to the inside. If the ball stays in the tackle box, he should squeeze and constrict the cutoff. If the defender is a squeeze player and the ball bounces outside the tackle box, he can drop step, power rip, swim, or wipe, and pursue flat down the line of scrimmage. If the defender is a contain player, he should trail and look for BCR. BCR is an acronym for bootleg, counter, reverse.

Defensive Line Shades

Thickness of shades depends upon many factors, including offensive and defensive talent levels and game situations. Base alignment has the defender's shaded foot down the crotch of the offensive linemen. The defender uses an attack-read step. Talent level or game situation may call for a wide shade. In this shade, the defender aligns with his shaded foot on the near foot of the offensive lineman, again using the attack-read step. In both base and wide alignments, linemen play run first and react to pass. A jet alignment has the defensive lineman aligned with his shaded foot outside the offensive lineman in a sprinter's stance and gets vertical on the snap. This technique is used for passing situations. The defender will play pass first and react to run.

13

Linebacker Play

This chapter explores the mental and physical qualifications plus fundamentals needed for linebackers to successfully implement and execute the schemes and techniques covered in this playbook.

Mental Qualifications

- Leadership is probably the number-one mental qualification linebackers need. Linebackers are in the middle of the defense. They are sandwiched between the defensive line and the back end, the secondary. As a result, they must take charge of the huddle and be able to effectively communicate with both ends of the defense. Linebackers must lead by example. They must model hustle, alertness, and coachability.
- Linebackers—specifically Mike—must declare formation strength and offensive changes of strength.
- Recognition of formation cheats and line splits is paramount.
- Linebackers must possess refined instincts such as reacting correctly to keys, knowing where the ball is, and seeing the whole picture, and must have the ability to diagnose the play and make the tackle. They must have a nose for the football.

Physical Qualifications

- *Quickness:* Effective linebackers posses quick feet, acceleration, catch-up speed, and the ability to flash to the ball.
- *Change of direction:* Linebackers must be able to diagnose counter concepts and adjust quickly to break down offensive blocking angles.
- *Range:* Linebackers must be able to run. Linebackers must be able to play from sideline to sideline. Linebackers also have to be able to break on the ball on passes and execute proper cutoff angles versus runs or passes.
- *Field vision:* This would include formation and blocker awareness. Anticipation is also a plus, which would come from effective pre-game study.
- *Strength at the point of attack:* Linebackers must have the physical ability to strike a blocker and know what edge of the blocker to be on according to the position of the ballcarrier, assigned gap, and where help will come from. Linebackers must exert pad control on the blocker and proper use of his legs and hands.
- *Pass coverage:* All linebackers must be proficient in pass coverage. Linebackers must have receiver and pattern awareness. Linebackers have to effectively communicate with fellow linebackers and the secondary versus pass plays. Linebackers must physically position themselves in 1-on-1 coverage and have knowledge of where the helpside is.

Fundamentals

Following are the basic techniques and fundamentals needed to be an effective linebacker. These basics are needed to excel and execute the schemes illustrated in this playbook.

- *Stance:* The feet should be shoulder-width apart with toes pointing straight ahead. The weight should be on the insteps of both feet with a little daylight under the heels. Linebackers should never be flat-footed. Unlike linemen or secondary players, linebackers don't know which of their feet will have to move first. They may have to react right or left on each play. Knees should be flexed with hands lightly on the thigh boards and elbows kept close to the body. Knees should be over the toes with the shoulders back and the tail down. The head should be up with eyes focused on the appropriate key. Linebackers must keep their body under control at all times. Balance is one of the most important fundamentals in football, especially for two-point stance players. To help with balance, upper body movement should be kept to a minimum.
- *Steps:* The first step is a 6- to 12-inch step downhill at a 45-degree angle. The heel replaces the toe with the shoulders square to the line of scrimmage. The shoulders should not rise as the linebacker steps. The feet should be kept close to the ground cutting the grass.

- *Pursuit:* Linebackers should keep their feet moving as they follow their key. They should shuffle if the ball is in the box, keeping hips and shoulders square as long as possible and keeping assigned leverage on the ballcarrier. The shuffle technique is a controlled movement when the ball is moving slow and stays in the box in the high-contact area. A correct shuffle has the linebacker sliding his feet while staying low and keeping good flexion in the knees, hips, and ankles. He should stay on the backside hip of the runner, keeping the ball at arm's length. Linebackers should never follow the same color. He must stay one yard deeper than a teammate in front of him. The farther the ball is away, the deeper the angle of pursuit. If the ball is fast flow and out of the box in the alley, the linebacker will have to use a scrape technique. The scrape technique is used on wide plays when the shuffle cannot keep up. When the ball leaves the box, the linebacker will turn his hips and run, keeping the shoulders square to the box to maintain leverage on cutbacks. This is a defensive run technique. When the ball gets outside the box very quickly, the backer must take a flatter angle. However, the flatter the angle, the more susceptible the defender is to a cutback.

- *Keys and reads:* The base linebacker read is the near back under keying the guard and tackle area. Backers key the back on his first step only (i.e., the six-inch directional step). First step keys are broken down into three read types: slow, fast, and divide (Figures 13-1 through 13-3). The A, B, and C gaps are considered slow reads. Cutbacks are a distinct possibility. The D gap is considered a fast read with a cutback unlikely.

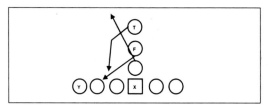

Figure 13-1. Slow read

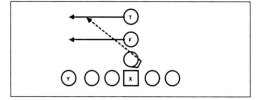

Figure 13-2. Fast read

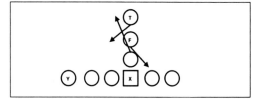

Figure 13-3. Divide read

Play Flow Definition

The generic term *flow* means ball action. Flow to means ball action to a particular linebacker, while flow away means ball action away from a particular backer. Figure 13-4 shows action to Will and away from Sam. Flow toward strength is termed *flow action* (Figure 13-5). Flood action is run action away from strength (Figure 13-6).

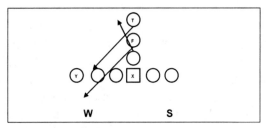

Figure 13-4. Flow to Will and away from Sam

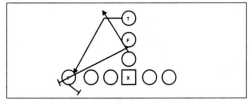

Figure 13-5. Flow action

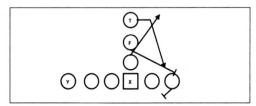

Figure 13-6. Flood action

Under Keys

The second phase of key progression is the recognition of blocking schemes. Since linebackers key the back for only the first step, attention should next go to the offensive linemen. In reality this doesn't mean two separate reads, but one. In essence, the linebacker reads the onside back *through* linemen. Pulling linemen override any other key. This is also determined by game plan. Vision is a vital part of reading and play recognition. Players must look at the right things in the correct places. This is a large part of the read progression. Key progression is based on looking at the correct people, reacting to what they are doing and playing to daylight and where the ball is.

Fill Techniques

These techniques are used to attack assigned gap responsibilities and determine what leverage to use on the blocker.

Flow To

Vertical

Vertical is used when a linebacker has A gap responsibility. A vertical read occurs with an A gap point attack. The linebacker will spill all blocks. Figure 13-7 shows Sam spilling the block in under China. Spilling requires the backer taking on the block with inside leverage. Linebackers spill in all coverages.

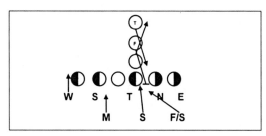

Figure 13-7. Sam spilling the block in under China

Scrape

Scrape is used when the backer has a 3 technique lineman to his side. Scrape occurs when he reads a D point attack (Figure 13-8).

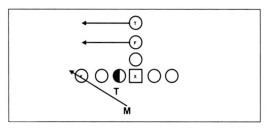

Figure 13-8. Scrape

Shuffle

Shuffle is used when the linebacker reads a B or C point attack. The backer stays in the box while the ball is in the box. Shuffle is also used on slow flow runs away.

Plug

The plug technique used with a C technique end and an A technique tackle. The backer plays to daylight. This technique may occur to an open or closed end side. Gap responsibility is determined by the block scheme.

Flow Away

On flow away, linebackers have one of three responsibilities:
- *Backside fill:* When backside A is unoccupied
- *Free:* When backside A is occupied
- *Hitter:* When both A gaps are occupied

Linebackers must shuffle to the assigned gap with pads square. After checking the assigned gap, the backer becomes a running linebacker, checking and filling holes on the run.

Physical check is used whenever the linebacker gets an A or B gap angle by key on plays away. The backer must physically get up in the gap for a cutback. He will use a shuffle technique. Mental checks are used whenever the linebacker gets a C or D gap angle by the key on a play away. The linebacker works downhill toward his assigned gap, but since cutback possibilities are minimal, he doesn't enter the gap but instead will flatten out and pursue.

Counter Technique

On plays away, linebackers pick up the offside guard and tackle area, looking for linemen pulling toward their side of the ball. The linebacker must read the blur and give a pull call. If to the playside, the backer should shuffle to the widest offensive man expecting a bounce out. If backside, the linebacker should see offensive linemen leaving and shuffle inside-out and take the first open seam. Figure 13-9 shows a flow counter.

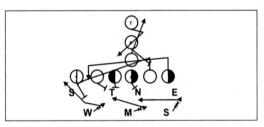

Figure 13-9. Flow counter

Stunt Technique

Backers should run a basic stunt from a depth of three and a half to four yards. Some stunts may call for a deeper depth or in some cases from the line of scrimmage. As a basic rule, linebackers should time up the stunt and hit the line of scrimmage full-speed. They should key the back to the side of the stunt and expect the ball to be in the stunt gap. Linebackers should never allow the running back through the gap unmolested. They should determine if the play is a pass or run when one yard deep. While the running back is behind the quarterback, they should expect a run or draw. They should not run past the ball.

Blow Delivery

Linebackers have the use of two blow delivery systems: hand shiver and a forearm lift. Linebackers must be proficient with both. A crucial coaching point for both blows is the linebacker must keep his hips back at the junction point and avoid a hip roll except when tackling. Different circumstances call for one or the other blow delivery. Regardless of the blow used, general characteristics are required for both styles. Following are the general parameters for both a forearm lift and the hand shiver:

- All movement with hands and arms are forward and should be delivered with quickness. Defenders should not wind up.
- Defenders should defeat the offensive lineman on or near the line, and shed as quickly as possible.
- Defenders should obtain operating space by gaining separation with the blocker by fully extending the arms with low hips.
- Defenders should end up with hips and shoulders parallel with the line of scrimmage, working with the inside leg slightly forward. Linebackers do not want to fully extend their legs anytime other than short yardage or goal line.
- Linebackers want their feet under them and moving.
- Linebackers should keep their face mask lower than the blocker's face mask.

The forearm lift is used mainly in defending isolation-type plays. Following are the key coaching points for a forearm lift:

- The blow is struck with the back of the hand and forearm into the pit of the stomach, chest, or head of the offensive man.
- The backer should strike and step with the staggered foot simultaneously. The backer should hit with the same arm as the staggered foot. For example, with a right arm shiver, the right foot should be forward.
- It is important that all movement of the arm is forward with quickness on movement of ball or offensive man. The backer should not wind up.
- As the forearm is being delivered, the other hand (the off hand) is brought up, attacking the blocker's near shoulder.
- As the blow is struck, the defensive man should bull his neck and snap his head back to ensure that his weight is over the feet, and the big muscles are involved with a straight line of force from the foot up through the upper body of the blocker.
- It is very important that the forearm is delivered up through the man and beyond. The backer should follow through to gain operating space and shed the blocker.

Following are the key coaching points for the hand shiver:

- The blow is delivered with the palms and heels of the hands to the chest, shoulders, or head of the offensive lineman. The defender should use the hard part of the hand.

- The initial step is with the staggered foot, squaring up the feet as the blow is struck. The defender should lead with the hands, and bring the feet. Hands and staggered foot should come simultaneously.
- Movement of the hands must be all forward, locking the elbows as the blow is struck. Thumbs should be at 12:00. The defender should not wind up.
- As the hands strike and the staggered foot is brought forward, it is crucial for the linebacker to drop or roll the hips and snap the head back to ensure balance.
- The blow must be delivered through the man and beyond to give operating space. The defender should follow through to gain separation.

Blocks

This section deals with how to take on different types of blocks. Covered will be base, reach, cut, and crackback blocks.

Base Block

The blocker goes straight at the linebacker. The backer should stay square, keeping his outside shoulder free. He should concentrate on a quick powerful punch, squeezing the blocker into the inside gap, gaining separation. He should not allow the blocker to latch on. As the backer locates the ball, he disengages the blocker as quickly as possible.

Base block don'ts:
- Do not turn the shoulders.
- Do not give ground.
- Do not spin off the blocker.
- Do not let the blocker turn his shoulder pads and hips to get between the backer and the ball.

Reach Block

The blocker comes at the backer at an angle. The linebacker should work to drive his helmet through the blocker's inside throat while getting his hands on the blocker's pads as quickly as possible. Linebackers should never lose sight of the ballcarrier. Linebackers have a three-way go. They can go over the top, go through the blocker, or slip the block. If slipping the block, the linebacker must stay butt-to-butt.

Reach block don'ts:
- Do not let the blocker get his shoulders turned back upfield. As long as the blocker is parallel to—or at an angle to—the line of scrimmage, he has lost a lot of his power. Once the blocker gets turned upfield, he is strong again.
- Do not stop, wait, or look for the blocker. Don't take him on unless it is necessary.
- Do not lose sight of the ballcarrier.

Vision

An effective defensive back cannot have tunnel vision. Pre-snap vision includes recognizing formations, offensive personnel, motions, shifts, and so forth. Post-snap vision includes seeing keys, pass-actions, routes, and the like. Also, vision is a large part of effective ball skills.

Fundamentals

Stance

Corners assume a comfortable stance with the outside foot forward and pointed straight ahead. The inside foot should be toe-to-instep with the outside foot. The body is slightly cocked inside with the eyes focused at a point halfway between the quarterback and receiver. Hips should be low, the back arched, and the head up. Weight should be over the front foot. Safeties have a more parallel stance and are more upright.

Alignment

Depth and vertical alignment depend upon the coverage called. As a basic rule, corners align inside in man coverage and cover 8. An outside alignment is used by corners in cover 2. Corners, as a rule, align 1x7 inside in cover 8 and 1x5 outside in cover 2. In man coverage, depth is determined by ability level. With a press call, the defender lines up on the line of scrimmage with inside leverage. Safeties, in cover 8, with no displaced #2, align nine yards deep on the edge of the box. With a displaced #2, they line up 1x9 inside #2. Cover 2 alignment has the safeties at a depth of 12 yards.

Start

Corners will backpedal, keying the three-step drop. They must eliminate false steps, which would allow a receiver to eat up the defensive back's cushion. The corner pushes off his front foot. Safeties, as a start trigger, will bounce step in cover 8. A bounce step is a moving-in-place foot action. This serves to get the safeties feet moving. Safeties will not backpedal in cover 8. Safeties will backpedal in man coverage or cover 2.

Backpedal

The backpedal technique is used to maintain vertical position on the receiver. This technique is activated by pushing off the front foot and reaching back with hips lowered, shoulders over the knees, ankle bones close, and feet skimming the grass. Good arm action is important. The backpedal starts out slowly and progressively gets faster. Early in the backpedal, the defensive back will key the three-step drop by the quarterback. If the quarterback is in the gun, the defensive back will read a quick pass when the quarterback has the ball at his ear and his front hand comes off the ball.

Weave

The weave is used to maintain horizontal leverage on the receiver. The defensive back must not allow the receiver to gain a head-up position. To weave inside, the defensive back pushes off the outside foot and reaches inside at a 45-degree angle. To weave outside, he will push off the inside foot at a 45-degree angle. When a defensive back weaves left, the right foot will be slightly behind the left foot. Conversely, when he moves to the right, the left foot will be behind the right foot. When weaving, the defensive back must keep his shoulders square and gain ground by gaining width and depth.

Transition

Transition involves a movement from the backpedal and weave to a forward break or a turn-and-run technique. The key to an effective transition is to keep the feet moving. The feet must not stop. Forward movement for pass or run can be either a stick foot or a speed break. A stick foot transition is executed by getting the foot opposite the break in the ground and pushing off that foot to drive. The stick foot should be at a 45-degree angle. A speed break is executed by pointing the toes in the desired direction and accelerating the feet. A transition backward involves a plant foot and a point foot. The plant foot is the foot opposite the turn, and the point foot is the foot toward the turn. The point foot must clear the turnside hip.

In Phase

When the defensive back transitions from a backpedal to a man turn, he should be low shoulder on the receiver and hip-to-hip and close enough to get the near hand on the receiver. This is called the A position. When the defensive back looks up on a ball call, he should look up at a 45-degree angle.

Press Coverage

Press coverage can be used with any coverage package. Press coverage can be used to take away the quick passing game, disrupt timing, keep the receiver off the safety in cover 8, and as a change-up. Pressing forces the receiver to bubble release and redirect. The receiver's release will give tips on the route to be run. An outside release indicates a fade, back shoulder fade, comeback, or an out-and-up. An inside release leads to a slant, sluggo, post, or a dig.

Press Technique

The corner will assume an inside position, splitting the receiver's crotch. He must be careful not to line up offside. The corner faces the receiver with his shoulders square to the line of scrimmage, focusing only on the receiver. This is called the mirror position. The corner can move to this position late; however, he should not be moving when the ball is snapped. He should take a denial step on the snap and read the receiver's release. He should not attack the receiver, but read his release. He should deliver a hand shiver in a rising manner, which is done as a catch technique. If the receiver releases outside, the corner will shiver him with the inside hand and play low shoulder, keying his inside hip. If the receiver releases inside, the corner will shiver with the outside hand and play low shoulder and squeeze him inside. The corner must not reach. Contact should be made within the framework of the corner's body. He should catch, not lunge. With a short route, the corner gets depth and midpoints the smash. The five-yard no-cover rule is still in effect.

Bail Technique

The corner aligns press on #1. He will open step inside just before the snap, with eyes looking inside. This open step will create a half turn. The corner will cross over and run. This technique is used by the corner in cover 8 flat.

Rock and Roll

This technique is used in man coverage when a safety's assigned man goes in motion. When this happens, the man coverage defender will spin to the hole, and the hole player assumes man coverage on the motion man. In essence, the safeties swap assignments. Figure 14-1 shows how this effectively stops a speed sweep. Figure 14-1 illustrates a China coverage call.

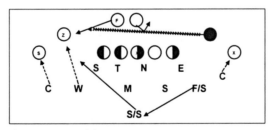

Figure 14-1. China coverage

Man Coverage vs. Bunch Formations

Lock (Figure 14-2)

In lock, there are no switch-offs. Each defender will stay with his assigned man. Defenders will align at different levels so they will not get picked.

Lock Rules:
#2 defender: Presses man on the #2 receiver.
#1 defender: Aligns deeper than #2 defender. Takes the #1 receiver man-to-man.
#3 defender: Aligns deepest of all. Takes the #3 receiver man-to-man.

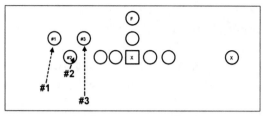

Figure 14-2. Lock

Banjo

With a banjo call, defenders #1 and #3 will switch off certain route combinations. The #2 defender will press #2 with no switch-off.

Banjo Rules:

#2 defender: Presses man on the #2 receiver.

#1 and #3 defenders: Align deeper than the #2 defender, but at the same level with each other. They will in and out on the #1 and #3 receivers. The #1 defender will take the first out cut, and the inside defender will take the first in cut. Figure 14-3 shows reaction to a #1 and #3 receiver cross. Should both receivers go out, the #1 defender will take the first out cut, and the #3 defender will take the second out cut (Figure 14-4). Conversely, if both receivers run in cuts, the inside defender takes the first in cut, and the outside defender takes the second in cut (Figure 14-5).

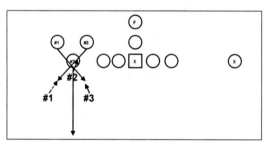

Figure 14-3. #1 and #3 receivers crossing

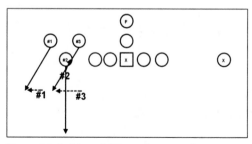

Figure 14-4. #1 and #3 receivers running out cuts

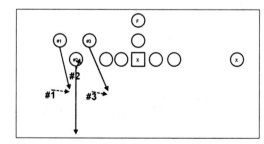

Figure 14-5. #1 and #3 receivers running in cuts

15

Designing and Implementing a Defensive Practice Plan and Drills

This chapter gives guidelines for planning drills, play competency, defensive practice notes, and actual drills to use in implementing the playbook.

Guidelines for Planning Drills

- Know how much practice time is available. Obviously, teams which do not two-platoon have less defensive time than teams which have one-way players.
- Prioritize and make the most efficient use of the available time.
- Determine the skills that are needed. Specificity is crucial.
- Determine whether the drill is instructive or competitive. Usually, competitive drills do not foster learning. Competitive drills should not be used in the formative or introductory phase of a new technique. Learning speed is desired in stage one of implementing a new technique or skill.
- Make sure service players understand the role that is expected of them.
- Specify the attire to be used (full pads, shells, or shorts).
- Make sure the drill fits into the team's defensive system.
- Relate each drill to a game situation.
- Follow the basic teaching progression of: hear it, see it, do it. Use sequence teaching. Use a systematic approach that will build on previous learning—A, B, C learning.

- Inform players what they will be doing in practice and why they will be doing it. Post the practice schedule. The purpose of each drill should be clear. Inform players the intensity level desired. Is it a walk-through, run-through, learning speed, or game speed?
- Demand a high level of performance no matter the drill speed. Insist that players concentrate.
- Periodically evaluate the effectiveness of the drill. Are the taught skills showing up on game film?

Play Competency

There are three levels of play competency. Level 1 is pre-snap. Levels 2 and 3 are both post-snap. Levels 2 and 3 should be the focus of practice time. Levels 2 and 3 require teaching, fundamentals, and technique. The majority of practice time should be spent on these areas.

Level 1

Teach alignment, assignment, and stance. These occur before the ball is snapped. Alignment and assignment are mental. If coaches spend an inordinate amount of time on those two aspects of level 1, the defensive scheme may be too complicated.

Level 2

Level 2 happens after the ball is snapped. Taking on blocks, breaking on balls, and correct angles (to name a few) are considered level 2 skills.

Level 3

Interceptions, fumbles, big hits, tackles, and incompletions are examples of level 3 activities. These are a few ways a particular offensive play ends.

Defensive Practice Notes

- Fundamentals are paramount. Schemes are no good if players can't run, defeat blocks, and tackle.
- Use two-a-days to master physical techniques. The mental aspect of the playbook should already be installed before pads are put on.
- Have up-tempo practices. Fast tempo practices serves to shorten practice, increase functional conditioning, and maximizes repetitions. Also, up-tempo defensive practices prepares the defense to play the up-tempo style of offensive play.
- Walk-through is better than board work.
- Review the tougher looks (e.g., empty, unbalanced, tight bunch, quads, etc.).

- Quiz players orally on alignment and assignment.
- Coach effort. Demand great effort. Reward hustle, and punish loafs.
- Emphasize the importance of individual roles. "Do your job!" is the motto.
- "Play fast, play hard" should be the mantra.

The following drills are tailored to be used in the installation of the playbook. Figures are used when appropriate.

Defensive Line Drills

Stance Drill

Purpose: Develops functional stances.

Procedure: Linemen will squat down, lean on the back foot, and reach out with the shaded arm. They should have a flat back and toe-to-instep stagger and should be looking through their eyebrows.

- Attack read stance: 60-40 weight distribution with 60 percent on the down hand. The defenders should play run first, and react to pass. They should stab and grab the blocker. They should attack the blocker's chest plate and shoulder cup.
- Jet stance: 90-10 weight distribution with 90 percent on the down hand. The defenders should play pass first, and react to run.
- Tough stance: Four-point low charge used on short-yardage and goal-line plays.
- Two-gap stance: Parallel stance. Step, shuffle, shuffle are the steps used.

Stance on Command

This drill is a spin-off of the stance drill just described. Any stance may be used. On the stagger command, the linemen will set their feet. On ready, the defensive linemen will put their hands on their knees, and on down, the linemen will get into the appropriate stance.

Takeoff Drill

Purpose: Develops aggressive takeoff.

Procedure: Numerous takeoff drills are available. All these drills are triggered by movement. The coach can incorporate sound to try to get a defensive lineman to jump offside.

- Air: Linemen jet.
- Mat take-off: Linemen lunge out onto the mat.
- Tennis balls: Linemen lunge and try to catch a tennis ball before it hits the ground.
- Cones: Linemen jet.
- Redirect: Linemen get depth, and then are redirected by the coach. The redirect should be sharp and not rounded. Allow no fish hooks.

- Stick with redirect
- Prowl: Linemen move from a right-handed stance to a left-handed stance and vice versa.
- Chutes: Linemen take off in the chute.
- Barrels: Linemen stab and grab. sUse actual fronts in this drill.
- Bodies: Linemen work on hand placement—stab and grab.
- Line step: Linemen must step straight ahead using a yard mark.
- Jet close: Linemen are on a jet and must read a down block. On a down block, the linemen must close.
- Garden gate: This simulates a draw block. Linemen must retrace their steps.
- Fronts across the field: Linemen line up in various fronts and take off. The groups rotate from offense to defense as they work up the field.
- Tough charge versus bags

Hands Drill

The most successful defensive line coaches are masters at teaching effective hand techniques.

Purpose: Develops hand skills.

Procedure: The following hands progression can be executed against a sled or bodies. Have the linemen perform all three steps first from a six-point stance, then from a three-point stance.

- Lock out: Linemen fit their hands on the target. On command, they will go from having a bend in their arms to locking out. This movement will give the defensive linemen the feel of using the big muscle groups. The defender has his thumbs up and gains separation.
- Lock out and roll hips: Linemen repeat step one, but this time they will roll the hips as they lock out.
- Strike the blow: The linemen put it all together by striking with the hard part of the hand. The linemen will follow up the strike with a lockout and rolling the hips. The force of the blow comes from the quickness of the blow. There must not be a windup.

Blow Delivery Drill

Purpose: Develops aggressive hand strikes.

Procedure: Blow delivery skills are executed against sleds and bodies. Place jerseys on the sleds.

Sled Drills

Various types of sleds may be used. Also, live bodies may be used to drill correct hand placement.

- Six-point with quick hands
- Six-point rapid fire
- Six-point fire out (land on belly)
- Six-point fire out against popsicle sled

Body Drills

- Quick draw: Two- and six-point stances with both players on defense. Players go on movement. Who has the quickest hands?
- Rag doll: Defender grabs the service man and violently shakes him. This drill develops violent hands.
- 1-on-1 on short board: Coach uses a quick whistle. Which man has the best pop?

Steer Drill

Purpose: Teaches linemen how to take on blocks, lock out, and separate
Procedure: Drills can be done from a pre-lock-up or from a stance and start.

❏ Base Block

- Pre-lock-up and escape: Defender uses an inside snatch.
- Three-point fire out: Defender focuses on extension and separation. He turns the blocker's shoulders inside.
- Three-point fire out: Defender uses an outside snatch.
- Three-point fire out: Defender uses an inside snatch.

Coaching Points:
- The defender should hold the point.
- The defender must get the inside hand locked out quickly.

❏ Reach Block

- Pre-lock-up: Blocker and defender start locked up. Defender focuses on extension and separation. He forces the blocker's shoulders outside.
- Pre-lock-up and escape: Defender uses an outside snatch.
- Pre-lock-up and escape: Defender uses an inside snatch.
- Three-point fire out: Defender focuses on extension and separation.
- Three-point fire out: Defender focuses on extension and separation.

- Three-point fire out: Defender uses an outside rip.
- Three-point fire out: Defender uses an outside snatch.

Coaching Points:
- The defender should keep his hips in the gap.
- The defender should keep his hips to the heat.
- If being reached, the defender should throw his hips outside.
- The tackle has a 2x1 rule. This rule says the tackle, against a reach block, must end up two yards deep and one yard outside the blocker.
- The end has a 4x1 rule. The end must end up four yards deep and one yard outside the blocker.

❏ Double-Team Block

- Pre-lock-up
- Live

Coaching Points:
- The defender should keep his head in the crack.
- The defender should grab the post man and drive the hips to the drive man.
- The defender should turn his shoulders inside to make himself small.
- The defender should crossface the drive man if his head is in front.
  The defender should collapse as a last resort.

Spider Reactions

Purpose: Teaches defensive linemen how to play 1-on-1 blocks.
Procedure: The offense can use base, down, reach, pass, pass cut, and draw blocks. The defender will use the correct technique for each type of block.

- 1-on-1 (Figure 15-1): The coach directs the blocker on the type of block.
- 1-on-1 Boink (Figure 15-2): The blocker chooses the type of block to use. The defender chooses to use an attack read, jet, or stick technique.
- 1-on-1 Stick Boink (Figure 15-3): The blocker chooses the block and the defender will stick.
- 1-on-1 Jet Boink (Figure 15-4): The blocker chooses the type of block. The defender will react to the block off a jet move.

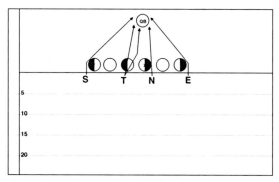

Figure 15-6. Base pass rush lanes

Hoop With a Blocker

Purpose: Teaches the rusher to rush the quarterback while attacking the outside half of the blocker.

Procedure: The rusher will run the hoop with a blocker inside the hoop, riding him as he runs the hoop. The drill can be done live, or the blocker can use a shield.

Hoop With a Blocker and Quarterback

The previous drill can be used, but add a quarterback, which will allow the rusher to develop a quarterback strip at the end.

Catch Him (Figure 15-7)

Purpose: Teaches the pass rusher to get to the blocker as quickly as possible so he can make a pass rush move.

Procedure: Have a blocker face the rusher, and at the snap have the blocker backpedal. See how quickly the rusher can get his hands on the blocker. A cover element may be added to the drill.

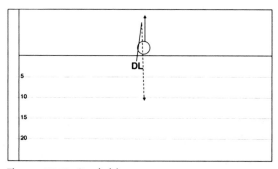

Figure 15-7. Catch him

Bend the Corner (Figure 15-8)

Purpose: Teaches the rusher to bend the corner by leaning in to potential blockers.

Procedure: Have the rusher come off the edge and hug the cones on the way to the quarterback.

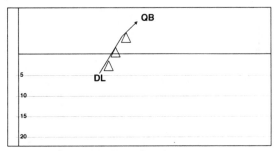

Figure 15-8. Bend the corner

Cover Angles From a Base Pass Rush (Figure 15-9)

Purpose: Teaches defensive linemen how to properly run to the pass from a base pass rush. Also, the drill fosters a "cover the pass" mentality.

Procedure: Have the quarterback throw the ball to a receiver who is in the flat. The quarterback can throw to either flat.

Coaching Point: Defenders should not follow the same color.

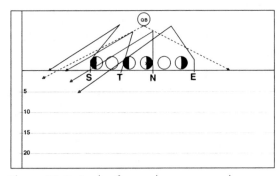

Figure 15-9. Angles from a base pass rush

Sprint Pass

Purpose: Develops the defensive line's ability to cover a sprint pass.

Procedure: The quarterback can sprint to either edge. The offensive linemen can either reach or turnback protect. Versus turnback protection, the tackles "play the piano." Playing the piano has the tacklers crossfacing blockers instead of running upfield and allowing the offensive linemen to shield them from the quarterback.

Front Hands Up (Figure 15-10)

Purpose: Teaches rushing linemen when to get their hands up. Also teaches defensive linemen when to keep working to the quarterback and not put their hands up.

Procedure: Have linemen on a base rush. If the quarterback's front hand comes off the ball and the quarterback is facing a rusher, the rusher will get his hands up. Defenders away from the quarterback's face keep rushing.

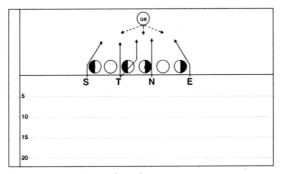

Figure 15-10. Front hands up

Stay in the Game (Figure 15-11)

Purpose: Shows rushers how to pressure the quarterback and not end up in the worst place for a rusher to be: behind the quarterback.

Procedure: Have two blockers set up at the quarterback depth, and start two rushers deep in the backfield. When the rushers get to quarterback level, they must not get washed past the quarterback. Rushers, at this time, point their toes to the quarterback and bull rush.

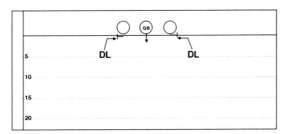

Figure 15-11. Stay in the game

Linebacker Drills

Stance

Purpose: Schools linebackers on how to get in a good functional stance, which allows them to get a good takeoff.

Procedure: The coach will give a series of commands, and the linebackers respond:

- "Ready": On ready, the linebackers will concentrate on foot placement. They will get their feet shoulder-width apart with weight on the inside balls of their feet. Knees are bent at 45 degrees and pointed straight ahead. If the knees tend to point out, have the linebacker kick his heels out.
- "Bend": On bend, the linebackers will move to a flat back with the gut out and the butt back. The shoulders should be slightly in front of the knees. Hands are on the thigh board.
- "Stance": On stance, the linebacker will drop his hands with wrists in front of the knees.

First Step (Figure 15-12)

Purpose: Develops the linebacker's first step.

Procedure: The coach will give direction. Linebackers will take the first step. The step is a six-inch step with the heel replacing the toe. The step should be downhill toward the line of scrimmage. The shoulders should not come up as the linebacker steps.

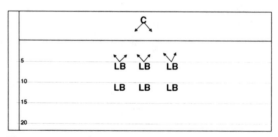

Figure 15-12. First step

Jab Shuffle (Figure 15-13)

Purpose: Trains the linebackers the first two steps in the shuffle technique.

Procedure: Shuffle steps are used whenever the ball is in the box. For this two-step drill, the first step is followed by a drag step.

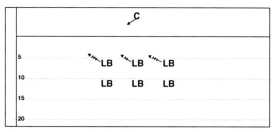

Figure 15-13. Jab shuffle

Shuffle (Figure 15-14)

Purpose: Trains the linebackers how to correctly shuffle step for five yards.
Procedure: Linebackers will shuffle for five yards. The coach will give direction.

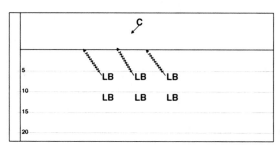

Figure 15-14. Shuffle

Shuffle Press (Figure 15-15)

Purpose: Teaches linebackers how to shuffle and attack a running play in the box.
Procedure: The coach will give direction. Linebackers shuffle and, on the command of "press," will burst upfield.

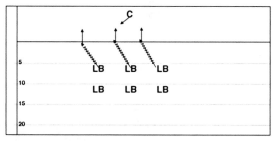

Figure 15-15. Shuffle press

Shuffle Alley (Figure 15-16)

Purpose: Schools linebackers on how to shuffle and convert to a defensive run when the ball leaves the box to the alley.

Procedure: Linebackers shuffle and, on the command of "alley," will burst to the alley.

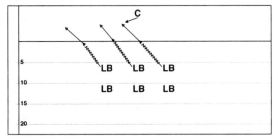

Figure 15-16. Shuffle alley

Fast Flow (Figure 15-17)

Purpose: Teaches linebackers how to attack the alley on a fast flow play.

Procedure: On key, linebackers will immediately run to the alley. No shuffle steps are used. The linebackers use a defensive run technique where the upper body stays square to the line of scrimmage with the hips tilted toward the alley.

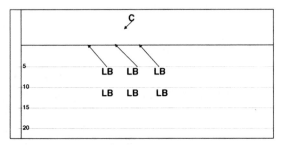

Figure 15-17. Fast flow

Counter (Figure 15-18)

Purpose: Teaches linebackers how to react to counter-type plays.

Procedure: Linebackers shuffle then redirect to a defensive run. All linebackers must yell, "Pull, pull." The onside linebacker thinks over the top of a potential block. Mike thinks under or over the top of a potential block, and backside linebacker visualizes keeping the ball on his playside shoulder.

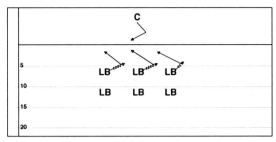

Figure 15-18. Counter

Direct Read (Figure 15-19)

Purpose: Prepares linebackers on how to react when the ball attacks their primary gap on plays such as dive options or isolations.

Procedure: The coach steps straight ahead. Linebackers attack with no false steps and simulate spilling the play.

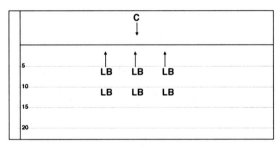

Figure 15-19. Direct read

Play-Action Pass (Figure 15-20)

Purpose: Trains linebackers how to read run or play-action pass.

Procedure: The coach will simulate mesh action. The offensive line will show high helmets with a pass block or low helmets with a simulated run block. Linebackers drop on pass or explode forward on a run read.

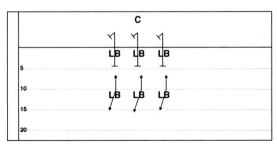

Figure 15-20. Play-action pass

Over the Falls (Figure 15-21)

Purpose: Develops the linebacker's ability to play inside-out while navigating over debris on or near the line of scrimmage.

Procedure: Linebackers work over the bags, playing inside-out. They will tag off or fit up on the runner at the end. A variation of this drill would be to put a blocker at the end of the last bag. The blocker can go at a variety of speeds. He can simulate a block as an offensive lineman, back, or a receiver on a crackback block.

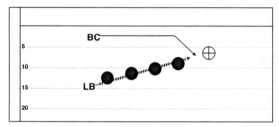

Figure 15-21. Over the falls

Linebacker Eye-Opener (Figure 15-22)

Purpose: Teaches linebackers to play inside-out on a ballcarrier.

Procedure: Linebackers work downhill, playing inside-out. They tag off or fit in on the ballcarrier. The ballcarrier stretches to the near bag before cutting back.

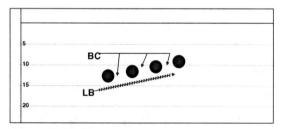

Figure 15-22. Eye-opener

1-on-1 Advantage Shed (Figure 15-23)

Purpose: Develops linebackers' ability to take on and shed a block.

Procedure: The linebacker lines up slightly outside a blocker who fires out and tries to block him. The drill can be done with a one-yard separation or from a pre-lock-up position.

Coaching Points:
- The defender should keep the playside foot back.
- The defender should plant the inside foot. He should avoid the pancake position of having the inside foot back.

- The playside hand is the power hand. The backside hand is the trail hand. The power hand should be on the blocker's outside shoulder, and the trail hand should be down the middle. The defender should play half man on the blocker.
- Elbows should be in with thumbs up.
- The defender should work low to high.
- The defender should use a quick steer and finish with a rip. He should get off quickly. He should avoid extended contact.
- The defender should stay square.
- The defender should press the line of scrimmage after defeating the block.

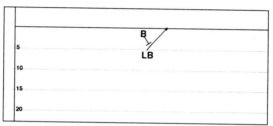

Figure 15-23. 1-on-1 advantage shed

1-on-1 Disadvantage Shed (Figure 15-24)

Purpose: Teaches linebackers to play a block when the offensive man has an angle.

Procedure: The mechanics used in the 1-on-1 advantage shed drill are used for this drill.

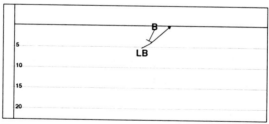

Figure 15-24. 1-on-1 disadvantage shed

Three-Way Go (Figure 15-25)

Purpose: Teaches linebackers how to play inside-out on a ballcarrier with the availability of going under, over, or through a blocker. The blocker cannot be allowed to get comfortable knowing how the linebacker will get to the ball.

Procedure: The blocker will climb to the linebacker depth and try to block the linebacker as he works inside-out on the ballcarrier. Should the linebacker go under the block, he must ensure the tackle.

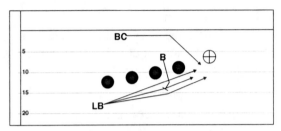

Figure 15-25. Three-way go

Run the Stripe (Figure 15-26)

Purpose: Teaches linebackers how to play a flat or flat-and-up route by #2 in cover 8.

Procedure: A receiver runs a flare or flat route. The backer will run the stripe. As he goes, he will take a peek at #1, which is done to ensure that he will not be picked by #1.

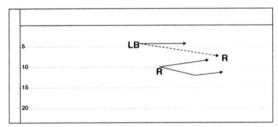

Figure 15-26. Run the stripe

Boot (Figure 15-27)

Purpose: Schools linebackers on how to play boot action in cover 2 and 8.

Procedure: The offense will give boot action. The frontside linebacker will run the stripe. Mike will gain depth, looking for a drag. The backside backer will take the fake back man-to-man looking for a screen or wheel.

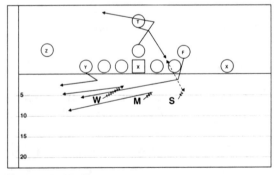

Figure 15-27. Boot

Onside Read (Figure 15-28)

Purpose: Teaches linebackers to read pulling linemen on action to them.

Procedure: The back will give an onside read. Have the offensive linemen either step forward or have one or both pull. The linebacker must key the onside back, but see the offensive with the bottom of their eyes. When linemen pull, the linebacker must yell. "Pull, pull."

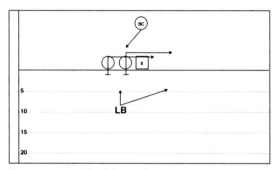

Figure 15-28. Onside read

Offside Read (Figure 15-29)

Purpose: Teaches linebackers to read the offside area for pullers on counter-type plays.

Procedure: The back will give an offside read with offensive linemen either stepping forward or pulling toward the linebacker. One or both linemen can pull. The backer must give a "Pull, pull" call when linemen pull.

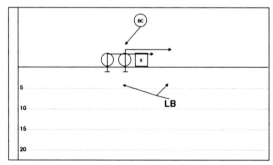

Figure 15-29. Offside read

Daylight Dark (Figure 15-30)

Purpose: Trains linebackers how to read if a gap is closed (dark) or open (daylight).

Procedure: A back will give action to a particular gap. The outside lineman will either step down toward the linebacker or out. If the gap is closed, the backer will fit over the top. If the gap is open, the linebacker will fill.

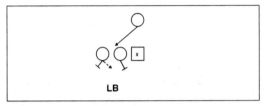

Figure 15-30. Daylight dark

Secondary Drills

Safety Bounce Steps (Figure 15-31)

Purpose: Teaches safeties correct stance and start in cover 8.

Procedure: The coach will give the safety a simulated snap. On the snap, the safety will bounce in place. Safeties do not backpedal in cover 8. The coach will also give the safety one of three reads. He will give a run cue, double cue, or a zone the quarter cue. These are the three basic reads for the safety in cover 8.

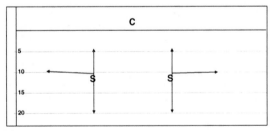

Figure 15-31. Safety bounce steps

Safety Bounce and Go (Figure 15-32)

Purpose: Trains the safety to read a run block or pass release by #2 in cover 8.

Procedure: Place two defenders in front of two offensive players. If the offensive players block, the safety will bounce and explode to stack. Mix in pass releases by the offensive players. On a vertical release, the safeties take them man-to-man with inside leverage.

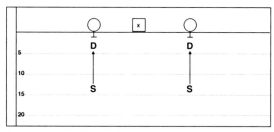

Figure 15-32. Safety bounce and go

Safety Arc (Figure 15-33)

Purpose: Teaches the safety to defeat an arc block on the way to pitch.

Procedure: Have a runner run a pitch route with a blocker arc blocking the safety. The safety must keep outside leverage on the blocker and rip through to the ballcarrier.

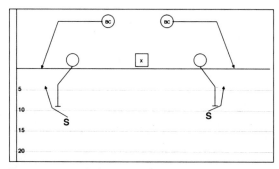

Figure 15-33. Safety arc

Safety Stack (Figure 15-34)

Purpose: Prepares safeties to be able to play a run that breaks inside or outside their stack position.

Procedure: The running back will run inside or outside at a landmark. The safety will go to stack and be able to leverage the ball.

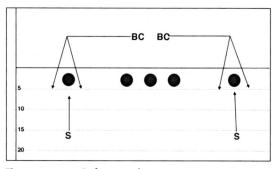

Figure 15-34. Safety stack

Safety Spin Alley Fill (Figure 15-35)

Purpose: Teaches safeties how to spin in stunt and man-free coverages.

Procedure: One safety will dive to a cone or man. This safety has man responsibility. The other safety will spin to the hole. The ballcarrier can go either way, and the hole player must play the ball inside-out.

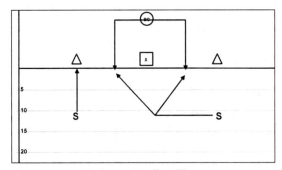

Figure 15-35. Safety spin alley fill

Safety Spin Hole Pitch (Figure 15-36)

Purpose: Teaches the safety spinning to the hole how to play pitch inside-out.

Procedure: One safety will spin to a cone or man. This safety has man responsibility. The other safety will spin to the hole and plays pitch inside-out to either side.

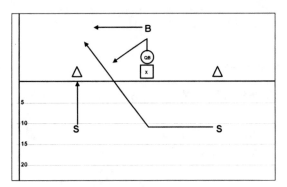

Figure 15-36. Safety spin hole pitch

Defensive Back Two-Yard Buddy (Figure 15-37)

Note: This drill can also be done with corners.

Purpose: Teaches a defensive back how to hold a proper cushion in man-to-man coverage.

Procedure: A safety aligns with inside leverage two yards from a receiver. The receiver will then sprint for seven yards. The defensive back must hold the cushion for five yards.

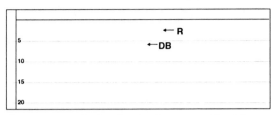

Figure 15-37. Defensive back two-yard buddy

Defensive Back Weave (Figure 15-38)

Purpose: Schools defensive backs how to maintain inside leverage on a receiver in man coverage.

Procedure: A receiver, at half to three-quarter speed, tries to get head-up position on the defensive back. The drill can also be run at game speed after the defender gets a feel on how to weave correctly.

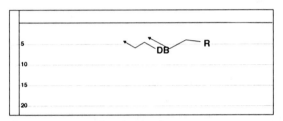

Figure 15-38. Defensive back weave

Defensive Back Crossover and Run (Figure 15-39)

Purpose: Teaches defensive backs how to maintain a low shoulder position on a receiver with their eyes on the receiver's inside hip. Also develops good footwork.

Procedure: The coach gives the two defenders a three-rep weave. After the third weave, the coach will point to one side. The defensive back to that side becomes the receiver, and the other defensive back becomes the defender. The receiver can run a go, stutter go, or stutter out. On the stutter out, the defender will hook and swat.

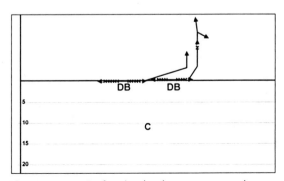

Figure 15-39. Defensive back crossover and run

Defensive Back Late Man-Turn and Burst (Figure 15-40)

Purpose: Schools a defensive back on how to collision and run with a receiver who has eaten the defender's cushion.

Procedure: A defensive back starts out with a five-yard cushion on a receiver. The receiver goes first and tries to run past the defender. The defender will get an off hand jam and sprint to regain position. The defender must gain a low shoulder position with his eyes on the receiver's hip.

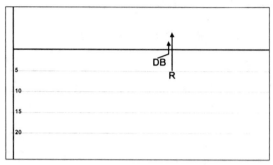

Figure 15-40. Defensive back late man turn and burst

Corner Cover 8 Stance and Start (Figure 15-41)

Purpose: Teaches corners how to backpedal while keying the three-step drop.

Procedure: The corner will start out slowly on his backpedal. The coach will simulate a quick pass. On this signal, the corner will stick foot or speed break to an imaginary receiver. If the coach clears the three-step, the corner will get his eyes back on the imaginary receiver. The coach can give a smash signal. On a smash, the corner will midpoint two imaginary receivers while pointing to the short receiver while yelling, "Smash, smash." On a deep signal by the coach, the corner will man-turn on an imaginary receiver.

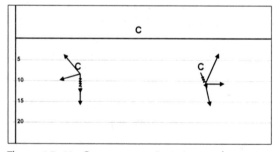

Figure 15-41. Corner cover 8 stance and start

Corner Cover 2 Stance and Start (Figure 15-42)

Purpose: Teaches corners the correct way to play cover 2.

Procedure: This drill is similar to the corner cover 8 stance and start drill. However, in this drill, the corner will line head-up on an imaginary receiver and, just before the ball is snapped, will slide outside at five yards depth. He will key the three-step with no backpedal. The coach can give the following signals:

- Run: The corner gets up.
- Quick pass: The corner drives.
- Clear the three-step: The corner gets his eyes on a receiver and gains depth.
- Smash: The corner will midpoint, point at the flat receiver, and yell, "Smash, smash."

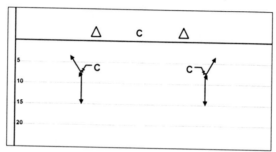

Figure 15-42. Corner cover 2 stance and start

Corner Kick-Out (Figure 15-43)

Purpose: Teaches the corner the correct way to force in cover 2.

Procedure: The corner faces two blockers. Either blocker can move forward. The corner will take on the blocker with the appropriate shoulder. The corner will set the edge aggressively.

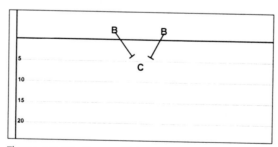

Figure 15-43. Corner kick-out

Corner Dig Block on Cutback to Cutoff (Figure 15-44)

Purpose: Teaches corners the correct way to execute cutback to cutoff duties.

Procedure: A ballcarrier will start away from the corner who has a blocker assigned to him. The ballcarrier can cutback at any point. The corner must keep the ball on his inside shoulder. A second blocker may be added. The coach can blow the whistle at any point to simulate a tackle on the ballcarrier. The corner will go all the way to the pile, keeping the ball on his inside shoulder.

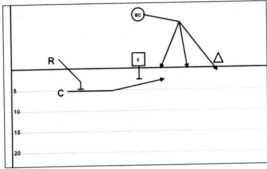

Figure 15-44. Corner dig block on cutback to cutoff

Corner Smash Shuffle (Figure 15-45)

Purpose: Teaches corners how to midpoint the smash.

Procedure: Place one receiver in the flats and one receiver in the flag area. Have the corner midpoint both receivers. The coach can throw to either receiver. The corner must point to the flat receiver and yell, "Smash, smash."

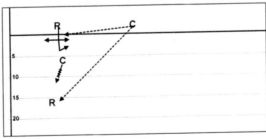

Figure 15-45. Corner smash shuffle

Turnover Drills

Country Fumble (Scoop and Score)

Purpose: Teaches defenders the proper technique to use on a country fumble (i.e., a fumble with no one around).

Procedure: Place four footballs on the ground with four lines of defenders. On command, four defenders scoop and score.

Coaching Points:
- The defender should play off to the side of the ball so it won't get accidentally kicked.
- The defender should get his hands under the ball and his knuckles on the ground.
- Defenders only get one attempt to scoop. If the defender muffs the first chance, he must fall on the ball.
- The defender should cover the front tip of the ball and "chin" the ball. He should get it high and tight. He should not fumble it back to the offense.
- Coaches should mix in a victory fumble scenario when running this drill. A victory fumble situation would occur late in the game when the defense has a lead on the opponent. In this situation, possession of the ball is the issue. Defenders should not attempt to scoop and score.

City Fumble (Fall On)

Purpose: Exposes the correct way to fall on and cover the ball.

Procedure: The setup is the same as the country fumble drill, except defenders will fall on the ball since there is a lot of traffic, hence the name of city fumble.

Coaching Points:
- The defender should cover both tips of the ball. This technique will prevent the ball from getting leveraged out in a pile.
- The defender should get in a fetal position with the top leg over the ball.

1-on-1 Ballside Strip (Figure 15-46)

Purpose: Teaches defenders how to attack the ball on a ballside tackle.

Procedure: The runner and defender start out with a five-yard separation. The defender will secure the tackle and tomahawk and rip the ball. Declare the fumble to be a city, country, or victory fumble.

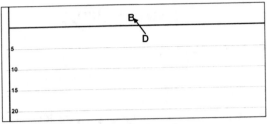

Figure 15-46. 1-on-1 ballside strip

1-on-1 Offside Strip (Figure 15-47)

Purpose: Teaches defenders how to attack the football when behind or offside the football.

Procedure: The setup is the same as the ballside strip drill, except the defender is trailing or offside the ball. Behind the ballcarrier is considered offside. The defender will use an upper cut on the ball as he secures the tackle. Declare the fumble to be a city, country, or victory fumble.

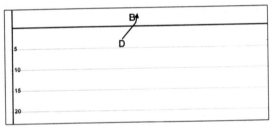

Figure 15-47. 1-on-1 offside strip

2-on-1 Strip (Figure 15-48)

Purpose: Teaches defenders how to use a tomahawk or punch, depending upon their position on the ballcarrier.

Procedure: Two defenders are placed behind the ballcarrier. One defender is ballside, with the other defender placed offside. There is a five-yard separation from them and the ballcarrier. After everyone starts, the coach will point to the stripper, who will use the appropriate technique. The non-stripper will recover the fumble. Determine if the fumble is a country, city, or victory fumble.

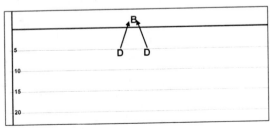

Figure 15-48. 2-on-1 strip

2-on-1 Tackle Strip (Figure 15-49)

Purpose: Helps defenders perfect a straight on tackle and a strip.

Procedure: Two defenders line up 10 yards apart with a ballcarrier between them. The ballcarrier will spin in place, and then take off toward one of the defenders. The defender to the ballcarrier becomes the tackler. He uses the correct straight-on technique of getting either his face or shoulder on the ball. He must tackle at ball level. The second defender becomes the stripper. He will use either a punch or tomahawk. Determine the type of fumble and the appropriate technique.

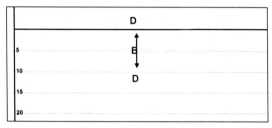

Figure 15-49. 2-on-1 tackle strip

3-on-1 Strip (Figure 15-50)

Purpose: Teaches defenders how to strip the ballcarrier after the ballcarrier has been wrapped up.

Procedure: Two tacklers fit up on the runner, with the third defender placing both hands on the ball and doing a 360-degree turn to rip it out.

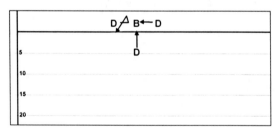

Figure 15-50. 3-on-1 strip

Hockey

Purpose: Teaches defenders how to correctly scoop a ball in a crowd.

Procedure: Place two defenders in a six-point stance, facing each other. The coach will drop the ball between them just like a faceoff in hockey.

Coaching Points:
- Defenders must be quick.
- After a defender gets his hands on the ball, he should get his back turned quickly to the other defender.
- Defenders should cover the tips of the ball with the top leg over.

Blind Man's Bluff

Purpose: Teaches defenders how and where to look for a fumble.

Procedure: The coach will stand behind a defender, who is in a football position with his eyes closed. The coach will then roll the ball through the defender's legs, to either side, or behind. Other defenders in the drill yell, "Ball, ball." This alerts the defender that the ball is on the ground. He will immediately scan the ground until he finds the ball. Determine the type of recovery desired.

Tackling Drills

Form Tackling

Purpose: Exposes the tackler to proper tackling form.

Procedure: This drill has four steps:
- Step 1: Fit the face or shoulder on the ball.
- Step 2: Shoot the hands and slide the head.
- Step 3: Shoot the hands, slide the head, and roll the hips.
- Step 4: Put it all together from one step away.

Coaching Point: The defender should emphasize hip roll, with the eyes or shoulder at ball level.

Giant Lift Tackle (Figure 15-51)

Purpose: Teaches tacklers the proper way to tackle.

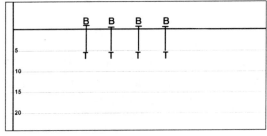

Figure 15-51. Giant lift tackle

Procedure: This drill can be done in shorts. Two speeds are used: walk or jog. Three angles are used: straight on, angle, or cutback. Tacklers face ballcarriers. The tackler will grab the runner at hip level. This gets the tackler in a football position. The tackler exaggerates the hip roll and picks up the runner and accelerates his feet, carrying the ballcarrier backward. The ballcarrier can help by placing his hands on the tackler's shoulders and jumping. This drill is tailored for the skill positions. Defensive linemen may be a little hard to pick up.

Six-Point Hip Roll Tackle (Figure 15-52)

Purpose: Develops good hip roll when tackling.

Procedure: Tacklers are in a six-point stance, facing a stand-up dummy. On command, they will explode through the pads.

Coaching Points:
- Defenders should hit with the chest on the rise.
- Defenders should sky the eyes.
- Defenders should explode through the hips.
- Defenders should rip the arms.

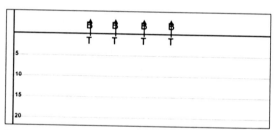

Figure 15-52. Six-point hip roll tackle

Square Tackle (Figure 15-53)

Purpose: Teaches tacklers how to use inside-out leverage.

Procedure: Runners run to the designated cone. The drill incorporates a cutback option. The tackler must play inside-out. The tackler contacts the near number of the runner, and then slides his head across.

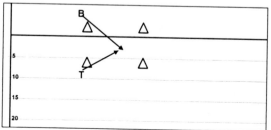

Figure 15-53. Square tackle

All-Position Eye-Opener (Figure 15-54)

Purpose: Teaches all tacklers how to use inside leverage.

Procedure: The ballcarrier has the option of cutting back in one of four gaps. He should stretch the tackler by going almost all the way to a marker before cutting back.

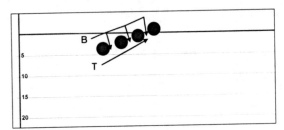

Figure 15-54. Eye-opener

2-on-1 Leverage Tackle (Figure 15-55)

Purpose: Teaches defenders how to use leverage on the tackle.

Procedure: One defender is placed outside the runner, and the other starts out inside the runner. The ballcarrier will then run between the two tacklers or try to get around a tackler. Defenders must tackle, depending upon their leverage.

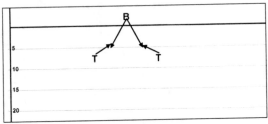

Figure 15-55. 2-on-1 leverage tackle

Georgia Tackle (Figure 15-56)

Purpose: Teaches proper hip roll and wrap-up.

Procedure: The coach is between a ballcarrier and the tackler. He places his hands on the tackler and runner. All three walk together, and on "hit," the tackler angle tackles the runner.

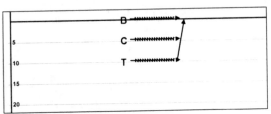

Figure 15-56. Georgia tackle

16

Defensive Call Sheet

This chapter is a compendium of defensive calls, wrinkles, and adjustments covered in the playbook. After a coach studies the upcoming opponent, he can consult the call sheet and cherry-pick calls and strategies that would be effective.

Personnel Groups

- ❏ Nickel
- ❏ Dime
- ❏ Quarter
- ❏ Normal (4-3)
- ❏ NASCAR
- ❏ Mustang
- ❏ Goal line

Shades

- ❏ Base
- ❏ Wide
- ❏ Jet

4-3 Personnel

- ❏ Over 8
- ❏ Over pirate
- ❏ Over spike
- ❏ Over end
- ❏ Zorro
- ❏ Yo-yo
- ❏ Squeeze
- ❏ Steeler
- ❏ Flat
- ❏ Combinations (yo-yo flat)
- ❏ Press
- ❏ 8 match (21 personnel)
- ❏ Over 2
- ❏ 2 loose
- ❏ Spy 2 middle
- ❏ 2 man
- ❏ 2 lurk
- ❏ 2 lurk quarterback
- ❏ 2 cone
- ❏ 2 deuce
- ❏ 2 Mike
- ❏ 2 trap
- ❏ 2 swipe (82 swipe, cover 8 vs. 2 backs, cover 2 swipe vs. empty or one back)
- ❏ 3Y
- ❏ 3X

Checks

- ❏ Tampa
- ❏ Toledo
- ❏ Tucson
- ❏ Baseball

Eight-Men-in-the-Box Man Coverage

- ❏ Under China (use nickel)
- ❏ Over China (use nickel)

- ❏ Under white
- ❏ Under pirate
- ❏ Under Stud

Game Plan on How to Use the Plugger

- ❏ Russian
- ❏ Cut
- ❏ Double (by backfield set)
- ❏ Spy
- ❏ Oregon black
- ❏ Pirate
- ❏ Spike
- ❏ End

Cover 0

- ❏ (Stem/move to) Storm
- ❏ (Stem) Under storm
- ❏ Green storm
- ❏ Green storm robber
- ❏ Hurricane (sell the farm)
- ❏ Storm pick-pop-change
- ❏ Blizzard
- ❏ 22 Storm (third-and-one or fourth-and-one)
- ❏ Storm tango

Bullets

- ❏ Over bullets 0
- ❏ Under (opposite) bullets 0
- ❏ Oregon bullets 0
- ❏ Green bullets 0
- ❏ Short yardage

Cover 4 Stunts

- ❏ Cover 4 Will stunts (flip-flop alert)
- ❏ Cover 4 Mike stunts
- ❏ Cover 4 Sam stunts (special alert)

- ❏ Cover 4 strong safety stunts
- ❏ Cover 4 free safety stunts
- ❏ Cover 4 weak safety stunts
- ❏ Cover 4 strong corner stunts (viper)

Peel Blitzes

Strongside

- ❏ Under Will buccaneer
- ❏ Mug under Will buccaneer
- ❏ Under Will buccaneer bracket
- ❏ Under Will buccaneer X
- ❏ Under strong safety shark
- ❏ Mug under strong safety shark
- ❏ Under strong safety shark bracket
- ❏ Under strong safety shark X

Weakside

- ❏ Over Sam blackbeard
- ❏ Mug over Sam blackbeard
- ❏ Over Sam blackbeard bracket
- ❏ Over Sam blackbeard X
- ❏ Over free safety dolphin
- ❏ Mug over free safety dolphin
- ❏ Over free safety dolphin bracket
- ❏ Over free safety dolphin X
- ❏ Over cat
- ❏ Mug over cat
- ❏ Over cat bracket
- ❏ Over cat X

Middle

- ❏ Green Sam maroon (mug)
- ❏ Green Sam cross
- ❏ Over Sam cross
- ❏ Under Sam gallows

Green Package

- ❏ Pick
- ❏ Pop
- ❏ Change
- ❏ Twist
- ❏ Tango
- ❏ Read twist
- ❏ Spike
- ❏ Nail
- ❏ Double spike
- ❏ Pick-pop strong
- ❏ Pick-pop weak
- ❏ Yellow

Over-Under Pass Rush Games

- ❏ Over pirate wrap
- ❏ Under pirate wrap
- ❏ Pick (double-weak-strong-delayed)
- ❏ Pop (double-weak-strong-delayed)
- ❏ Change
- ❏ Twist
- ❏ Tango
- ❏ Read twist
- ❏ Robber
- ❏ Mixer
- ❏ Over mirror

Red Zone Defense

- ❏ Over pirate 2
- ❏ Over spy 2 middle
- ❏ Over pirate 2 loose
- ❏ Over pirate 2 cone
- ❏ Oregon pirate black
- ❏ Under China
- ❏ Oregon-under cram lightning 4
- ❏ Cover 4 family
- ❏ Storm package cover 0

Goal Line Package: Base

- ❏ Double easy
- ❏ Pinch
- ❏ Rebel
- ❏ Rifle
- ❏ Pittsburgh

Mustang

Rush 3

- ❏ Sun-eon 2 middle
- ❏ Sun-eon 8 spy
- ❏ Sun-eon 2 spy
- ❏ Sun-eon 2 man spy

Rush 4

- ❏ Weak (eon)
- ❏ Strong (sun)
- ❏ Strong jet (sun)
- ❏ Weak jet (eon)
- ❏ Weak-strong China

Rush 5

- ❏ Will buccaneer 4
- ❏ Will buccaneer eon 4
- ❏ Will buccaneer bracket (eon) 4
- ❏ Strong safety shark 4
- ❏ Strong safety shark eon 4
- ❏ Strong safety shark bracket (eon) 4
- ❏ Sam blackbeard 4
- ❏ Sam blackbeard sun 4
- ❏ Sam blackbeard bracket (sun) 4
- ❏ Free safety dolphin 4
- ❏ Free safety dolphin sun 4
- ❏ Free safety dolphin bracket (sun) 4
- ❏ Cobra 4
- ❏ Cobra sun 4

- ❏ Cobra bracket (sun) 4
- ❏ Sam gallows 4
- ❏ Sam gallows eon 4
- ❏ Will swap 4
- ❏ Will swap eon 4
- ❏ +/− Blast 1
- ❏ +/− Tab 1
- ❏ Bear 1

Special Situations

- ❏ Punt safe (single-double)
- ❏ Field goal safe (pigtail-unbalanced)
- ❏ Swinging gate
- ❏ Loco
- ❏ Unbalanced
- ❏ Big Ben
- ❏ Armageddon
- ❏ Emory & Henry
- ❏ Halfback pass
- ❏ Reverse
- ❏ Fake reverse
- ❏ Reverse pass
- ❏ Flea flicker
- ❏ Hitch and pitch
- ❏ Spike
- ❏ Watch
- ❏ Throwback to quarterback
- ❏ Interception return
- ❏ Two-minute ahead
- ❏ Four-minute behind
- ❏ Scramble

Versus Bunch Sets

- ❏ Toledo
- ❏ Tampa
- ❏ Lock
- ❏ Banjo

Glossary

A

Absorb: Linemen spy technique on back in peel.

Action away: Running play away from a particular linebacker.

Action to: Running play toward a particular linebacker.

Alley: Run fit for the hole player. He must first get a pass or run read from uncovered linemen before he commits. Once he commits, he will play aggressively inside-out. He must read slow and act fast, and never allow the ball to crossface.

Attack read stance: Basic lineman stance. 60-40 weight distribution. Lineman plays run first, and reacts to pass.

B

Backdoor: Technique where a lineman slips a block underneath.

Backer: Linebacker in a 9 technique. Primary run support man.

Bail: Defensive back shows press coverage, but turns and runs on the snap.

Banana: Close technique off the jet look (green package).

Banjo: In-out coverage on adjoining receivers. Defenders read the inside receiver to determine responsibility. Used in zone or man coverages.

Baseball: Check for over end cover 2.

BCR: Bootleg, counter, and reverse responsibility. Assumed is a tight end delay.

Bear technique: Playing the tight end man from a 7 technique.

Big stick: Lineman sticks three gaps.

Bird: Pass alert call. Can use any bird.

Blitz: Five-man (or more) rush.

Blitz cage: Stunt defender has cage on quarterback.

Blitz engage: Used in man coverage. Defender rushes to his assigned back, reading his eyes. If the receiver releases, the defender covers him. If he blocks, the defender rushes the quarterback.

Blitz the back: Used by a linebacker in blitz packages. The backer stunts to his assigned back.

Blizzard technique: Will and Sam bluff a stunt. They take the quarterback on options and the flats versus passes.

Bluff: Defender faking a stunt.

Boss: Backers over strong. Cover China.

Bow: Backers over weak. Cover black.

Box: Defender takes on all inside-out blocks with the inside shoulder and forces the ball inside.

Boy: Backer man coverage on the tight end. Used in cover China.

Bracket: End is hard upfield with a stunter (or stunters) underneath. The end has peel anytime he brackets.

Bull: Call to defensive linemen versus empty sets. Linemen thicken their alignment and mush (slow) rush the quarterback. They must be aware of quarterback draw.

Bump trips call: Call given versus 3x1 sets. The Will goes halfway, with Mike and Sam moving to 30 alignments.

Bumper car: Ricochet technique off an opponent into flow on a stick.

Butch: Call for Stud to get hold up on the tight end before he rushes the quarterback. Automatic in Ohio front.

C

Cadence alert: Warning to expect a hard count.

Cage: Quarterback pass contain responsibilities.

Carry fold: Technique by seam player on run away.

Catch man: Man coverage from five- to six-yard cushion.

Center technique: The hole player aligns or rocks to midpoint between the widest #1 receivers.

Cha, cha, cha: Timing device on delayed stunts (e.g., delayed pick).

Chase: End-of-line defender on run away is responsible for bootleg, counter, and reverse (BCR).

Checkdown technique: Used by linebackers to snug up on receivers as they check down.

City fumble: Fumble in a crowd. Defenders use the fall-on technique.

Claw: Technique by defensive lineman when driving his hands through the breastplate of the offensive lineman.

Closed side: Side to strength call. May declare to the tight end or in some cases to the numbers.

Cloud: Corner force.

Color in the hole: A blocker is in an assigned gap on a run away. The linebacker is free to go to playside.

Contain blitz: Man on outside track of zone blitz is a cage player on the quarterback.

Cop: Linemen spy the back. Used in peel blitzes.

COS motion: Change of strength motion.

Counter flow: Backs start in one direction, then redirect.

Country fumble: A fumble in open space. Defenders use a scoop-and-score technique.

Crack replace: The corner will replace the primary force man when the receiver blocks inside on the force man.

Credit card alignment: A tight alignment on the ball without being offside.

Cut: Coverage places the free defender on a designated receiver. Used in trio coverages. Also a call for the 1 technique to work to the near shoulder of the guard.

Cutback gap: A gap on the backside of a running play (e.g., cutback B−).

Cutback threat: Linebacker can read the running back's numbers on run away.

Cutback to cutoff: On runs away, a defender, usually the corner, leverages the cutback to the corner of the goal line.

D

Dark: A blocker in the linebacker's assigned frontside gap.

Dash: Quarterback will drop to level three then attack the edge. Usually a two-receiver route with #3 pinning the cage player. Also, there will be a crossing receiver opposite the dash side.

David alignment: Taking an inside position on a receiver.

Daylight: No blocker in linebacker's assigned frontside gap.

Dead call: Call by the corner when he has a tight end only or a wing set. The strongside will run a pirate stunt. This call sends Will to playside on a flood run. The corner will play flat-footed and will chase flat on flood runs.

Diamond: 4x1 receiver alignment with the receivers in a diamond configuration.

Dime: Defensive back in for Sam.

Direct read: Ball and back attacking the linebacker's primary gap.

Distribution: Release of the backs into the pass route.

Dive flood: Run to openside with a dive back.

Dive flow: Run to the closed side with a dive back.

Divide: Backfield action with the fullback and the tailback going in opposite directions. Can be a divide belly or divide dive. Divide low equals no flow. Linebackers have primary gap responsibilities.

Dot: A running back aligned behind the quarterback.

Draw technique: On level-three pass, linebackers eyeball the quarterback and running back area for a draw until the quarterback passes the deepest back.

E

Easy technique: Technique used in the goal line package, where the weak tackle lines up in the B gap. A double easy call places both tackles in the B gap.

End: Weakside end. Also, an end stick stunt.

End it: A stunt where the ends charge through the V of the neck of the offensive tackle.

Exchange: Linebacker and defensive back match up on receivers. Used when the receiver aligns inside with the back or the tight end outside. The offense is seeking to get a mismatch.

Expressway handoff: Fast flow handoff (e.g., speed sweep).

F

Fallback: A defender backside of a pirate or divide action can go to frontside, but be able to redirect should the ball cut back.

Fast flow/flood: Action without a dive. There is no cutback threat. Linebackers cross over and run. They mirror the running back.

Fire pass: A play-action pass to the closed side with the tight end on a drag.

Fishhook: Poor pursuit angle off upfield charge.

Fit the funnel: Versus one-back motion, the man on him follows and is still assigned to him. The linebackers still Reggie the back.

Five-yard no-cover rule: Defenders do not cover a receiver man who runs a route within five yards of the line of scrimmage.

Flat: The area from the inside leg of a wide receiver to the sideline to a depth of 8 to 16 yards. Also, a change-up in cover 8.

Flip-flop: Used in cover 4 Will stunts against wide 3x1 sets where Mike will assume the stunt and Will takes #3.

Flood: A run to the openside. Fast flood has no cutback threat. Dive flood has a cutback component.

Flood distribution: Both backs release away from the closed side.

Flood pass: A play pass to the openside.

Flow: A run to the closed side. Fast flow has a cutback threat. Dive flow has a cutback component.

Flow distribution: Both backs release to the closed side.

Flow pass: A play-action pass to the closed side with the tight end vertical.

Fly motion: In-the-box running back motion to the tight end side.

Fold: Technique on running plays away. If aligned in the seam, the defender will carry fold.

Force: Defender turns the ballcarrier back inside.

Free rush: A linebacker technique when he is on a stunt and doesn't have cage responsibility.

Free rusher: The plugger in trio or Reggie coverage will rush the quarterback instead of plugging.

Free safety: The safety away from the closed side.

G

G: Tag to a front call. This puts the 1 technique in a 2 technique.

Game: Defensive line pass rush lane change-ups.

Gap: Defensive linemen align in the gap to their shade and explode upfield on the snap (e.g., over gap).

Gather: A press technique with the corner working off the line of scrimmage to allow the wide receiver to declare his release.

Get-off: Lineman movement on snap. Linemen generate power and speed on what moves first.

Ghost block: Offensive lineman pass sets then allows the rusher to pass to the quarterback. A ghost block equals a screen or draw.

Gilligan: A hard inside alignment with no hole help (e.g., cover 0). The defender is on an island.

Goal line: Minus five to goal line defense.

Green: An automatic jet package.

Green dog: Linebacker inserts on the quarterback when his man assignment pass blocks.

H

Halfway: Linebacker splits the difference from a displaced #2 and the end man on the line of scrimmage (EMLOS).

Hang: Opposite of hug. A defender responsible for a back who pass blocks covers him from the defensive side of the line of scrimmage. He is a possible helper on crossing routes or can spy on the quarterback.

Hat in the crack (HIC): Defensive lineman keeps his head in his assigned gap.

Heads: Tackles align head-up and stick to the assigned shade (e.g., over heads).

Hole: The deep middle third. The defender splits the distance between the widest receivers.

Hook: The area from the ball to a tight end or ghost tight end 8 to 16 yards deep.

Hot: Defensive lineman goes under a pass set. The stunter has cage (e.g., spike Will, the Stud is hot).

Hug: Linebacker goes to get his assigned back, who blocks. This inserts the defender to the quarterback (green dog).

I

I'm here: The safety tells the linebackers he is coming to the box. Used in covers China and black.

Indicator: Represents the eyes, head, shoulders, and free arm of the quarterback. Determines the timing of the break by the defender.

J

Jayhawk: Coverage of a tight end from a depth of five yards instead of a bear technique.

Jet close: Even though the defensive lineman is on a jet charge, he must still close versus a down block.

Jet stance: Defensive linemen on a hard upfield rush through their assigned gap. They play pass first and react to runs.

Jump: Adjustment in cover 8 where the free safety takes a shallow crosser man-to-man.

K

Kamikaze: Linebacker will turn and run to a collision point with the receiver on a three-step drop.

Key blitz: Used in the peel blitz package. As the Mike stunts, he will read the offensive tackle. If the offensive tackle blocks down, Mike will fit outside. If the offensive tackle blocks or steps outside, Mike goes under.

L

Lock: Man-to-man coverage with no banjo.

Long stick: Defensive lineman sticks two gaps.

Looper: Second man in a pass rush game.

Lurker: Robber in cover 2 lurk.

M

Man under: Defender aligns David and stays low shoulder, keying the inside hip. Technique used in cover 2 man.

Match: Linebackers match up or pair up with backs and receivers as they distribute into the route.

Match coverage: Corners cover wide receivers.

Mayday: Defense repeats the last defensive call.

Mental chase: Defender will be responsible for chase while folding on play away.

Middle read: Receiver splitting the safeties in cover 2.

Middle run-through: Mike carries a receiver through centerfield in cover 2.

Mike: Middle linebacker.

Move to: Coordinated group movement. Mike will make a move call (e.g., move to storm).

Mug: Linebackers play at the heel line of defensive linemen. They can stunt or play technique from there.

Mustang: 3-3-5 package.

N

Nail: A nose stick.

NASCAR: Four speed rushers.

Natural: End may go inside the offensive tackle on a pass rush if the tackle oversets or opens up the inside. The nose will assume cage whenever he sees the defensive end cross his face.

Nickel: Defensive back in for Will.

Nose: Weakside tackle.

Nub: Tight-end-side-only formation or only a two-man surface.

O

Ohio: Front with Stud in a 6 technique.

Once-dead always-dead rule: Once a pirate is checked to, it stays on regardless of motion.

One-gap football: Linebackers have run fit in the gap aligned in. Used versus one-back sets.

Openside: Side away from the closed call.

Opposite: Call where tackles align in the opposite shade and stick to the assigned shade (e.g., over opposite).

Opposite cover rule: Cover rule for the man on the tight end. The defender will adjust to Stud's alignment as he covers the tight end. If Stud is outside the tight end, the defender will walk up in a bear alignment. If the Stud lines up inside the tight end, the defender will cover the tight end from the outside.

ORCA: Call given by the corner versus a minus split by the receiver. ORCA is an acronym for: out, reverse, crack, across. The defender will automatic press in man coverage.

Oregon: Defensive front with Stud in a 7 technique.

Over: Defensive front with Stud in a 9 technique.

Over the top: Gap fit on a play when all playside gaps are covered.

P

Pair: Tight end wing set.

Peel: Defender on an outside rush checks backfield action. If the back flares, the defender jumps him man-to-man. Interior rushers will cop the back.

Peel motion: In-the-box back motion away from the tight end.

Peg leg: Used in one-gap football when a linebacker's gap is closed due to a stick. This term means slow down and leverage the ball. Linebacker moves as if he had a peg leg.

Penetrator: First man in a pass rush game.

PGR: Draw technique where the defender will plant, grab, and retrace.

Physical chase: Defender will trail a play away on the offensive side of the line of scrimmage.

Pirate: Tackle and end combination stick.

Pirate wrap: Tackle and end stunt with the nose on a predetermined wrap.

Pittsburgh: Check in goal line versus one-back sets. Defense goes from zone to man.

Play it: Defenders run the defense called. There are no checks.

Plug: Short hole pass responsibility. Used in covers black and China.

Plugger: The defender who has short hole responsibility in the trio and Reggie packages.

Post stick: Linemen line up in the appropriate shade instead of sticking to it. Used in the mustang package.

Press bail: Corners bail from a press position. Can tag coverages with a bail call (e.g., cover 4 bail).

Press man: Man-to-man coverage from the line of scrimmage.

Prowl: Individual movement by defensive lineman from one shade to another.

Punch pedal: Corner starts out slow keying the three-step drop. He gains speed as he goes.

Pursue: Defender on play away runs to the ball with no BCR responsibility. He should not follow the same color.

Q

Quads: 4x1 receiver alignment.

Quarter: Defensive back in for Mike.

R

Rabbit: Run alert call. Can use any walking animal.

Radar: Linemen scramble in a two-point stance and hit the assigned gap on the snap.

Ram: Call and technique by the strong safety in cover 2 versus slot sets. The strong safety is more aggressive versus run than normal in cover 2. The strong safety plays a tight cover 2 technique. He is over the top on a flood run and D+ on flow run. He is responsible for reverse.

Read: Technique in cover 8 where the safeties key and react off #2. Also when the Stud and strong safety react to the block of the tight end in determining option responsibilities.

Recage: Linebacker run through on the quarterback on sprint passes when he breaks the end's cage.

Red zone: Refers to the area between the −20 and the −5.

Reenter motion: An offensive player motioning to a backfield position.

Reggie: Two linebackers have read man coverage on one back.

Reload: Adjustment of the front and secondary versus a tight end trade.

Reset: Mike recalls the defense when two or more offensive men move to new positions pre-snap.

Ricochet: Redirection by a defensive lineman off a stick.

Robber: Stunt with the tackle on a jet and the end on a long stick.

Rock and roll: A linebacker's steps on a counter play. Also, when the hole player and defensive back in man coverage swap responsibilities versus cross motion.

Rock back: Safety rolls back to the hole when the other safety rocks down. The hole defender will sprint to the midpoint and square up. This happens on the snap.

Rock down: Safety moves to an underneath zone. This happens on the snap.

Rocket technique: Used by Stud versus a tight end and wing set. He blows up the D gap.

Rover: The fifth defensive back in the mustang package.

Russian: Plugger rushes the quarterback instead of plugging. He finds a crack and goes. Used with trio coverage.

S

Salesman: Second defender in a pass rush game. He must sell a 1-on-1 pass rush move.

Sam: Weakside outside linebacker.

Scatter: Two or more offensive men move pre-snap followed by motion.

Scramble: Two or more offensive men move pre-snap with no motion.

Seam: Alignment where defender splits the distance between #2 and EMLOS (end man on the line of scrimmage).

Secondary contain: The corner doesn't come up until the ball crosses the line of scrimmage. He must defend the play-pass.

Seed of speed: Basis of a defensive end's pass rush success. The offensive tackle must fear the end's speed. This fear will make inside and counter moves successful.

Seed of strength: Basis of a defensive tackle's pass rush success. The offensive guard must fear the tackle's power and strength. Planting this seed will open up other moves.

Set and club: Offensive linemen draw block technique.

Shoot your gun: If the man a defender has in man coverage blocks, the defender must explode toward the line of scrimmage. He should read slow and react fast.

Short hole: Area from offensive tackle to offensive tackle to a depth of 8 to 10 yards. Usually a plugger drops to this area.

Skate: Slow chase technique by the end.

Slam release: Tight end initially blocks then pass releases.

Slant technique: Used by a corner away from 3x1 formations. He aligns David at six yards. Used when the corner has no inside help.

Sluggo: Slant and go route.

Smash: #1 receiver is on a quick route, and #2 receiver is on a corner route.

Smell a rat: Detecting an offensive lineman influence block on draw or screen.

Special: Man-to-man adjustment versus one-back sets.

Spike: 3 technique stick.

Spill: Trap closing technique using the outside shoulder to make the play bounce. The defender closes, wrong arms, and pivots upfield, making the ball run the hump. Also a linebacker technique where he forces the ballcarrier from his intended direction to the sideline by taking on the blocker with his outside shoulder.

Split distribution: Backs split on a pass release.

Split the pair: The stunter goes between a tight end-wing or a slot-tackle combination.

Spy: Tag to a call that puts the nose over #3 on a pass drop (e.g., over spy 2 middle).

Squeeze: Cover 8 check for an empty or as a change-up in cover 8.

Stack: Linebacker alignment behind a defensive lineman (e.g., stack B+).

Steeler: Coverage change-up in cover 8.

Stem: Defensive line aligns in an over front and linemen individually move to the called front (e.g., stem storm).

Stick: Lineman slants one gap. A long stick is a two-gap movement. A big stick involves three gaps.

Strong safety: Safety to the closed side.

Stud: Strongside end.

Stunt: Linebacker and defensive line game.

Stunt man: Service personnel mimicking an opponent.

Submarine: Corner force technique. The corner will take on blocks at knee level and spill the play. This is a goal line technique.

Swim: Over front with a lane exchange. Defensive linemen not on a stunt will jet.

T

Tackle: Strongside tackle.

Tailback stunt: The stunter aims for the deepest back. The defender has pitch responsibilities.

Tampa: Check for over 2.

Tan: Linebacker alignment head-up on offensive tackle at a five-yard depth.

Toledo: Check for green 2.

Top: Strong safety technique in cover 8 versus empty.

Tough charge: Low four-point stance and charge used in the goal line and hurricane packages.

Track: Linebackers key the onside back through the guard.

Trade: Tight end switches sides pre-snap.

Trail technique: Inside press and hard underneath coverage. Defender is one yard inside and low shoulder on the receiver. He focuses his eyes on the hip of the receiver. Used in cover 2 man.

Trailer technique: Aggressive hug technique. The back must be in the box. The trailer will follow a stunter to hug his assigned man.

Transfer: Gap exchange based on the blocking scheme.

Trio coverage: Three defenders on two backs with read man coverage. The free man can plug, Russian, cut, double, or spy. Can predetermine assignments to help on bootleg.

Triple call: Used in peel blitzes. Sam has #3 on 3x1 formations.

Tucson: Check for over pirate 2.

Turn in: Linebackers take on blocks at the point of attack with the inside shoulder. They force the ball back to help.

Two-way go: 3 technique can rush the A or B gap when playing base.

V

Visual trail: Used with back away rule. Defender's eyes go to fullback to offside back when man on motions away or goes away on the snap.

W

Waggle: Play-pass off divide action with the fullback in the flat and the tight end on a drag.

Walk down: Safety working down pre-snap into the box as opposed to a rock down.

Water ski: Defensive lineman grabbing and trailing a pulling offensive lineman on runs.

Wheel rules: Corner runs with the second man through his zone, taking him man-to-man.

Wide: Front with the tackle in a 4i.

Wide and go: The end aligns wide and jets. Used in the peel package.

Will: Strongside outside linebacker.

Willful separation: Influence block used for screens and draws.

Wrap: Defensive tackle assumes cage to cover up a line game.

n cover 8.

ht end trade.